REVISION GUIDE

AQA Religious Studies A (9 – 1)

Christianity & Judaism

Marianne Fleming
Peter Smith
Harriet Power

OXFORD
UNIVERSITY PRESS

OXFORD
UNIVERSITY PRESS

Great Clarendon Street, Oxford, OX2 6DP, United Kingdom

Oxford University Press is a department of the University of Oxford. It furthers the University's objective of excellence in research, scholarship, and education by publishing worldwide. Oxford is a registered trade mark of Oxford University Press in the UK and in certain other countries

British Library Cataloguing in Publication Data
Data available

978-019-843254-8

10 9 8 7 6

Paper used in the production of this book is a natural, recyclable product made from wood grown in sustainable forests. The manufacturing process conforms to the environmental regulations of the country of origin.

Printed in India by Multivista Global Pvt. Ltd.

Links to third party websites are provided by Oxford in good faith and for information only. Oxford disclaims any responsibility for the materials contained in any third party website referenced in this work.

Please note that the Practice Questions in this book allow students a genuine attempt at practising exam skills, but they are not intended to replicate examination papers.

Acknowledgements

Cover: Image Source/Getty Images & Lisa F. Young/Alamy Stock Photo

Artworks: QBS Learning & Jason Ramasami

Photos: p18: Renata Sedmakova/Shutterstock; p19: GrahamMoore999/ iStockphoto; p48: Ira Berger/Alamy Stock Photo; p50: Gapper/Alamy Stock Photo; p64: Oleksandr Rupeta/Alamy Stock Photo; p67: Rhonda Roth/Shutterstock; p70: Design Pics Inc/Alamy Stock Photo; p94: mshch/ iStock; p96: janrysavy/iStock; p99: zendograph/Shutterstock; p109: cinoby/iStock; p128: querbeet/iStock; p144 (T): Nick Savage/Alamy Stock Photo; p144 (B): Gary Perlmutter.

Carrotflower font © Font Diner – www.fontdiner.com

We are grateful to the authors and publishers for use of extracts from their titles and in particular for the following:

Scripture quotations [marked NIV] taken from the **Holy Bible, New International Version Anglicised** Copyright © 1979, 1984, 2011 Biblica. Used by permission of Hodder & Stoughton Ltd, an Hachette UK company. All rights reserved. 'NIV' is a registered trademark of Biblica UK trademark number 1448790.

Excerpts from **Tanakh: The Holy Scriptures** (Jewish Publication Society Inc., 1991). © 1985, The Jewish Publication Society, Philadelphia. Reproduced with permission from University of Nebraska Press.

AQA: *Paper 1A: Specimen question paper*, (AQA 2017). Reproduced with permission from AQA.

AQA: *Paper 1A: Additional specimen question paper*, (AQA 2017). Reproduced with permission from AQA.

The Church of England: Lines from the Creeds, the Lord's Prayer, the marriage rite and the baptism rite. (The Archbishops' Council, 2017). © **The Archbishops' Council**. Reproduced with permission from The Archbishops' Council.

The Church of England: *Marriage, Family & Sexuality Issues,* https://www. churchofengland.org/our-views/marriage,-family-and-sexuality-issues/ family.aspx (The Archbishops' Council, 2010). © **The Archbishops' Council**. Reproduced with permission from The Archbishops' Council.

S. Hucklesby: 'Mutual cooperation, not mutual destruction' say Churches, The Methodist Church in Britain website, 23rd May 2015. http://www.methodist.org.uk/about-us/news/latest-news/all-news/mutual-cooperation-not-mutual-destruction-say-churches/ (The Methodist Church in Britain, 2015). © Trustees for Methodist Church Purposes. Reproduced with permission from The Methodist Church in Britain.

Rabbi D. Saperstein: *Statement on the Nuclear Reduction/Disarmament Project's Release of Its Joint Statement.* (Religious Action Center of Reform Judaism, 2000). Reproduced with permission from Rabbi Saperstein.

Father L. Serrini: *The Christian Declaration on Nature,* (Alliance of Religions and Conservation (ARC), 1986). Reproduced with permission from ARC.

Pope Francis: *Address to a Meeting at the Pontifical Academy of Sciences,* October 2014. (The Vatican, 2014) © Libreria Editrice Vaticana. Reproduced with permission from The Vatican.

Rabbi Lord J. Sacks: *The Great Partnership: Science, Religion and the Search for Meaning,* (Hodder & Stoughton, 2012). Copyright © 2011 Jonathan Sacks. Reproduced with permission from Hodder Faith, a division of Hodder and Stoughton Limited and from Schocken Books, an imprint of the Knopf Doubleday Publishing Group, a division of Penguin Random House LLC.

The Salvation Army: *Positional Statement: Euthanasia and Assisted Suicide,* July 2013 http://www.salvationarmy.org/ihq/ipseuthanasia (The Salvation Army, 2013). Reproduced with permission from the General of The Salvation Army.

The United Nations: *The Universal Declaration of Human Rights,* (UDHR) (United Nations, 1948). Reproduced with permission from United Nations.

E. Wiesel: *Nobel Acceptance Speech, 1986* http://www.nobelprize.org/nobel_prizes/ peace/laureates/1986/wiesel-acceptance_en.html (Nobel Foundation, 1986). © The Nobel Foundation.

We have made every effort to trace and contact all copyright holders before publication, but if notified of any errors or omissions, the publisher will be happy to rectify these at the earliest opportunity.

The publisher would like to thank Rabbi Benjy Rickman for his advice and guidance.

Contents

Introduction 7

PART ONE: THE STUDY OF RELIGIONS   14

Chapter 1: Christianity: Beliefs and teachings 14

1.1	The nature of God	14
1.2	God as omnipotent, loving and just	15
1.3	The Oneness of God and the Trinity	16
1.4	Different Christian beliefs about creation	17
1.5	The incarnation and Jesus, the Son of God	18
1.6	The crucifixion	19
1.7	The resurrection and ascension	20
1.8	Resurrection and life after death	21
1.9	The afterlife and judgement	22
1.10	Heaven and hell	23
1.11	Sin and salvation	24
1.12	The role of Christ in salvation	25
	Exam practice	26

Chapter 2: Christianity: Practices 30

2.1	Worship	30
2.2	Prayer	31
2.3	The sacraments: Baptism	32
2.4	The sacraments: Holy Communion	33
2.5	Celebrating Holy Communion	34
2.6	Pilgrimage	35
2.7	Celebrating festivals	36
2.8	The role of the Church in the local community: Food banks	37
2.9	The role of the Church in the local community: Street Pastors	38
2.10	The place of mission and evangelism	39
2.11	Church growth	40
2.12	The importance of the worldwide Church	41
2.13	Christian persecution	42
2.14	The Church's response to world poverty	43
	Exam practice	44

PART ONE: THE STUDY OF RELIGIONS *(continued)*

Chapter 3: Judaism: Beliefs and teachings 48

3.1	The nature of God: God as One	48
3.2	The nature of God: God as creator	49
3.3	The nature of God: God as lawgiver and judge; the divine presence	50
3.4	Life after death, judgement and resurrection	51
3.5	The nature and role of the Messiah	52
3.6	The Promised Land and the covenant with Abraham	53
3.7	The covenant at Sinai and the Ten Commandments	54
3.8	Key moral principles in Judaism	55
3.9	Sanctity of life	56
3.10	Free will and mitzvot	57
	Exam practice	58

Chapter 4: Judaism: Practices 62

4.1	The importance of the synagogue	62
4.2	Interior features of a synagogue	63
4.3	Worship in Orthodox and Reform synagogues	64
4.4	Daily services and prayer	65
4.5	Shabbat in the synagogue	66
4.6	Shabbat in the home	67
4.7	Worship in the home; the written and oral law	68
4.8	Ceremonies associated with birth	69
4.9	Bar and Bat Mitzvah	70
4.10	Marriage	71
4.11	Mourning for the dead	72
4.12	Dietary laws	73
4.13	Rosh Hashanah and Yom Kippur	74
4.14	Pesach	75
	Exam practice	76

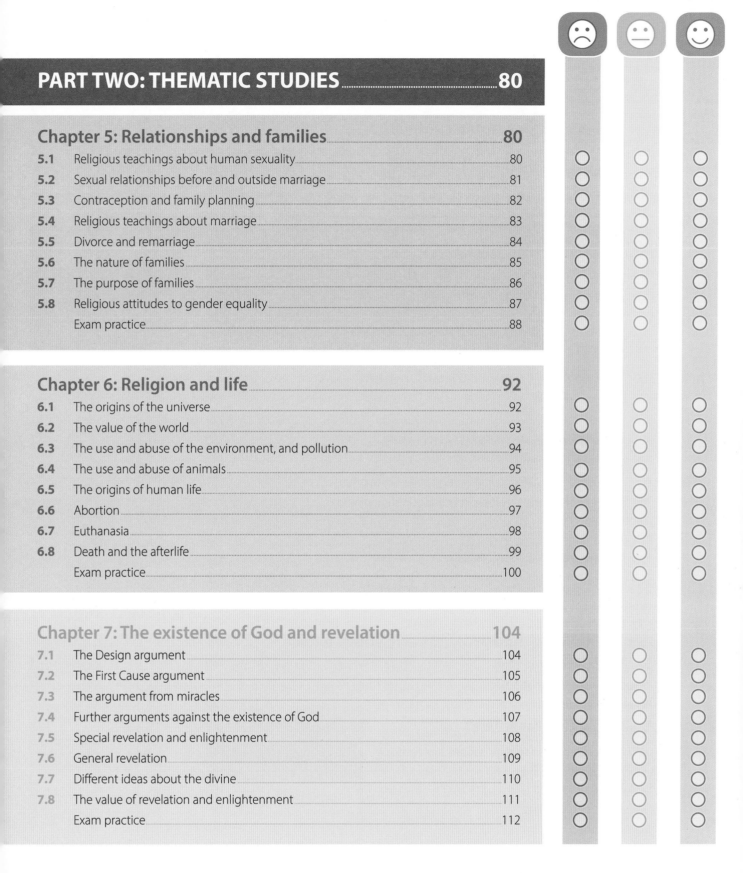

PART TWO: THEMATIC STUDIES 80

Chapter 5: Relationships and families 80

5.1	Religious teachings about human sexuality	80
5.2	Sexual relationships before and outside marriage	81
5.3	Contraception and family planning	82
5.4	Religious teachings about marriage	83
5.5	Divorce and remarriage	84
5.6	The nature of families	85
5.7	The purpose of families	86
5.8	Religious attitudes to gender equality	87
	Exam practice	88

Chapter 6: Religion and life 92

6.1	The origins of the universe	92
6.2	The value of the world	93
6.3	The use and abuse of the environment, and pollution	94
6.4	The use and abuse of animals	95
6.5	The origins of human life	96
6.6	Abortion	97
6.7	Euthanasia	98
6.8	Death and the afterlife	99
	Exam practice	100

Chapter 7: The existence of God and revelation 104

7.1	The Design argument	104
7.2	The First Cause argument	105
7.3	The argument from miracles	106
7.4	Further arguments against the existence of God	107
7.5	Special revelation and enlightenment	108
7.6	General revelation	109
7.7	Different ideas about the divine	110
7.8	The value of revelation and enlightenment	111
	Exam practice	112

PART TWO: THEMATIC STUDIES *(continued)*

Chapter 8: Religion, peace and conflict 116

8.1	Introduction to religion, peace and conflict	116
8.2	Violent protest and terrorism	117
8.3	Reasons for war	118
8.4	Nuclear war and weapons of mass destruction	119
8.5	The just war	120
8.6	Holy war and religion as a cause of violence	121
8.7	Pacifism and peacemaking	122
8.8	Religious responses to victims of war	123
	Exam practice	124

Chapter 9: Religion, crime and punishment 128

9.1	Crime and punishment	128
9.2	Reasons for crime	129
9.3	Attitudes to lawbreakers and different types of crime	130
9.4	Three aims of punishment	131
9.5	Religious attitudes to suffering and causing suffering to others	132
9.6	The treatment of criminals – prison, corporal punishment and community service	133
9.7	Religious attitudes to forgiveness	134
9.8	Religious attitudes to the death penalty	135
	Exam practice	136

Chapter 10: Religion, human rights and social justice 140

10.1	Social justice and human rights	140
10.2	Prejudice and discrimination	141
10.3	Religious freedom	142
10.4	Prejudice and discrimination – race	143
10.5	The status and roles of women in religion	144
10.6	Teachings about wealth	145
10.7	Exploitation of the poor	146
10.8	Giving money to the poor	147
	Exam practice	148

Answers		152

Introduction

What will the exam be like?

For your GCSE Religious Studies exam, you will sit two papers.

- **Paper 1 will cover the study of religions.** You will need to answer questions on the beliefs and teachings, and practices, of **two** world religions. There will be separate question and answer booklets for each religion. Chapters 1 and 2 of this revision guide will help you to answer questions on Christianity for Paper 1. Chapters 3 and 4 will help you to answer questions on Judaism.

- **Paper 2 will cover thematic studies.** There are six themes on the paper. You will need to **choose four themes**, and answer all the questions for each chosen theme. You will need to know about religious beliefs and viewpoints on themes and issues. Except in those questions where the main religious tradition of Great Britain is asked for, you can use beliefs from any religion in your answer. For example, you might want to focus on Christianity, including viewpoints from different traditions within Christianity, such as Catholic or Protestant views. Or you might want to include beliefs across six religions, including Christian, Buddhist, Hindu, Muslim, Jewish or Sikh viewpoints. Chapters 5 to 10 of this revision guide cover the six themes, focusing on Christian and Jewish perspectives.

If you are studying **St Mark's Gospel**, then the six themes will appear in Section A of Paper 2. You will need to choose **two themes**. You will then also need to answer the **two questions on St Mark's Gospel** from Section B.

> TIP
>
> Each paper is 1 hour and 45 minutes long, and you'll need to answer four full questions. Aim to spend 25 minutes on each question.

What kind of questions will be on the exam?

Each question on the exam will be split into five parts, worth 1, 2, 4, 5 and 12 marks.

The 1 mark question

The 1 mark question tests knowledge and understanding.

It is always a **multiple-choice question** with four answers to choose from. It will usually include the command words: **'Which one of the following...'**

> Which **one** of the following is the idea that God is three-in-one?
>
> Put a tick (✔) in the box next to the correct answer.
>
> A   Atonement   ☐
>
> B   Incarnation   ☐
>
> C   Salvation   ☐
>
> D   Trinity   ☐
>
> **[1 mark]**

How is it marked?

1 mark is awarded for a correct answer.

The 2 mark question

The 2 mark question tests knowledge and understanding.

It always begins with the command words 'Give two...' or 'Name two...'

Give **two** ways in which religious believers help victims of war.

[2 marks]

How is it marked?

1 mark is awarded for 1 correct point.
2 marks are awarded for 2 correct points.

TIP

The examiner is expecting two simple points, not detailed explanations. You would get 2 marks if you answered "1) praying for victims; 2) providing food and shelter". You don't need to waste time by writing in full sentences and giving long explanations.

The 4 mark question

The 4 mark question tests knowledge and understanding.

It always begins with the command words '**Explain two...**'

It might test your knowledge of how a religion influences individuals, communities and societies. Or it might ask for similarities or differences within or between religions.

TIP

Here, 'contrasting' means different. The question is asking you to explain two different ways in which Holy Communion is celebrated.

Explain **two** contrasting ways in which Holy Communion is celebrated in Christianity.

[4 marks]

How is it marked?

For the first way, influence or similar/contrasting belief:

- 1 mark is awarded for a simple explanation
- 2 marks are awarded for a detailed explanation.

For the second way, influence or similar/contrasting belief:

- 1 mark is awarded for a simple explanation
- 2 marks are awarded for a detailed explanation.

So for the full 4 marks, the examiner is looking for two ways/influences/ beliefs and for you to give detailed explanations of both. The examiner is expecting you to write in full sentences.

What is a detailed explanation?

An easy way to remember what you need to do for the four mark question is:

But how do you develop a point? You might do this by:

- giving more information
- giving an example
- referring to a religious teaching or quotation.

The 'Great Britain' question

Sometimes there may be additional wording to the 4 mark question, asking you to **'Refer to the main religious tradition of Great Britain and one or more other religious traditions.'**

> Explain **two** similar religious beliefs about abortion.
>
> In your answer you should refer to the main religious tradition of Great Britain and one or more other religious traditions.
>
> **[4 marks]**

The main religious tradition of Great Britain is Christianity, so in your answer **you must refer to Christianity**. You can refer to **two different denominations within Christianity**, or you can compare **a Christian belief with that from another religion**, such as Buddhism, Hinduism, Islam, Judaism or Sikhism.

For theme C: the existence of God and revelation, the wording will say: 'In your answer you should refer to the main religious tradition of Great Britain **and non-religious beliefs.'** You must refer to Christianity and a non-religious belief.

This type of question will only be asked about certain topics. We point them out in this revision guide using this feature:

> You might be asked to compare beliefs on contraception between Christianity (the main religious tradition in Great Britain) and another religious tradition.

TIP

One point you might make to answer this question is to say "Catholics celebrate Holy Communion by receiving offerings of bread and wine." This would get you 1 mark. For a second mark you could develop the point by giving further information: "During the service they believe the bread and wine become the body and blood of Jesus Christ." There is more you could probably say, but as you'd get 2 marks for this, it would be better to turn your attention to thinking about a second contrasting way in which Holy Communion is celebrated, and then developing that second point.

TIP

You can't, for example, refer to two different groups within Buddhism, or compare Buddhism and Islam. There must be a reference to Christianity or you won't get full marks for this question however detailed your answer is.

The 5 mark question

The 5 mark question tests knowledge and understanding.

Like the 4 mark question, it always begins with the command words '**Explain two…**' In addition it will also ask you to '**Refer to sacred writings or another source of religious/Christian belief and teaching in your answer.**'

> Explain **two** reasons why Christians pray.
>
> Refer to sacred writings or another source of Christian belief and teaching in your answer.
>
> **[5 marks]**

How is it marked?

For the first reason/teaching/belief:

- 1 mark is awarded for a simple explanation
- 2 marks are awarded for a detailed explanation.

For the second reason/teaching/belief:

- 1 mark is awarded for a simple explanation
- 2 marks are awarded for a detailed explanation.

Plus 1 mark for a relevant reference to sacred writings or another source of religious belief.

So for the full 5 marks, the examiner is looking for two reasons/teachings/beliefs and for you to give detailed explanations of both, just like the 4 mark question. **For the fifth mark, you need to make reference to a writing or teaching that is considered holy or authoritative by a religion.** The examiner is expecting you to write in full sentences. You might aim to write five sentences.

What counts as 'sacred writings or another source of religious belief and teaching'?

Sacred writings and religious beliefs or teachings might include:

- a quotation from a holy book, for example the Bible or the Tenakh
- a statement of religious belief such as the Apostles' Creed or 'God is One'
- a prayer such as the Lord's Prayer or the Amidah
- a statement made by a religious leader, for example the Pope
- a quotation from a religious text such as the Catechism of the Catholic Church or the Mishnah.

TIP

If you can quote exact phrases this will impress the examiner, but if you can't then it's fine to paraphrase. It's also ok if you can't remember the exact verse that a quotation is from, but it would be helpful to name the holy book, for example, to specify that it is a teaching from the Bible.

The 12 mark question

The 12 mark question tests analytical and evaluative skills. It will always begin with a statement, and then ask you to **evaluate the statement**. There will be bullet points guiding you through what the examiner expects you to provide in your answer.

From Paper 1:

'The Bible tells Christians all they need to know about God's creation.'

Evaluate this statement. In your answer you should:

- refer to Christian teaching
- give reasoned arguments to support this statement
- give reasoned arguments to support a different point of view
- reach a justified conclusion.

[12 marks]
[+3 SPaG marks]

From Paper 2:

'War is never right.'

Evaluate this statement. In your answer you:

- should give reasoned arguments in support of this statement
- should give reasoned arguments to support a different point of view
- should refer to religious arguments
- may refer to non-religious arguments
- should reach a justified conclusion.

[12 marks]
[+3 SPaG marks]

TIP

The examiners are not just giving marks for what you know, but for your ability to weigh up different sides of an argument, making judgements on how convincing or weak you think they are. The examiner will also be looking for your ability to connect your arguments logically.

TIP

For Paper 2, on thematic issues, you can use different views from one or more religions, and you can also use non-religious views.

TIP

This question is worth the same amount of marks as the 1, 2, 4 and 5 mark questions combined. Try to aim for at least a full page of writing, and spend 12 minutes or more on this question.

How is it marked?

Level	What the examiner is looking for	Marks
4	A well-argued response with two different points of view, both developed to show a logical chain of reasoning that leads to judgements supported by relevant knowledge and understanding. ***References to religion applied to the issue.***	10–12 marks
3	Two different points of view, both developed through a logical chain of reasoning that draws on relevant knowledge and understanding. ***Clear reference to religion.***	7–9 marks

2	One point of view developed through a logical chain of reasoning that draws on relevant knowledge and understanding. OR Two different points of view with supporting reasons. **Students cannot move above Level 2 if they don't include a reference to religion, or only give one viewpoint.**	4–6 marks
1	One point of view with supporting reasons. OR Two different points of view, simply expressed.	1–3 marks

Tips for answering the 12 mark question

- **Remember to focus your answer on the statement you've been given** – for example, 'War is never right.'

- **Include different viewpoints, one supporting the statement, one arguing against it** – for example, one viewpoint to support the idea that war is *never* right, and an alternative viewpoint to suggest that war is sometimes necessary.

- **Develop both arguments showing a logical chain of reasoning** – for example, draw widely on your knowledge and understanding of the subject of war, and try to make **connections** between ideas. Write a detailed answer and use evidence to support your arguments.

- **Be sure to include religious arguments** – a top level answer will explain how religious teaching is relevant to the argument.

- **Include evaluation** – you can make judgements on the strength of arguments throughout, and you should finish with a justified conclusion. If you want to, you can give your own opinion.

- **Write persuasively** – **use a minimum of three paragraphs** (one giving arguments for the statement, one for a different point of view and a final conclusion). The examiner will expect to see extended writing and full sentences.

Spelling, punctuation and grammar

Additional marks for **SPaG – spelling, punctuation and grammar** – will be awarded on the 12 mark question.

A maximum of 3 marks will be awarded if:

- your spelling and punctuation are consistently accurate

- you use grammar properly to control the meaning of what you are trying to say

- you use specialist and religious terminology appropriately. For example, the examiner will be impressed if you use appropriately the term 'resurrection' rather than just 'rising from the dead'.

In Paper 1, SPaG will be awarded on the Beliefs question for each religion.

In Paper 2, SPaG will be assessed on each 12 mark question, and the examiner will pick your best mark to add to the total.

TIP

Always try to use your best written English in the long 12 mark questions. It could be a chance to pick up extra marks for SPaG.

A note on the sacred texts used in this book:

'[NIV]' placed after a quote indicates that it has been taken from the Christian Holy Bible, New International Version. '[Tenakh]' shows that a quote has been taken from the Jewish sacred scriptures, the Tenakh. The Tenakh consists of 24 books which can all be found in what Christians call the Old Testament.

How to revise using this book

This revision guide takes a three step approach to help with your revision.

RECAP	This is an overview of the key information. It is not a substitute for the full student book, or your class notes. It should prompt you to recall more in-depth information. Diagrams and images are included to help make the information more memorable.
APPLY	Once you've recapped the key information, you can practise applying it to help embed the information. There are two questions after each Recap section. The first question will help you rehearse some key skills that you need for the questions on the exam that test your knowledge (the 1, 2, 4 and 5 mark questions). The second question will help you rehearse some key skills that you will need for the 12 mark question, which tests your evaluative skills. There are suggested answers to the Apply activities at the back of the book.
REVIEW	At the end of each chapter you will then have a chance to review what you've revised. The exam practice pages contain exam-style questions for each question type. For the 4, 5 and 12 mark questions, there are writing frames that you can use to structure your answer, and to remind yourself of what it is that the examiner is looking for. When you've answered the questions you can use the mark schemes at the back of the book to see how you've done. You might identify some areas that you need to revise in more detail. And you can turn back to the pages here for guidance on how to answer the exam questions.

The revision guide is designed so that alongside revising *what* you need to know, you can practise *how* to apply this knowledge in your exam. There are regular opportunities to try out exam practice questions, and mark schemes so you can see how you are doing. Keep recapping, applying and reviewing, particularly going over those areas that you feel unsure about, and hopefully you will build in skills and confidence for the final exam.

Good luck!

1.1 The nature of God

RECAP

Essential information:

- [ ] Christianity is the main religion in Great Britain.
- [ ] Christianity has three main traditions: Catholic, Protestant and Orthodox.
- [ ] Christianity is **monotheistic**, meaning that Christians believe in one Supreme Being, **God**.

Different branches of Christianity

CHRISTIANITY

- **Catholic** – based in Rome and led by the Pope.

- **Orthodox** – split from Catholic Christianity in 1054 CE and practised in Eastern Europe.

- **Protestant** – split from Catholic Christianity in the 16th century and branched out into different **denominations** (distinct groups), e.g. Baptist, Pentecostal, Methodist, United Reformed Churches. Protestants agree that the Bible is the only authority for Christians.

What do Christians believe about God?

- There is only one God:

> **" We believe in one God "**
>
> *The Nicene Creed*

- God is the creator and sustainer of all that exists.
- God works throughout history and inspires people to do God's will.
- People can have a relationship with God through prayer.
- God is spirit (John 4:24) – neither male nor female – but has qualities of both.
- God is **holy** (set apart for a special purpose and worthy of worship).
- Jesus is God's son – the true representation of God on earth (Hebrews 1:3).

TIP

If you are asked about similarities and differences in a religion, try to remember that even though Christianity has different denominations, they all share the same belief in God.

TIP

See page 15 for more Christian beliefs about God.

APPLY

A Christians believe that there is only one God. Refer to scripture or another Christian source of authority to support this idea.

B 'Christianity is a major influence on people's lives.'

Write a paragraph to **support this statement**.

1.2 God as omnipotent, loving and just

RECAP

Essential information:

Christians believe:

☐ God is **omnipotent**, almighty, having unlimited power.

☐ God is **benevolent**, all-loving and all-good.

☐ God is **just**, the perfect judge of human behaviour who will bring about what is right and fair or who will make up for a wrong that has been committed.

Some qualities of God

Omnipotent	Benevolent	Just
• God is the Supreme Being who is all-powerful. • God has unlimited authority.	• God uses his power to do good. • God shows his love by creating humans and caring for them. • God showed his love by sending God's Son, Jesus, to earth.	• God is a just judge of humankind. • God will never support injustice, ill-treatment, prejudice or oppression.

The problems of evil and suffering

The problems of evil and suffering challenge belief in these qualities of God:

- If God is benevolent, **why does God allow people to suffer**, and to hurt others?
- If God is omnipotent, **why does God not prevent evil and suffering**, such as the suffering caused by natural disasters?
- If God is just, **why does God allow injustice** to take place?

Christians believe a just God treats people fairly, so they trust God even when things seem to be going wrong.

TIP
See page 107 for more arguments in response to these challenges to belief in God.

APPLY

A Give **two** ways in which Christians believe God shows his benevolence.

B Write the response a Christian would make to someone who said that a loving God would not allow suffering. Think of **two** arguments and develop them.

TIP
In the 12 mark exam answer, using the key terms 'omnipotent', 'benevolent' and 'just' where appropriate, and spelling them correctly, may gain you more marks for SPaG.

1.3 The Oneness of God and the Trinity

RECAP

Essential information:

- ☐ Christians believe there are three persons in the one God: Father, Son and Holy Spirit. This belief is called the **Trinity**.
- ☐ Each person of the Trinity is fully God.
- ☐ The persons of the Trinity are not the same.

The Trinity

- God is understood by Christians as a relationship of love between Father, Son and Holy Spirit.
- In describing God as Trinity, 'person' does not mean a physical being, although Jesus did have a physical presence in history.

TIP

The Apostles Creed and/or the Nicene Creed, Christian statements of belief, are useful to know when discussing the Trinity. They begin 'I/We believe in one God' and include references to 'the Father Almighty', 'the Son' and 'the Holy Spirit'.

God the Father, the creator of all life, acts as a good father towards his children. He is all powerful (omnipotent), all loving (omnibenevolent), all knowing (omniscient) and present everywhere (omnipresent).

THE FATHER — IS NOT — IS — GOD — IS — THE SON — IS NOT — THE HOLY SPIRIT — IS NOT

God the Holy Spirit is the unseen power of God at work in the world, who influences, guides and sustains life on earth.

God the Son became incarnate through Jesus, who was both fully human while on earth and fully God at all times. Jesus is called the **Son of God** to show his special relationship to God the Father.

APPLY

 A Here are **two** Christian beliefs about the Trinity. Develop each point with further explanation or a relevant quotation:

1. *"The Trinity is the Christian belief that there are three persons in the one God."* _____
   _____

2. *"One of the persons of the Trinity is God the Father."* _____
   _____

B Here are some arguments that could be used to evaluate the statement, 'The Trinity is a helpful way of describing God.' Sort them into arguments in support of the statement, and arguments in support of different views. **Write your own justified conclusion.**

1. The Trinity is a helpful idea because it describes God as a loving relationship of persons.	5. If God is One, then how can God have three persons?
2. The love of God the Son is shown in Jesus' mission and sacrifice.	6. The Holy Spirit is the outpouring of love between Father and Son that encourages Christians to love their neighbour.
3. The Trinity seems contradictory.	7. Jesus was a Jew and believed in the oneness of God.
4. The love of God the Father is shown in his sending his Son to earth to save humankind.	8. The Trinity is not helpful to people of other faiths as they may think that Christians believe in three different Gods.

16

1.4 Different Christian beliefs about Creation

Essential information:

- [ ] Christians believe in **creation** by God, the act by which God brought the universe into being.
- [ ] God, the Father, chose to design and create the earth and all life on it.
- [ ] The Holy Spirit was active in the creation (Genesis 1:1–3).
- [ ] The **Word**, God the Son or Jesus, was active in the creation (John 1:1–3).
- [ ] The Trinity, therefore, existed from the beginning and was involved in the creation.

Creation: *Genesis 1:1–3*

> **In the beginning, God created the heavens and the earth**. Now the earth was formless and empty, darkness was over the surface of the deep, and the Spirit of God was hovering over the waters. And God said, "Let there be light," and there was light.
>
> *Genesis 1: 1–3* [NIV]

- Many Christians believe that the story of the creation in Genesis, while not scientifically accurate, contains religious truth.
- Some Christians believe that God made the world in literally six days.
- God created everything out of choice and created everything 'good'.
- Christians believe that God continues to create new life today.
- Although God the Father is referred to as the creator, the Holy Spirit was active in the creation, according to Genesis.

Creation: *John 1:1-3*

> In the beginning was the Word, and **the Word was with God, and the Word was God**. He was with God in the beginning. Through him all things were made; without him nothing was made that has been made.
>
> *John 1: 1–3* [NIV]

- In John's gospel, everything was created through the Word, who was both with God and was God.
- The Word refers to the Son of God who entered history as Jesus.
- Christians believe that the Son of God, the Word of God, was involved in the creation.

TIP

See pages 92 and 104–105 for more detail on different Christian beliefs about creation.

 A Explain **two** ways in which belief in creation by God influences Christians today.

 B Here is an argument in support of the statement, 'The Bible is the best source of information about the creation.'

Evaluate the argument. Explain your reasoning.

"The Bible contains the truth about the creation of the world by God. God is omnipotent, so God can just say 'Let there be light' and it happens. The Bible is God's word, so it is true. Other theories about the creation, like evolution and the Big Bang theory, have not been proved."

TIP

Show the examiner that you are aware of contrasting views within Christianity about the way Genesis 1 is interpreted, that is, between those who take the story literally and those who do not.

RECAP

Essential information:

☐ Christians believe that Jesus was God in human form, a belief known as the **incarnation** (becoming flesh, taking a human form).

☐ Christians believe that Jesus was the Son of God, one of the persons of the Trinity.

The incarnation

> **❝** This is how the birth of Jesus the Messiah came about: His mother Mary was pledged to be married to Joseph, but before they came together, **she was found to be pregnant through the Holy Spirit. ❞**
>
> *Matthew 1:18* [NIV]

- On separate occasions an angel appeared to Mary and Joseph explaining that it was not an ordinary conception and it was not to be an ordinary child.
- The gospels of Matthew and Luke explain that Mary conceived Jesus without having sex.
- The virgin conception is evidence for the Christian belief that Jesus was the Son of God, part of the Trinity.
- Through the incarnation, God showed himself as a human being (Jesus) for around 30 years.

> **❝ The Word became flesh** and made his dwelling among us. **❞**
>
> *John 1:14* [NIV]

Son of God, Messiah, Christ

- Jesus was fully God and fully human, which helps explain his miracles and **resurrection** (rising from the dead).
- His words, deeds and promises have great authority because they are the word of God.
- Most Jews expected a Messiah who would come to save Israel and establish an age of peace, but Jews do not believe that Jesus was that person.
- Christians believe that Jesus is the Messiah, but a spiritual rather than a political one.
- Gospel writers refer to Jesus as the Christ ('anointed one' or Messiah), but Jesus warned his disciples not to use the term, possibly because his opponents would have him arrested for **blasphemy** (claiming to be God).

Jesus — 'The Word' — Christ — Messiah — God the Son, one of the persons in the Trinity — Son of God

APPLY

A Explain **two** Christian beliefs about Jesus' incarnation. **Refer to sacred writings in your answer**.

B **Develop this argument** to support the statement, 'The stories of the incarnation show that Jesus was the Son of God' by explaining in more detail, adding an example, or referring to a relevant religious teaching or quotation.

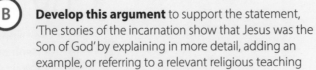
"The stories of the incarnation in the gospels of Matthew and Luke show that his mother, Mary, was a virgin. Joseph was not the natural father of Jesus. Jesus' conception was through the Holy Spirit, so really God was his father. That is why he is called the Son of God."

TIP

In a 5 mark question, you need to give a detailed explanation of each belief and then support your answer by quoting from scripture or sacred writings for full marks. The sacred writings may refer to just one of the beliefs or to both of them.

RECAP

Essential information:

- [ ] Jesus was sentenced to death by Pontius Pilate, a death by **crucifixion** (fixed to a cross).
- [ ] Jesus forgave those who crucified him and promised one of the men crucified with him that he would join God in paradise.
- [ ] Jesus' body was buried in a cave-like tomb.

Jesus' crucifixion – what happened?

- Although Jesus was fully God, he was also fully human so suffered pain and horror.
- Jesus' last words before dying were:

> ❝ Father, into your hands I commit my spirit. ❞
>
> *Luke 23:46 [NIV]*

- A Roman centurion acknowledged Jesus was innocent, and said he was the Son of God (Mark 15:39).
- The Roman guards made sure Jesus was dead.
- Joseph of Arimathea was permitted to bury Jesus in a cave-like tomb, rolling a large stone to block the entrance.
- Jesus' burial was rushed because the Sabbath was about to begin.

Jesus' crucifixion – why is it important?

- Jesus' sacrifice on the cross gives hope to Christians that **their sins will be forgiven if they sincerely repent**.
- Christians believe that **God understands human suffering** because Jesus, who is God, experienced it.
- **Christians accept that suffering is part of life**, just as it was a part of Jesus' life.

TIP

See page 25 for more detail on why the crucifixion was important.

APPLY

(A) Here are two ways in which Jesus' crucifixion influences Christians today:

1) Their sins are forgiven.
2) They have hope when they are suffering.

Develop both points by **explaining in more detail or by adding an example**.

TIP

Keep rereading the statement to make sure you are answering the question asked.

(B) Read the following response to the statement, 'The crucifixion is the most important belief for Christians.' Underline the **two** best arguments. Explain how this answer could be improved.

"Jesus was arrested in the Garden of Gethsemane and brought to trial, first before the Jewish Council and then before the Roman Governor, Pontius Pilate. In the gospels it says that Pontius Pilate did not think Jesus was guilty of anything, so he didn't want to have him killed. Instead he had him flogged. The Jewish leaders called for Jesus' death, so Pilate gave in to their wishes and sentenced Jesus to death. After about six hours of agony on the cross, Jesus died. A Roman centurion said that because Jesus was innocent, he must surely be the Son of God. When Jesus died, he took the sins of everyone on himself. This is called the atonement. If Jesus had not died, he would not have risen from the dead."

1.7 The resurrection and ascension

RECAP

Essential information:

- [ ] The gospels say that after Jesus died and was buried, he rose from the dead. This event is known as the **resurrection**.
- [ ] The **ascension** of Jesus took place 40 days after his resurrection, when he returned to God the Father in **heaven**.
- [ ] There would be no Christian faith without the resurrection.

The resurrection of Jesus – what happened?

- Early on Sunday morning, some of Jesus' female followers, including Mary Magdalene, visited the tomb to anoint Jesus' body.
- Jesus' body was not there.
- Either a man or two men, who may have been angels, told the women to spread the news that Jesus had risen from the dead.
- Over the next few days, Jesus appeared to several people including Mary Magdalene and his disciples. He told them he had risen from the dead, as he predicted he would before the crucifixion.

> **"** And if Christ has not been raised, our preaching is useless and so is your faith. But Christ has indeed been raised from the dead […] For as in Adam all die, so in Christ all will be made alive. **"**
>
> *1 Corinthians 15:14, 20, 22* [NIV]

The ascension of Jesus – what happened?

- After meeting with his disciples and asking them to carry on his work, Jesus left them for the last time, returning to the Father in heaven. This event is called the ascension.

> **"** While he was blessing them, he left them and was taken up into heaven. **"**
>
> *Luke 24:51* [NIV]

The significance of these events for Christians today

The significance of the **resurrection**:

- Shows the power of good over evil and life over death.
- Means Christians' sins will be forgiven if they follow God's laws.
- Means Christians will be resurrected if they accept Jesus, so there is no need to fear death.

The significance of the **ascension**:

- Shows Jesus is with God in heaven.
- Paves the way for God to send the Holy Spirit to provide comfort and guidance.

> **TIP**
> This quote shows that Christianity would not exist without the resurrection. It also shows that the resurrection is important because it is significant evidence for Christians of the divine nature of Jesus.

APPLY

 A Give **two** reasons why the disciples believed Jesus was alive after his resurrection. (AQA Specimen question paper, 2017)

B 'The resurrection is the most important belief for Christians.'

Develop this response to the statement, by adding a relevant religious teaching or quotation.

"Without the resurrection, there would be no Christian faith. Jesus' death would have been the end of all the hopes the disciples placed on him. He would have been just like all the other innocent victims put to death for their beliefs."

1.8 Resurrection and life after death

RECAP

Essential information:

- [ ] Jesus' resurrection assures Christians that they too will rise and live on after death.
- [ ] Christians have differing views about what happens when a person who has died is resurrected.
- [ ] Belief in resurrection affects the way Christians live their lives today.

Different Christian views about resurrection

Some Christians believe a person's soul is resurrected **soon after death**.	Other Christians believe the dead will be resurrected at **some time in the future**, when Jesus will return to judge everyone who has ever lived.
Catholic and Orthodox Christians believe in bodily resurrection. This means resurrection is **both spiritual and physical**: the physical body lost at death is restored and transformed into a new, spiritual body.	Some other Christians believe resurrection will **just be spiritual**, not physical as well.

> " So will it be with the resurrection of the dead. The body that is sown is perishable, it is raised imperishable; it is sown in dishonour, it is raised in glory; it is sown in weakness, it is raised in power; it is sown a natural body, it is raised a spiritual body. If there is a natural body, there is also a spiritual body. "
>
> *1 Corinthians 15:42–44 [NIV]*

TIP
This quote explains some of the differences between a living body and a resurrected body. For Catholics and Orthodox Christians, it suggests there is a physical element to resurrection, as it talks about the resurrected body being a 'body', even if it is a spiritual one.

Impact of the belief in resurrection

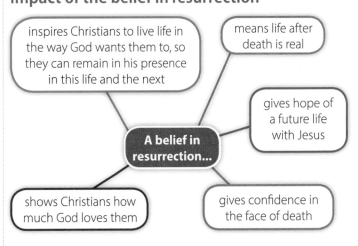

- inspires Christians to live life in the way God wants them to, so they can remain in his presence in this life and the next
- means life after death is real
- gives hope of a future life with Jesus
- **A belief in resurrection...**
- shows Christians how much God loves them
- gives confidence in the face of death

APPLY

A Explain **two** ways in which a belief in resurrection influences Christians today.

B The table below presents arguments for and against the belief in bodily resurrection. **Write a paragraph** to explain whether you agree or disagree with bodily resurrection, having evaluated both sides of the argument.

TIP
If you need to give different points of view in your answer to an evaluation question, you could include contrasting non-religious perspectives as well as religious perspectives.

For	Against
Jesus rose from the dead and appeared to his disciples.	Science has shown the body decays after death, so there cannot be a physical resurrection.
The gospels insist he was not a ghost, as he ate with them and showed his wounds to them.	Some people are cremated so their bodies no longer exist.
Yet he could appear and disappear suddenly, so it seems that his body was transformed.	Stories of the resurrection appearances may have been exaggerated.
Paul says 'the body that is sown is perishable, it is raised imperishable', suggesting the natural body is raised as a spiritual body, but a body nevertheless.	The disciples may have felt Jesus' presence spiritually rather than seeing him physically.
Catholic and Orthodox Christians believe people's bodies are transformed into a glorified state in which suffering will not exist.	Christians believe in the soul and it is the soul that rises again, not the body.

RECAP

Essential information:

- [ ] Christians believe in an **afterlife** (life after death) that depends on faith in God.
- [ ] The afterlife begins at death or at the **Day of Judgement**, when Jesus will come to judge the living and the dead.
- [ ] Judgement will be based on how people have behaved during their lifetimes, as well as their faith in following Jesus. This has an effect on how Christians choose to live their lives today.

The afterlife

Christian beliefs about life after death vary, but many believe that:

- They will be **resurrected** and receive **eternal life** after they die.
- This is a gift from God, and **dependent on faith** in God.
- They will be **judged by God** at some point after they die, and either rewarded by being sent to heaven or punished by being sent to hell.
- This judgement will happen either **very soon after death** or **on the Day of Judgement**. This is a time in the future when the world will end and Christ will come again to judge the living and the dead.

Some of these beliefs about the afterlife are found in the **Apostles' Creed**, which is an important statement of Christian faith.

> **"**He ascended into heaven, and is seated at the right hand of the Father, and he will come to judge the living and the dead: I believe in […] the resurrection of the body; and the life everlasting. **"**
>
> *The Apostles' Creed*

Judgement

- Christians believe that after they die, God will judge them on their **behaviour and actions** during their lifetime, as well as their **faith in Jesus** as God's Son.
- In the Bible, Jesus' **parable of the Sheep and the Goats** describes how God will judge people.
- This parable teaches Christians that **in serving others**, **they are serving Jesus**, so this is the way they should live their lives.

JUDGEMENT

for good actions and behaviour

for faith in God and Jesus

> **"**For I was hungry and you gave me something to eat, I was thirsty and you gave me something to drink, I was a stranger and you invited me in, I needed clothes and you clothed me, I was ill and you looked after me, I was in prison and you came to visit me. **"**
>
> *Matthew 25:35–36* [NIV]

- Before he died, Jesus told his disciples he would prepare a place for them in heaven with God. He also made it clear that **having faith in him and following his teachings** was essential for being able to enter heaven when he said:

> **"**I am the way and the truth and the life. No one comes to the Father except through me. **"**
>
> *John 14:6* [NIV]

APPLY

(A) Explain **two** Christian teachings about judgement. **Refer to sacred writings or another source of Christian belief and teaching in your answer.**
(AQA Specimen question paper, 2017)

(B) **Evaluate the statement**, 'The afterlife is a good way to get people to behave themselves and help others.' Refer to two developed Christian arguments, and two developed non-religious arguments. **Write a justified conclusion.**

TIP

When writing a justified conclusion, do not just repeat everything you have already said. Instead, weigh up the arguments and come to a personal view about their persuasiveness.

1.10 Heaven and hell

RECAP

Essential information:

- [ ] Many Christians believe God's judgement will result in eternal reward or eternal punishment.
- [ ] **Heaven** is the state or place of eternal happiness and peace in the presence of God.
- [ ] **Hell** is the place of eternal suffering or the state of being without God.

What happens after God's judgement?

- After God's judgement, Christians believe they will either **experience eternal happiness in the presence of God** (heaven), or **be unable to experience God's presence** (hell).
- Catholics believe some people might enter an intermediate state, called purgatory, before they enter heaven.
- Knowledge of these states is limited and linked to imagery from the past.

Heaven and purgatory

- **Heaven** is thought to be either a **physical place** or **spiritual state** of peace, joy, freedom from pain and a chance to be with loved ones.
- Traditional images of heaven often show God on a throne with Jesus next to him and angels all around him, or a garden paradise.
- Christians differ in their views about **who is allowed into heaven**, where there may be:
  - only Christians (believers in Jesus)
  - Christians and other religious people who have pleased God by living good lives
  - baptised Christians, regardless of how they lived their lives.
- However, many Christians believe heaven is a reward for **both faith and actions** – not just one of these – as the parable of the Sheep and the Goats seems to show (see page 22).
- **Purgatory** is an intermediate state where souls are cleansed in order to enter heaven. This is a Catholic belief.

Hell

- **Hell** is seen as the opposite of heaven – a state of existence without God.
- It is often pictured as a **place of eternal torment** in a fiery pit ruled by Satan (a name for the Devil), who is the power and source of evil.
- However, many people question whether a loving God would condemn people to eternal torment and pain in hell.
- Christians who believe God would not do this see hell as an **eternal state of mind** of **being cut off from the possibility of God**.
- Hell would then be what awaits someone who did not acknowledge God or follow his teachings during their life.

APPLY

(A) Give **two** reasons why some people do not believe in hell.

(B) **Make a list of arguments** for and against the idea that heaven and hell were invented to encourage people to behave themselves.

TIP
If this question said 'some Christians', you should offer Christian objections to the idea of hell. 'Some people' means you can give non-religious reasons if you wish.

23

1.11 Sin and salvation

Essential information:

☐ **Sin** is any thought or action that separates humans from God.

☐ **Original sin** is the in-built tendency to do wrong and disobey God, which Catholics believe all people are born with.

☐ The ways Christians can be saved from sin to gain salvation include following God's **law**, receiving God's **grace**, and being guided by the **Holy Spirit**.

The origins and meanings of sin

A sin is any **thought or action that separates humans from God**. Sinful thoughts (such as anger) can lead to sinful actions (such as murder).

- Some sins, like murder or assault, are illegal.
- Other sins, like adultery, are not illegal but are against the laws of God.

Christians believe that all humans commit sins. Some Christians (particularly Catholics) also believe humans are born with an in-built tendency to sin, called **original sin**.

- The idea of original sin comes from Adam and Eve's disobedience of God, when they ate the fruit of the tree of knowledge of good and evil which was forbidden by God. This was the first (original) sin.
- The result of their sin was separation from God, and the introduction of death into the world.

Christians believe **God gave people free will**, but they should use their freedom to make choices God would approve of, otherwise they will separate themselves from God. God provides people with the guidance to make good choices in his law, for example the Ten Commandments (Exodus 20:1–19), the Beatitudes (Matthew 5:1–12) and other Christian teachings.

Salvation

- **Salvation** means to be saved from sin and its consequences, and to be granted eternal life with God.
- Salvation **repairs the damage caused by sin**, which has separated people from God.

There are two main Christian ideas about how salvation can come about:

- Through **doing good works** – the Old Testament makes it clear that salvation comes through faith in God and obeying God's law.

> 66 In the same way, faith by itself, if it is not accompanied by action, is dead. 99
>
> *James 2:17* [NIV]

- Through **grace** – salvation is given freely by God through faith in Jesus. It is not deserved or earned, but is a free gift of God's love.

> 66 For it is by grace you have been saved 99
>
> *Ephesians 2:8* [NIV]

- Christians believe it is the **Holy Spirit** who gives grace to Christians and continues to guide them in their daily lives, to help them achieve salvation.

A Explain **two** Christian teachings about the means of salvation. **Refer to sacred writings or another source of Christian belief and teaching in your answer.**
(AQA Specimen question paper, 2017)

B 'As nobody is perfect, it is impossible not to sin.' **Evaluate this argument** and explain your reasoning.

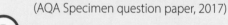

"It is perfectly possible to live a good life without sin. Jesus lived his life without sin. Many saints have lived good lives without acting badly to other people. It is true that nobody is totally perfect, but that's different. Sin separates you from God and goes against God's law, and there are many people who stay close to God and keep his commandments, so I disagree with the statement."

RECAP

Essential information:

☐ Christians believe that salvation is offered through the life and teaching of Jesus.

☐ Jesus' resurrection shows that God accepted Jesus' sacrifice as **atonement**. This means that through the sacrifice of his death, Jesus restored the relationship between God and humanity that was broken when Adam and Eve sinned.

> **TIP**
> To remember the meaning of 'atonement', think of it as 'at-one-ment', because Jesus' death and resurrection make people at one with God.

The role of Jesus in salvation

Christians believe Jesus' life, death and resurrection had a crucial role to play in God's plan for salvation because:

- Jesus' crucifixion **made up for the original sin** of Adam and Eve.
- The death of Jesus, as an innocent man, was necessary to **restore the relationship between God and believers**, to bring them salvation.
- Jesus' resurrection shows the goodness of Jesus defeated the evil of sin. It was proof that God had accepted Jesus' sacrifice on behalf of humankind.
- Jesus' resurrection means humans can now receive forgiveness for their sins.
- Jesus' death and resurrection made it possible for all who follow his teachings to **gain eternal life**.

> **❝** For the wages of sin is death, but the gift of God is eternal life in Christ Jesus our Lord. **❞**
> *Romans 6:23* [NIV]

> **TIP**
> This quote shows the Christian belief that death came into the world as a punishment for sin, but salvation is offered through the life and teaching of Jesus.

Atonement

- Atonement **removes the effects of sin** and allows people to restore their relationship with God.
- Many Christians believe that through the sacrifice of his death, Jesus took the sins of all humanity on himself and paid the debt for them all. He **atoned for the sins of humanity**.
- This sacrifice makes it possible for all who follow Jesus' teachings to **receive eternal life** with God.

> **❝** […] if anybody does sin, we have an advocate with the Father – Jesus Christ, the Righteous One. He is the atoning sacrifice for our sins, and not only for ours but also for the sins of the whole world. **❞**
> *1 John 2:1–2* [NIV]

Jesus' death + grace and good works

sin — atonement

APPLY

(A) Give **two** reasons why the death and resurrection of Jesus is important to Christians.

(B) Here are some sentences that could be used to evaluate the statement, 'Salvation is God's greatest gift to humans.'

Sort them into arguments in support of the statement, and arguments in support of different views. Try to put them in a logical order. What do you think is missing from these statements to make a top level answer? Explain how the answer could be improved.

1. Atheists do not consider salvation important because they do not think there is a God who saves people.	5. Without salvation, humankind would have to pay the price of human sin.
2. God shows his great love for people by sending his Son to save us.	6. People may doubt the truth of Jesus' resurrection so they don't see the need for a belief in salvation.
3. Even some religious people may think there are greater gifts to humans, such as nature or life itself.	7. Some people may question whether God is loving if God demands the death of his Son in payment for human sin.
4. Everyone needs forgiveness from God.	8. Humans should be grateful every day of their lives for Jesus' sacrifice on their behalf.

Test the 1 mark question

1   Which **one** of the following is the idea that God became human in Jesus?

   A | Atonement   B | Incarnation   C | Resurrection   D | Creation   **[1 mark]**

2   Which **one** of the following is the idea that God is loving?

   A | Omniscient   B | Omnipotent   C | Benevolent   D | Immanent   **[1 mark]**

Test the 2 mark question

3   Give **two** ways that Christians believe salvation can come about.   **[2 marks]**

   1) _____

   2) _____

4   Give **two** Christian beliefs about life after death.   **[2 marks]**

   1) _____

   2) _____

Test the 4 mark question

5   Explain **two** ways in which a belief in Jesus' crucifixion influences Christians today.   **[4 marks]**

● **Explain one way.**	One way in which a belief in Jesus' crucifixion influences Christians today is that they believe that the crucifixion was a sacrifice Jesus chose to make for them
● Develop your explanation with more detail/an example/ reference to a religious teaching or quotation.	in order to give them the opportunity to be granted forgiveness by God, so they can live in confidence that their sins have been forgiven.
● **Explain a second way.**	A second way in which a belief in Jesus' crucifixion influences Christians today is that it helps Christians who are suffering because they know Jesus suffered as well.
● Develop your explanation with more detail/an example/ reference to a religious teaching or quotation.	For example, Christians who are suffering persecution for their faith will be comforted to know that Jesus understands what they are going through because he too was innocent and suffered for his beliefs.

6   Explain **two** ways in which the belief in creation by God influences Christians today.   **[4 marks]**

● **Explain one way.**	
● Develop your explanation with more detail/an example/ reference to a religious teaching or quotation.	
● **Explain a second way.**	
● Develop your explanation with more detail/an example/ reference to a religious teaching or quotation.	

TIP

The student has explained the influence a belief in Jesus' crucifixion has on a Christian's **attitude** (their confidence in being forgiven and their comfort in dealing with their own suffering). You could also discuss the influence of this belief on a Christian's **life** (e.g. it might encourage them to spread the message of Jesus or to make the sign of the cross when they pray to remind themselves of Jesus' sacrifice).

7   Explain **two** ways in which the belief that God is loving influences Christians today.   **[4 marks]**

1 Exam practice

Test the 5 mark question

8 Explain **two** Christian beliefs about salvation.

Refer to sacred writings or another source of Christian belief and teaching in your answer.   **[5 marks]**

● **Explain one belief.**	One Christian belief about salvation is that salvation can be gained through good works.
● Develop your explanation with more detail/an example.	These good works may be following teachings such as the Ten Commandments, the Golden Rule and 'love your neighbour'. Worshipping and praying regularly also help Christians to earn salvation.
● **Explain a second belief.**	A second Christian belief about salvation is that it is gained through grace.
● Develop your explanation with more detail/an example.	God gives salvation to people who have faith in Jesus. It is a gift for the faithful.
● Add a reference to sacred writings or another source of Christian belief and teaching. If you prefer, you can add this reference to your first belief instead.	Paul wrote in his letters that it is through grace, which is a gift from God, that people are saved, not simply through their good works.

> **TIP**
> The references to scripture here count as development of your first point.

9 Explain **two** Christian teachings about God.

Refer to sacred writings or another source of Christian belief and teaching in your answer.   **[5 marks]**

● **Explain one teaching.**	
● Develop your explanation with more detail/an example.	
● **Explain a second teaching.**	
● Develop your explanation with more detail/an example.	
● Add a reference to sacred writings or another source of Christian belief and teaching. If you prefer, you can add this reference to your first teaching instead.	

> **TIP**
> You only need to make one reference to scripture in your answer. It can support either your first or your second point.

10 Explain **two** Christian teachings about atonement.

Refer to sacred writings or another source of Christian belief and teaching in your answer.   **[5 marks]**

Test the 12 mark question

11 'The stories of the incarnation prove that Jesus was the Son of God.'

Evaluate this statement. In your answer you should:

- refer to Christian teaching
- give reasoned arguments to support this statement
- give reasoned arguments to support a different point of view
- reach a justified conclusion.

[12 marks]
[+3 SPaG mark

REASONED ARGUMENTS IN SUPPORT OF THE STATEMENT ● **Explain why some people would agree with the statement.** ● Develop your explanation with more detail and examples. ● Refer to religious teaching. Use a quote or paraphrase or refer to a religious authority. ● **Evaluate the arguments.** Is this a good argument or not? Explain why you think this.	*Christians believe in the incarnation. This means that God took human form in Jesus. The stories of Jesus' birth show he was not conceived in the normal way. The fact he was conceived through the actions of God and born of a virgin proves that he was special and if God was involved it is likely that Jesus was his son. However, even though he was a physical person, he was also God at the same time. John's gospel calls Jesus 'the Son of God' and says he was the Word made flesh, living among us. This supports the idea that Jesus was both God and human.*
REASONED ARGUMENTS SUPPORTING A DIFFERENT VIEW ● **Explain why some people would support a different view.** ● Develop your explanation with more detail and examples. ● Refer to religious teaching. Use a quote or paraphrase or refer to a religious authority. ● **Evaluate the arguments.** Is this a good argument or not? Explain why you think this.	*Many people do not agree that Jesus was conceived through the actions of God and believe that Mary, his mother, was not a virgin. If the stories of the incarnation are not correct, they cannot be used as evidence that Jesus was the Son of God although his actions showed he was very special.*
CONCLUSION ● **Give a justified conclusion.** ● Include your own opinion together with your own reasoning. ● **Include evaluation.** Explain why you think one viewpoint is stronger than the other or why they are equally strong. ● Do not just repeat arguments you have already used without explaining how they apply to your reasoned opinion/conclusion.	*It may be true that the title 'Son of God' does not mean that there is such a close relationship between Jesus and God. It is possible that he was chosen by God, maybe when he was baptised, to do good works on earth and tell people about Christianity without there being a family relationship between himself and God. If this is true, there is no such thing as incarnation as far as Jesus is concerned.*

TIP
The question is about stories (plural) so it would improve the answer to mention details of Jesus' conception in the gospels of Matthew and Luke.

TIP
This argument could be developed further for more marks. For example, after the sentence that ends 'not a virgin' you might add 'Mary was engaged to Joseph, making it possible that Joseph was Jesus' father.'

TIP
The conclusion shows logical chains of reasoning. It evaluates different interpretations of the title 'Son of God' in relation to the stories of the incarnation. The examiner will want to see that you can link ideas together when developing your argument, and not just repeat what you have said already.

12 'There is no such place as hell.'

Evaluate this statement. In your answer you should:

- refer to Christian teaching
- give reasoned arguments to support this statement
- give reasoned arguments to support a different point of view
- reach a justified conclusion.

TIP

Spelling, punctuation and grammar is assessed on each 12 mark question, so make sure you are careful to use your best written English.

[12 marks]
[+3 SPaG marks]

REASONED ARGUMENTS IN SUPPORT OF THE STATEMENT ● **Explain why some people would agree with the statement.** ● Develop your explanation with more detail and examples. ● Refer to religious teaching. Use a quote or paraphrase or refer to a religious authority. ● **Evaluate the arguments.** Is this a good argument or not? Explain why you think this.	
REASONED ARGUMENTS SUPPORTING A DIFFERENT VIEW ● **Explain why some people would support a different view.** ● Develop your explanation with more detail and examples. ● Refer to religious teaching. Use a quote or paraphrase or refer to a religious authority. ● **Evaluate the arguments.** Is this a good argument or not? Explain why you think this.	
CONCLUSION ● **Give a justified conclusion.** ● Include your own opinion together with your own reasoning. ● **Include evaluation.** Explain why you think one viewpoint is stronger than the other or why they are equally strong. ● Do not just repeat arguments you have already used without explaining how they apply to your reasoned opinion/conclusion.	

TIP

It's essential to include evaluation because this is the key skill that you are being tested on in the 12 mark question. You can evaluate after each viewpoint, and/or at the end as part of your justified conclusion.

13 'The best way to gain salvation is to obey God's law.'

Evaluate this statement. In your answer you should:

- refer to Christian teaching
- give reasoned arguments to support this statement
- give reasoned arguments to support a different point of view
- reach a justified conclusion.

[12 marks]
[+3 SPaG marks]

Check your answers using the mark scheme on pages 158–159. How did you do?
To feel more secure in the content you need to remember, re-read pages 14–25.
To remind yourself of what the examiner is looking for, go to pages 7–13.

2.1 Worship

RECAP

Essential information:

☐ **Worship** is the act of religious praise, honour or devotion. It is a way for Christians to show their deep love and honour to God.

☐ Worship can take different forms, including liturgical, non-liturgical and informal worship.

☐ **Private worship** is when believers praise or honour God in their own home.

Why do Christians worship?

| To praise and thank God | To ask for forgiveness | To seek God's help for themselves or others | To deepen their relationship with God and strengthen their faith |

Different forms of worship

Type of worship	What form does it take?	Examples	Why is it important for Christians?
liturgical worship is a church service that follows a set structure or ritual	• takes place in a church • priest leads the congregation and may perform symbolic actions • formal prayers with set responses • Bible passages are read out, there may be a sermon • music and hymns	the Eucharist for Catholic, Orthodox and Anglican Churches	• worldwide set order for service that is familiar to everyone • ritual passed down through generations gives a sense of tradition • Bible readings follow the Christian calendar and teach Christian history and faith
non-liturgical worship is a service that does not follow a set text or ritual	• takes place in a church • often focused on Bible readings followed by a sermon • may also have prayers and hymns but there is no set order, the number and type can change from week to week	services in non-Conformist churches, e.g. Methodist, Baptist, United Reformed	• services can be planned and ordered to suit a certain theme • non-Conformist churches place an emphasis on the word of God in the Bible
informal worship is a type of non-liturgical worship that is 'spontaneous' or 'charismatic' in nature	• community or house churches meet in private homes and share food • Quaker worship is mainly silent, people speak when moved by God to offer their thoughts or read from the Bible • 'charismatic' worship may involve dancing, clapping, calling out and speaking in tongues	community or house churches, Quaker worship, charismatic ('led by the spirit') worship of the Pentecostal Church	• the style of worship in house churches is similar to the worship of early Christians • people can share readings and prayers and can take an active part in church by calling out or speaking without formal training • service may have an emotional impact with a feeling of personal revelation from God

APPLY

 A Going on pilgrimage, celebrating festivals and religious art are also forms of worship. Give **two** more ways that Christians worship.

B 'Worship is most powerful when believers follow a set ritual.'

List arguments to support this statement and arguments to support a different point of view.

TIP
The arguments should apply to Christianity. Try to use religious language (see key terms in red).

RECAP

Essential information:

☐ **Prayer** is communicating with God, either silently or through words of praise, thanksgiving or confession, or requests for God's help or guidance.

☐ Christians may use **set prayers** that have been written down and said more than once by more than one person. An example is **the Lord's Prayer**, which is the prayer Jesus taught to his disciples.

☐ Christians may also use **informal prayers** (made up by an individual using his or her own words) to communicate with God. Some Christians find they can express their needs to God more easily by using their own words.

The importance of prayer

encourages reflection in the middle of a busy life

enables Christians to talk and listen to God

gives strength in times of trouble

Why is prayer important?

helps Christians to keep a close relationship with God

gives a sense of peace

helps Christians to accept God's will even if it means suffering

The Lord's Prayer

> ❝Our Father in heaven, hallowed be your name,
> your Kingdom come, your will be done,
> on earth as in heaven.
> Give us today our daily bread.
> Forgive us our sins
> as we forgive those who sin against us.
> Lead us not into temptation, but deliver us from evil.
> For the kingdom, the power, and the glory are yours
> now and for ever. Amen.❞
>
> *The Lord's Prayer*

- When Jesus' disciples asked him to teach them how to pray, he answered with the Lord's Prayer.
- Christians see it as a **model of good prayer**, as it combines praise to God with asking for one's needs.
- It reminds Christians to **forgive others in order to be forgiven**, since prayer is only effective if people's relationships with others are right.
- It reminds Christians that **God is the Father of the whole Christian community**, and it can create a sense of unity when everyone in the congregation says it together.
- The Lord's Prayer is often used in worship and is nearly always said at Holy Communion, baptisms, marriages and funerals. It is also used in schools and in commemoration services in Britain.

APPLY

A Give **two** reasons why the Lord's Prayer is important to Christians.

B 'Private worship has more meaning for a Christian than public worship.'
(AQA Specimen question paper, 2017)

Develop this argument to support the statement by explaining in more detail, adding an example, or referring to a relevant religious teaching or quotation.

"An individual Christian can choose how they want to worship in private, whereas in public worship they have to follow what everyone else is saying and doing. Therefore private worship has more meaning because they can put their heart and soul into it."

TIP
Always analyse the statement carefully. For example, here 'has more meaning' might depend on an individual's reasons for prayer.

RECAP

Essential information:

☐ **Sacraments** are holy rituals through which believers receive a special gift of grace (free gift of God's love). Some Christian denominations recognise seven sacraments while others acknowledge fewer.

☐ **Baptism** is the ritual through which a person becomes a member of the Church. It involves the use of water to symbolise the washing away of sin.

☐ **Infant baptism** is for babies and young children. **Believers' baptism** is for people who are old enough to understand the significance of the ritual.

The sacraments

- **Catholic and Orthodox** Christians recognise **seven** sacraments: baptism, confirmation, Holy Communion, marriage, Holy Orders, reconciliation and the anointing of the sick.
- Many **Protestant** churches recognise **two** sacraments – baptism and Holy Communion – because they believe Jesus taught people to undertake these.

- Some churches that practise believers' baptism consider it to be important but not a 'sacrament'.
- Some churches, like the Quakers or Salvation Army, do not see any ritual or ceremony as being a 'sacrament'.

Baptism

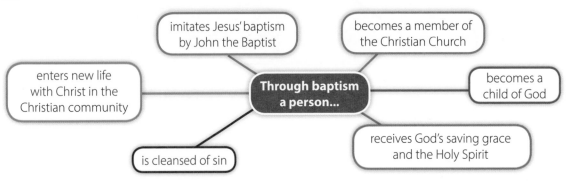

imitates Jesus' baptism by John the Baptist

becomes a member of the Christian Church

enters new life with Christ in the Christian community

Through baptism a person...

becomes a child of God

is cleansed of sin

receives God's saving grace and the Holy Spirit

Infant baptism and believers' baptism

	Practised by	Reasons why	What happens
Infant baptism	Catholic, Orthodox, Anglican, Methodist, and United Reformed Christians	• Removes original sin (Catholic and Orthodox belief). • Allows the child to be welcomed into the Church as soon as possible. • The parents can thank God for their new baby and celebrate with family and friends.	• The priest or minister pours blessed water over the baby's head and says, 'I baptise you in the name of the Father, and of the Son, and of the Holy Spirit.' • Godparents and parents promise to bring up the child as a Christian. • The child is welcomed into the Christian community.
Believers' baptism	Baptists, Pentecostalists	• People should be old enough to consciously make a mature decision about their faith. • The decision to live a life dedicated to Jesus is what saves a person, rather than the baptism itself.	• The person is fully immersed in a pool which symbolises cleansing from sin and rising to new life in Christ. • When asked whether they are willing to change their lives, the person gives a brief testimony of their faith in Jesus. • The person is baptised 'in the name of the Father, and of the Son, and of the Holy Spirit.'

APPLY

A Explain **two** contrasting ways in which Christians practise baptism and develop each point.

B 'Parents should not have their children baptised if they have no intention of bringing them up as Christians.'

Evaluate this statement.

2.4 The sacraments: Holy Communion

RECAP

Essential information:

☐ **Holy Communion** (also known as the Eucharist) is the sacrament that uses bread and wine to celebrate the sacrifice of Jesus on the cross and his resurrection.

☐ It recalls the Last Supper of Jesus, using his words and actions.

☐ Christians interpret the meaning of Holy Communion in different ways, but all agree that it brings them closer to each other and to God.

The meaning of Holy Communion

Holy Communion is a service which celebrates and gives thanks for the sacrifice of Jesus' death and resurrection (see pages 19–20). It has different meanings for different Christians:

- **Catholics, Orthodox Christians** and **some Anglicans** believe the bread and wine become **the body and blood of Christ**. This means Jesus is fully present in the bread and wine. This is a divine mystery that helps believers share in the saving sacrifice of Jesus' death and resurrection.
- **Protestant Christians** celebrate Holy Communion as a **reminder of the Last Supper**. They do not believe the bread and wine become the body and blood of Christ. Instead, the bread and wine remain **symbols of Jesus' sacrifice**, which helps believers to reflect on its meaning today.

> **❝**For whenever you eat this bread and drink this cup, you proclaim the Lord's death until he comes. **❞**
>
> *1 Corinthians 11:26* [NIV]

The impact of Holy Communion

For many Christians, Holy Communion is at the centre of their lives and worship. It affects individuals, local communities and the wider society in a number of ways:

Individuals	Communities	Wider society
• Christians **receive God's grace** by joining in the sacrifice of Jesus. • This helps to strengthen their faith. • They become closer to God.	• Holy Communion **brings the community of believers together** in unity by sharing the bread and wine. • This can provide support and encouragement for those going through a difficult time.	• Holy Communion **acts as a call to love others in practical ways**. • It encourages Christians to work for equality and justice for all. • Many churches collect money during the service to help support those in need, such as the poor or homeless.

APPLY

(A) Explain **two** ways in which Holy Communion has an impact on the lives of believers.

(B) Use the table below with arguments about the statement, 'It is more important to help the poor than to celebrate Holy Communion.'

TIP

Decide on two ways and explain each. Do not simply list a number of ways without developing any of your points.

Write a paragraph to explain whether you agree or disagree with the statement, having evaluated both sides of the argument.

In support of the statement	Other views
The poor need urgent help, particularly if they are living in less economically developed countries, so of course it is more important to help them than to receive Holy Communion. Christians are taught to love their neighbour so that must come before their own needs. Remembering Jesus' death and resurrection through Holy Communion is nice, but not very useful to anyone. It's just focusing on the past when people should be thinking about the present.	It doesn't need to be such a stark choice. After all, when Christians break bread together at Holy Communion they remember that people in the world are starving and they try to help them. Many churches collect money for the poor during the service of Holy Communion, so celebrating this sacrament encourages people to care for others, not just themselves. 'Eucharist' means 'thanksgiving', so it makes Christians grateful for God's love and this makes them want to share it.

RECAP

Essential information:

☐ In most churches the Holy Communion service has two parts: the ministry of the Word (which focuses on the Bible), and the ministry of Holy Communion (the offering, consecrating and sharing of bread and wine).

☐ Christians have different practices when it comes to celebrating Holy Communion.

Differences between Holy Communion services

- In the **Orthodox Church**, Holy Communion is called the Divine Liturgy, and is believed to recreate heaven on earth. Much of the service is held at the altar behind the iconostasis, which is a screen that represents the divide between heaven and earth. The priest passes through the iconostasis using the Royal Doors.

- Holy Communion in the **Catholic and Anglican Churches** is very similar. The main difference is that Catholics believe the bread and wine turn into the body and blood of Christ, whereas many Anglicans believe Jesus is only present in a spiritual way when the bread and wine are being eaten.

Further examples of how Holy Communion services differ from each other include the following:

Orthodox Divine Liturgy	Catholic Mass and Anglican Holy Communion	Holy Communion in the United Reformed Church
Liturgy of the Word: • There are hymns, prayers and a Bible reading. • The priest comes through the Royal Doors to chant the Gospel. • There may be a sermon. **Liturgy of the Faithful:** • The priest receives wine and bread baked by church members. • Prayers are offered for the church, the local community and the world. • Behind the iconostasis, the priest says the words of Jesus at the Last Supper. • Most of the bread is consecrated as the body and blood of Christ. • The priest distributes holy bread and wine on a spoon. • Prayers of thanksgiving are said. • Unconsecrated pieces of bread are given to people to take home, as a sign of belonging to the Christian community.	**Liturgy of the Word:** • There are three Bible readings, a psalm and a homily. • The Creed is said. • Prayers are said for the Church, the local community, the world, and the sick and the dead. **Liturgy of the Eucharist:** • In the Anglican Holy Communion, people give a sign of peace to each other. • Offerings of bread and wine are brought to the altar. • The priest repeats the words of Jesus at the Last Supper over the bread and the wine. • People say the Lord's Prayer. • In the Catholic Mass, the sign of peace is given at this point. • People receive the bread and wine. • The priest blesses people and sends them out to live the gospel.	• The service begins with a hymn and prayer of praise and thanksgiving. • Bible readings and a sermon are given. • Prayers for the world and the needs of particular people are said. • The minister repeats the words and actions of Jesus at the Last Supper. • There is an 'open table' so anyone who wishes may receive Holy Communion. • Sometimes the bread is cut beforehand, other times it is broken and passed around by the congregation. • Wine is sometimes non-alcoholic and is usually distributed in small cups. • The service ends with a prayer of thanksgiving, a blessing, and an encouragement to go out and serve God.

APPLY

(A) Explain **two** contrasting ways in which Holy Communion is celebrated in Christianity. (AQA Specimen question paper, 2017)

(B) **Write a paragraph** in response to the statement, 'Holy Communion services should focus more on the Liturgy of the Word than on the Holy Communion itself.' **Develop your reasons** and include a reference to scripture or religious teaching in your answer.

TIP

Holy Communion services have many similarities. Be sure to choose aspects that show a real contrast.

RECAP

Essential information:

☐ A **pilgrimage** is a journey made by a believer to a holy site for religious reasons. As well as making a physical journey to a sacred place, the pilgrim also makes a spiritual journey towards God.

☐ A pilgrimage gives many opportunities for prayer and worship, and is itself an act of worship and devotion.

☐ Two popular pilgrimage sites for Christians are Lourdes (a town in France) and Iona (a Scottish island).

The role and importance of pilgrimage

meet others who share the same faith

grow closer to God

strengthen faith in God

experience a holy place

Why go on a pilgrimage?

be forgiven for sin

help other pilgrims who are disabled or ill

reflect on one's life

seek a cure for illness

thank God for a blessing

pray for something special

A pilgrimage can impact on a Christian's life in a number of ways. It can:

- give them a better understanding of their faith
- renew their enthusiasm for living a Christian life
- help them to see problems in a new light
- help them to feel cleansed from sin

- help them to feel more connected to the Christian community
- give them a good feeling about helping other pilgrims who are disabled or ill.

Places of Christian pilgrimage

Place	Significance	Activities
Lourdes (a town in France)	• Where Mary, Jesus' mother, is said to have appeared in a number of visions to a girl called Bernadette. • Mary told Bernadette to dig in the ground, and when she did a spring of water appeared. • The water is believed to have healing properties, and a number of healing miracles are claimed to have taken place here.	• Pilgrims go to Lourdes to bathe in the waters of the spring, or to help other pilgrims who are ill or disabled to bathe in the waters. • Pilgrims also pray for healing or forgiveness. • They may recite the rosary together.
Iona (an island off the coast of Scotland)	• Where St Columba established a monastic community in the 6th century AD. • The community now has an ecumenical centre where pilgrims can stay.	• Because it is quiet, peaceful and a place of natural beauty, pilgrims can spend time praying, reading the Bible, and reflecting or meditating. • Pilgrims can also attend services in the abbey church, take part in workshops, and visit the island's holy or historic sites.

APPLY

 A Explain **two** contrasting examples of Christian pilgrimage. (AQA Specimen question paper, 2017)

 B 'There is no difference between a pilgrimage and a holiday.'

Develop this argument against the statement by explaining in more detail, adding an example or referring to Christian teaching.

TIP

You need to explain why the examples are contrasting, rather than just describing the two places, so be sure to explain the different reasons why pilgrims go there.

"Although a pilgrimage can seem a lot like a holiday, especially if you travel abroad, there is a big difference. A pilgrimage is a spiritual journey that people undertake for religious reasons rather than just to sightsee."

RECAP

Essential information:

☐ A **festival** is a day or period of celebration for religious reasons.

☐ Festivals help Christians to remember and celebrate the major events in their religion – particularly the life, death and resurrection of Jesus.

☐ **Christmas** commemorates the incarnation and the birth of Jesus. Celebrations begin on 25 December and last 12 days, ending with Epiphany (which recalls the visit of the wise men).

☐ **Easter** celebrates the resurrection of Jesus from the dead. Celebrations begin before Easter Sunday and finish with the feast of Pentecost.

Christmas

Christmas **commemorates the incarnation of Jesus**, which is the belief that God became human in Jesus (see page 18). The celebrations reflect Christian beliefs and teachings in the following ways:

- **lights** represent Jesus as the light coming into the world of darkness
- **nativity scenes** show baby Jesus born into poverty
- **carol services** with Bible readings remind Christians about God's promise of a saviour and the events of Jesus' birth

- **Midnight Mass** reflects the holiness of the night and the joy Christians feel at Jesus' birth
- **Christmas cards and gifts** recall the wise men's gifts to Jesus
- Christians **give to charity** in this time of peace and goodwill because God gave humanity the gift of Jesus, his Son.

Easter

Easter is the most important Christian festival, which **celebrates Jesus' rising from the dead** (see page 20).

Holy Week (the week before Easter Sunday) remembers the events leading up to Jesus' crucifixion, including his arrest and trial.

- On **Saturday night**, some churches hold a special service to celebrate Christ's resurrection.
- Orthodox Christians walk with candles in procession, then enter the dark church as if going into Jesus' empty tomb.
- The priest announces 'Christ is risen!' to which people answer 'He is risen indeed.'
- Catholics and Anglicans have a vigil that begins in darkness, before the Paschal candle is lit to symbolise the risen Christ. The service ends with Holy Communion.

On **Good Friday** (the day Jesus was crucified), there are special services and processions led by a person carrying a cross.

- On **Easter Sunday**, churches are filled with flowers and special hymns are sung to rejoice at Jesus' resurrection.
- Services are held at sunrise, and shared breakfasts include eggs to symbolise new life.

> **"**Christ is risen from the dead, trampling down death by death, and upon those in the tombs bestowing life. **"**
>
> *Traditional Orthodox hymn at the Easter Divine Liturgy*

APPLY

A Give **two** ways in which Christians celebrate the festival of Easter.

B 'Christmas is no longer a religious festival.' **Evaluate this statement.**

RECAP

Essential information:

☐ **The Church** is the holy people of God, also called the Body of Christ, among whom Christ is present and active.

☐ **A church** is a building in which Christians worship.

☐ Individual churches and the Church as a whole help the local community in a variety of ways, including the provision of **food banks**. These give food for free to people who cannot afford to buy it.

What does the Church do?

Individual churches and the Church as a whole help the local community in many ways.

Individual churches:

- educate people about Christianity (e.g. Bible study groups)
- are meeting places for prayer and worship
- provide activities for younger people (e.g. youth clubs)
- are places where Christians can socialise and obtain spiritual guidance.

The Church:

- supports local projects such as food banks
- provides social services such as schooling and medical care
- helps those in need
- campaigns for justice.

> ❝And God placed all things under his [Jesus'] feet and appointed him to be head over everything for the church, which is his body. ❞
>
> *Ephesians 1:22–23 [NIV]*

TIP
You could use this quote in your exam to show that Christians think of the Church as the followers of Jesus, who together are the body of Christ on earth.

Examples of the Church helping the local community

The Trussell Trust and The Oasis Project are two organisations that help the local community by providing food banks and other services. The work of these charities is based on Christian principles (such as the parable of the Sheep and the Goats).

The Trussell Trust
• A charity running over 400 food banks in the UK.
• These provide emergency food, help and support to people in crisis in the UK.
• Non-perishable food is donated by churches, supermarkets, schools, businesses and individuals.
• Doctors, health visitors and social workers identify people in crisis and issue them with a food voucher.
• Their aim is to bring religious and non-religious people together to help end poverty and hunger.

The Oasis Project
• A community hub run by Plymouth Methodist Mission Circuit.
• Provides an internet café, creative courses, a job club, training opportunities, a meeting place and a food bank.
• Spiritual and practical help is given to those in need because of ill health, learning disabilities, domestic violence, substance abuse, low income and housing problems.

TIP
You will not be asked about these particular organisations in your exam, but if you learn what they do, you will be able to give detailed examples of how the Church helps in the local community.

APPLY

A Give **two** meanings of the word 'church'.

B Here is a response to the statement, 'There will always be a need to feed hungry people in Britain.' Can you **improve this answer** by including religious beliefs?

"At first this statement appears untrue. No one should be hungry in Britain as there is a welfare state. People who can't work to feed themselves or their families can apply for benefits."

"However, I agree with the statement because people can suddenly be faced with bills they can't pay, or lose their jobs, or become ill so they can't work. It may take many weeks to apply for benefits and be accepted, so what do they do in the meantime? If they don't have much savings they will be really hard up and need the help of food banks."

RECAP

Essential information:

☐ Christians should help others in the local community because Jesus taught that people should show **agape** love (a Biblical word meaning selfless, sacrificial, unconditional love).

☐ Christians believe it is important to put their faith into action. They do this through many organisations and projects that help vulnerable people in the community.

☐ **Street Pastors** are people who are trained to patrol the streets in urban areas. They help vulnerable people by providing a reassuring presence on the street.

The importance of helping in the local community

- Jesus taught that **Christians should help others by showing agape love** towards them. For example, in the parable of the Sheep and the Goats, Jesus teaches Christians they should give practical help to people in need (see page 22).
- Two examples of Christian organisations that provide practical help to local communities are Street Pastors and Parish Nursing Ministries UK.

> **"** Faith by itself, if it is not accompanied by action, is dead. **"**
>
> *James 2:17 [NIV]*

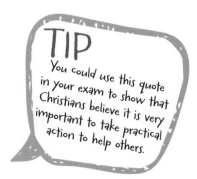

TIP
You could use this quote in your exam to show that Christians believe it is very important to take practical action to help others.

Street Pastors and Parish Nursing Ministries UK

Street Pastors	Parish Nursing Ministries UK
• An initiative started in London in 2003, by the Christian charity the Ascension Trust.	• This Christian charity supports whole-person healthcare through the local church.
• Adult volunteers are trained to patrol the streets in urban areas.	• They provide churches with registered parish nurses, who promote well-being in body, mind and spirit among the local community.
• The main aim originally was to challenge gang culture and knife crime in London.	• The nurses help to provide early diagnosis of health problems.
• The focus then widened to responding to drunkenness, anti-social behaviour and fear of crime.	• They train and coordinate volunteers to help combat loneliness or provide support during times of crisis.
• Street Pastors work closely with police and local councils.	• They give additional help to the NHS.
• They listen to people's problems, advise on where they might get help, and discourage anti-social behaviour.	• They encourage people to exercise and have a good diet.
• A similar group called School Pastors was set up in 2011 to discourage illegal drug use, bullying and anti-social behaviour in schools.	• They focus on the whole person, including listening to people and praying with them if asked. They also direct people to specific services if needed.

TIP
When using Christian charities as examples in your answers, focus on their work and why they do it, rather than details about when they were founded and by whom.

APPLY

 A Explain **two** ways in which Street Pastors carry out their Christian duty.

Refer to Christian teaching in your answer. (AQA Specimen question paper, 2017)

 B 'All Christians should do something practical to help their community, including praying for their neighbours.'

Develop two religious arguments in support of this statement, and **two** non-religious arguments against it.

RECAP

Essential information:

☐ A **mission** is a vocation or calling to spread the faith. The Church has a mission to tell non-believers that Jesus Christ, the Son of God, came into the world as its saviour.

☐ Christians spread the faith through **evangelism** (showing faith in Jesus by example or by telling others).

☐ They do this to fulfil Jesus' instructions to the disciples to spread his teachings (the **Great Commission**).

The Great Commission

> **"**Therefore go and make disciples of all nations, baptising them in the name of the Father and of the Son and of the Holy Spirit, and teaching them to obey everything I have commanded you. **"**
>
> *Matthew 28:19–20 [NIV]*

TIP

You can use this quote in your exam to show what the Great Commission involves. Jesus instructs his disciples to baptise people and to spread his teachings.

- Jesus gave a Great Commission to his disciples to **spread the gospel** and **make disciples of all nations through baptism**.
- The **Holy Spirit** at Pentecost gave the disciples the gifts and courage needed to carry out the Great Commission.
- All Christians have a duty to spread the gospel and tell others of their faith, but some become **missionaries** or **evangelists** (people who promote Christianity, for example by going to foreign countries to preach or do charitable work).
- The aims of missionary work and evangelism are to **persuade people to accept Jesus as their Saviour**, and to extend the Church to all nations.

Alpha

- Alpha is an **example of evangelism in Britain**.
- It was started in London by an Anglican priest, with the aim of helping church members understand the basics of the Christian faith.
- The course is now used as an **introduction for those interested in learning about Christianity**, by different Christian denominations in Britain and abroad.

- The organisers describe it as 'an opportunity to explore the meaning of life' through talks and discussions.
- Courses are held in homes, workplaces, universities and prisons as well as in churches.

APPLY

A   Give **two** ways in which the Church tries to fulfil its mission.

B   **Unscramble the arguments** in the table below referring to the statement, 'Every Christian should be an evangelist.' Decide which arguments could be used to support the statement and which could be used against it.

Write a paragraph to explain whether you agree or disagree with the statement, having evaluated both sides of the argument.

1. If Christians don't help to spread the faith, it might die out.	4. Not every Christian should be an evangelist because some people are just too shy.
2. Some Christians live in countries where they are persecuted, so if they spoke in public about their faith they would be risking death or imprisonment.	5. All Christians have received the Great Commission from Jesus to preach to all nations.
3. Evangelism can happen in small ways, for example Christians can spread their faith to people they meet in everyday life or just give a good example of loving their neighbours.	6. Christians who go around evangelising can annoy people, so it does not help their cause.

Essential information:

- [ ] Up to a third of the world's population claim to be Christian (including people who rarely attend church), and around 80,000 people become Christians each day.
- [ ] The Church expects new Christians to help spread the faith as part of their commitment to Jesus.
- [ ] Christ for all Nations is an example of a Christian organisation that promotes evangelism.

The growth of the Church

- The Church is growing rapidly in South America, Africa and Asia, but not in the USA, Europe and the Middle East (where Christians have been persecuted).
- Worldwide around 80,000 people become Christians each day, and over 500 new churches are formed.
- The Church's mission is to make disciples, not just new believers. This means **new Christians are also expected to help spread the faith**.
- Evangelism should therefore be followed up by training new **converts** (people who decide to change their religious faith) in the way of following Jesus.
- Every Christian has a role in **encouraging fellow believers**. They might do this in the following ways.

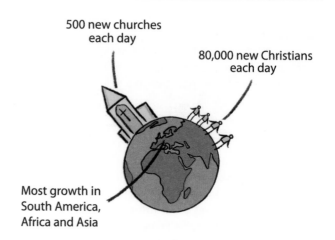

500 new churches each day

80,000 new Christians each day

Most growth in South America, Africa and Asia

advertising and using media (such as Facebook, Twitter or Premier Christian Radio)

sharing what God has done for them with others

Ways Christians can spread the faith

praying for others to accept God

inviting people to Christian meetings, fellowship meals and social events

Christ for all Nations

- Christ for all Nations is an example of a **Christian organisation promoting evangelism**. They do this by holding evangelistic meetings throughout the world, but particularly in Africa.
- They are led by the evangelists Richard Bonnke and Daniel Kolenda.
- Some of their large open-air rallies held in Africa have drawn crowds of up to 1.6 million people.
- It is claimed that many miracles of healing take place at the meetings.
- Christ for all Nations claims that 74 million people have filled in decision cards to follow Christ at their meetings.

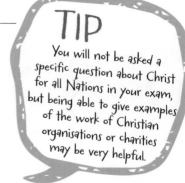

TIP

You will not be asked a specific question about Christ for all Nations in your exam, but being able to give examples of the work of Christian organisations or charities may be very helpful.

 A Give **two** ways in which the Church gets its message to people.

 B **Evaluate this argument** in response to the statement, 'Christians should just rely on evangelists for Church growth.' Explain your reasoning and suggest how you would improve the argument.

"Christians should not just rely on evangelists for Church growth because there are not that many specially trained evangelists to promote Christianity. People are more likely to be drawn to Christianity by the inspiration of someone they know, like a neighbour who is kind and considerate and demonstrates the love that Jesus taught."

Essential information:

☐ The worldwide Church has a mission to restore people's relationship with God and with one another.

☐ The Church therefore plays an important role in **reconciliation** (restoring harmony after relationships have broken down), through initiatives to develop peace and understanding.

Working for reconciliation

- Christians believe humans were **reconciled to God** through Jesus' death and resurrection. This means Jesus' death and resurrection helped to **restore the relationship between God and humanity**, which had been broken by sin (see page 24).
- For Catholics, the **sacrament of Reconciliation** also helps to restore people's relationship with God.
- Matthew 5:23–24 teaches that Christians should be **reconciled to each other**.
- Reconciliation is therefore an **important part of the Church's work**. This might involve anything from trying to restore relationships between individual people, to working for peace between different religious groups or nations at conflict.

> **❝** For if, while we were God's enemies, we were reconciled to him through the death of his Son, how much more, having been reconciled, shall we be saved through his life! **❞**
>
> *Romans 5:10 [NIV]*

TIP

You could use this quote in your exam to show that humanity's relationship with God was restored (or reconciled) through the death of Jesus.

Examples of organisations working for reconciliation

- The **Irish Churches Peace Project** brings Catholics and Protestants together in Northern Ireland.
- The project aims to develop peace and understanding between these two denominations.

- The **World Council of Churches** works for reconciliation between different Christian denominations and members of other faiths.
- For example, the Pilgrimage of Justice and Peace initiative supports inter-religious dialogue and cooperation.

- After the bombing of Coventry Cathedral in World War II, local Christians showed forgiveness to those responsible, and the cathedral became a world centre for peace and reconciliation.
- The cathedral is home to the **Community of the Cross of Nails**, which works with partners in other countries to bring about peace and harmony.

- The **Corrymeela Community** brings together people from different backgrounds, including people of different faiths or political leanings.
- They meet at a residential centre in Northern Ireland to build trust and explore ways of moving away from violence so they can work together constructively.

A Give **two** examples of how the Church has helped to work towards reconciliation.

B 'Reconciliation to God is more important than reconciliation to other people.'

Develop this argument to support the statement by explaining in more detail, adding an example, or referring to a relevant religious teaching or quotation.

"Reconciliation to God is more important because God is the Supreme Being. God will judge us when we die and if we are not sorry for our sins we will not receive eternal life with God in heaven."

RECAP

Essential information:

☐ Christians have faced **persecution** (hostility and ill-treatment) from the beginning of the Church, and Christians are still persecuted worldwide today.

☐ For some Christians, persecution can have positive effects: it can strengthen their faith, allow them to share in Jesus' sufferings, and even inspire others to become Christian.

☐ The Church helps those who are persecuted through prayer, practical help and financial support, and by raising awareness of persecution and campaigning against it.

What is persecution?

- The International Society for Human Rights estimates 80% of all acts of religious discrimination today are aimed at Christians.
- This persecution happens around the world, but particularly in countries such as North Korea, Somalia, Iraq and Syria.
- It might involve:
  - being forced to pay extra tax
  - job discrimination
  - being forbidden to build churches
  - attacks on Christian homes, churches and families, including murder.

TIP

These examples of the kinds of persecution Christians face will be helpful if you need to give an explanation of persecution in your exam.

Some Christian responses to persecution

Response	Supporting quote from scripture
• For some Christians, persecution can have a **positive effect**, as it strengthens their faith and conviction. • It also allows them to share in the suffering of Jesus.	**❝**I want to know Christ – yes, to know the power of his resurrection and participation in his sufferings **❞** *Philippians 3:10* [NIV] This quote shows that one way Christians can get to know Jesus is by sharing in his suffering.
• The Church believes it is important to **act against persecution**, by supporting persecuted Christians wherever possible and campaigning on their behalf.	**❝**If one part suffers, every part suffers with it **❞** *1 Corinthians 12:26* [NIV] This quote refers to the Church. It shows that helping individual Christians also helps the whole Church.
• Christians are **encouraged to show love and forgiveness** towards their persecutors.	**❝**Do not be overcome by evil, but overcome evil with good **❞** *Romans 12:21* [NIV] This quote shows that Christians should respond to evil with love.

Some ways the Church has helped persecuted Christians

- Christians have smuggled Bibles into the USSR (Russia) to strengthen and give comfort to persecuted Christians.
- The Barnabas Fund sends money to support people persecuted for their faith.
- Christian Solidarity Worldwide campaigns for religious freedom for all.

APPLY

(A) Give **two** ways in which Christians support those in countries where it is forbidden to follow Jesus.

(B) **Develop** one religious argument and one non-religious argument in response to the statement, 'It is not possible to "rejoice and be glad" if you are suffering persecution.'

TIP

'Develop' means you need to add some detail to your argument, for example by explaining it more fully and giving examples.

RECAP

Essential information:

- [ ] Christian charities follow the example and teaching of Jesus in working to relieve poverty.
- [ ] Christians believe they should show Jesus to the world through helping the disadvantaged.
- [ ] Three Christian charities that help the poor are Christian Aid, Tearfund and CAFOD.

Helping those in poverty

Christians try to help those living in poverty because Jesus taught that this was important. For example:

- Jesus once told a rich man to sell everything and give to the poor (Mark 10:21).
- The parable of the Rich Man and Lazarus (Luke 16:19–31) tells of a rich man who ends up in hell for ignoring a beggar.
- The parable of the Good Samaritan (Luke 10:30–37) teaches the importance of helping all people.
- Jesus helped outcasts such as lepers, tax collector and sinners.

> **"**If anyone has material possessions and sees a brother or sister in need but has no pity on them, how can the love of God be in that person? Dear children, let us not love with words or speech but with actions and in truth. **"**
>
> *1 John 3:17–18 [NIV]*

> **TIP**
> You only need to know about one of these organisations for your exam.

Three Christian charities that help those in poverty are Christian Aid, Tearfund and CAFOD (Catholic Agency for Overseas Development).

Charity	Examples of their work
Christian Aid	• Supports projects to encourage sustainable development. • Provides emergency relief, such as food, water, shelter and sanitation. • Campaigns to end poverty alongside organisations such as the Fairtrade Foundation, Trade Justice and Stop Climate Chaos.
Tearfund	• Works with over 90,000 churches worldwide to help lift people out of poverty. • Supplies emergency aid after natural disasters and conflict. • Provides long-term aid to help communities become more self-reliant, such as education or new farming equipment. • Supported by donations, fundraising events and prayer from churches in the UK.
CAFOD	• Works with local organisations to train, supply and support communities to work their own way out of poverty. • Gives short-term aid such as food, water and shelter during conflicts and disasters. • Lobbies UK government and global organisations for decisions that respect the poorest. • Encourages Catholic schools and parishes to pray, give money and campaign for justice.

APPLY

(A) Here are two ways in which a worldwide Christian relief organisation carries out its mission overseas. **Develop one of the points** by adding more detail and by referring to a relevant religious teaching or quotation.

"One way that Christian Aid carries out its mission overseas is to provide emergency relief when there is a disaster."

"Another way they help is by setting up longer-term programmes that encourage sustainable development."

> **TIP**
> Emergency aid gives help such as food, water and temporary shelter to people immediately after a disaster. In contrast, long-term aid tries to help people to become more self-sufficient over a longer period of time.

(B) **Write a paragraph** either supporting or against the statement, 'Religious charities should just concentrate on emergency aid.' Include a Christian teaching in your answer.

2 Exam practice

Test the 1 mark question

1. Which **one** of the following is a type of worship that follows a set pattern?

   A Informal worship   B Private worship

   C Non-liturgical worship   D Liturgical worship   **[1 mark]**

2. Which **one** of the following is the festival that celebrates the incarnation of Jesus?

   A Easter   B Good Friday   C Christmas   D Lent   **[1 mark]**

Test the 2 mark question

3. Give **two** ways in which the Church responds to world poverty.   **[2 marks]**

   1) _____

   2) _____

4. Give **two** reasons why prayer is important to Christians.   **[2 marks]**

   1) _____

   2) _____

Test the 4 mark question

5. Explain **two** contrasting ways in which Christians worship.   **[4 marks]**

● **Explain one way.**	Some Christians worship with other people in church on Sunday by going to a service called Holy Communion.
● Develop your explanation with more detail/an example/ reference to a religious teaching or quotation.	During the liturgy, they receive bread and wine that they believe is the body and blood of Jesus.
● **Explain a second contrasting way.**	Other Christians prefer informal worship, sometimes meeting in someone's home.
● Develop your explanation with more detail/an example/ reference to a religious teaching or quotation.	These Christians share their faith by reading and discussing a passage from scripture and praying together in their own words.

TIP
In this answer formal worship is contrasted with informal worship, but you could also contrast public worship with private worship or liturgical worship with charismatic worship.

6. Explain **two** contrasting ways in which Christians practise baptism.   **[4 marks]**

● **Explain one way.**	
● Develop your explanation with more detail/an example/ reference to a religious teaching or quotation.	
● **Explain a second contrasting way.**	
● Develop your explanation with more detail/an example/ reference to a religious teaching or quotation.	

TIP
The question asks for different 'ways' in which Christians practise baptism, not different beliefs about baptism. The clearest contrast is between believers' baptism and infant baptism, but you should focus your answer on the way each of these is carried out, not what people believe about them.

7. Explain **two** contrasting interpretations of the meaning of Holy Communion.   **[4 marks]**

2 Exam practice

Test the 5 mark question

8 Explain **two** ways that Christian charities help the poor in less economically developed countries.
   Refer to sacred writings or another source of Christian belief and teaching in your answer.   **[5 marks]**

● **Explain one way.**	One way that Christian charities help the poor in less economically developed countries is by providing emergency aid when there has been a natural disaster, like an earthquake or famine.
● Develop your explanation with more detail/an example.	For example, Tearfund, a Christian charity, was set up originally to provide emergency aid in response to the famine in Biafra, Nigeria, where it sent emergency food and clothing to refugees fleeing the famine-struck country.
● **Explain a second way.**	A second way that Christian charities help is by providing long-term aid that helps countries become self-sufficient or less dependent on aid.
● Develop your explanation with more detail/an example.	CAFOD, for example, works on development projects to give people access to education, healthcare, and clean water.
● Add a reference to sacred writings or another source of Christian belief and teaching. If you prefer, you can add this reference to your first belief instead.	These charities are inspired by Christian teachings such as the parable of the Rich Man and Lazarus, where Jesus taught that rich people who ignore the needs of the poor will be punished by God.

TIP
Here the student has used a parable from the Bible. Another 'source of Christian belief and teaching' could be official statements or documents by leaders of the Church.

9 Explain **two** reasons why Christians practise evangelism.
   Refer to sacred writings or another source of Christian belief and teaching in your answer.   **[5 marks]**

● **Explain one reason.**	
● Develop your explanation with more detail/an example.	
● **Explain a second reason.**	
● Develop your explanation with more detail/an example.	
● Add a reference to sacred writings or another source of Christian belief and teaching. If you prefer, you can add this reference to your first teaching instead.	

TIP
It is helpful to start by explaining the meaning of 'evangelism' before explaining why Christians practise it.

10 Explain **two** ways that Christians may work for reconciliation.
    Refer to sacred writings or another source of Christian belief and teaching in your answer.   **[5 marks]**

Test the 12 mark question

11 'The most important duty of the Church is to help people in need.'

Evaluate this statement. In your answer you should:

- refer to Christian teaching
- give reasoned arguments to support this statement
- give reasoned arguments to support a different point of view
- reach a justified conclusion.

[12 marks]

REASONED ARGUMENTS IN SUPPORT OF THE STATEMENT • **Explain why some people would agree with the statement.** • Develop your explanation with more detail and examples. • Refer to religious teaching. Use a quote or paraphrase or refer to a religious authority. • **Evaluate the arguments.** Is this a good argument or not? Explain why you think this.	'The Church' in this statement clearly stands for the Christian believers and not the actual building. So what does the Bible say about the duty of Christians? Jesus taught his followers that helping those in need is extremely important and he showed he believed that by the way he acted. If he saw a person suffering from an illness he healed them. He touched lepers in order that they might be cured, even though it was something other people would not do because it was against the law and they feared catching leprosy. He gave sight to the blind, healed the crippled and even cast out evil spirits that were tormenting a naked madman. Jesus did this because he had compassion and pity on those he saw were in need. Jesus also showed in his teaching that Christians should help people in need. In the parable of the Good Samaritan it is the traveller who showed pity on the wounded man and helped him that is the hero of the story. Furthermore Jesus warns that those who do not help will face the anger of God on judgement day in the parable of the Sheep and the Goats. The sheep represented the people who helped and were given the reward of eternal life, but the goats did not and were thrown out of God's presence. So you could argue that it is the most important duty of the Church to help people who are in need.
REASONED ARGUMENTS SUPPORTING A DIFFERENT VIEW • **Explain why some people would support a different view.** • Develop your explanation with more detail and examples. • Refer to religious teaching. Use a quote or paraphrase or refer to a religious authority. • **Evaluate the arguments.** Is this a good argument or not? Explain why you think this.	On the other hand, Jesus summed up the duty for Christians and the Church in two commandments. He said that the first, most important commandment is to love God. The second is to love our neighbour as ourselves. If that is the case, then the most important duty of the Church (Christians) is to love and worship God, and this is more important than helping those in need.
CONCLUSION • **Give a justified conclusion.** • Include your own opinion together with your own reasoning. • **Include evaluation**. Explain why you think one viewpoint is stronger than the other or why they are equally strong. • Do not just repeat arguments you have already used without explaining how they apply to your reasoned opinion/conclusion.	In conclusion I would say that the statement is wrong and I would argue that the most important duty is to love God. The only way the Church can show love of God is by loving human beings who need help. So that is also important, but not the most important duty. It merely follows on from the most important duty.

TIP The student has developed this argument by referring to the Bible. Although there are no direct quotations the answer shows excellent knowledge of Jesus' actions and teaching and uses these to support the statement.

TIP This argument could be developed further for more marks. For example, it could go into more detail about other important duties of the Church (such as preaching the gospel or administering the sacraments), and explain why these are equally or more important than helping people in need.

12 | 'The best way for Christians to grow closer to God is to go on a pilgrimage.'
Evaluate this statement. In your answer you should:
- refer to Christian teaching
- give reasoned arguments to support this statement
- give reasoned arguments to support a different point of view
- reach a justified conclusion.

TIP
Look for the key words in questions. Here it is 'best'. The answer should focus on whether or not a pilgrimage is the best way for Christians to grow closer to God or whether there are other ways that might be better.

[12 marks]

REASONED ARGUMENTS IN SUPPORT OF THE STATEMENT ● **Explain why some people would agree with the statement.** ● Develop your explanation with more detail and examples. ● Refer to religious teaching. Use a quote or paraphrase or refer to a religious authority. ● **Evaluate the arguments.** Is this a good argument or not? Explain why you think this.	
REASONED ARGUMENTS SUPPORTING A DIFFERENT VIEW ● **Explain why some people would support a different view.** ● Develop your explanation with more detail and examples. ● Refer to religious teaching. Use a quote or paraphrase or refer to a religious authority. ● **Evaluate the arguments.** Is this a good argument or not? Explain why you think this.	
CONCLUSION ● **Give a justified conclusion.** ● Include your own opinion together with your own reasoning. ● **Include evaluation**. Explain why you think one viewpoint is stronger than the other or why they are equally strong. ● Do not just repeat arguments you have already used without explaining how they apply to your reasoned opinion/conclusion.	

13 | 'A Christian's most important duty is to tell others about their faith.'
Evaluate this statement. In your answer you should:
- refer to Christian teaching
- give reasoned arguments to support this statement
- give reasoned arguments to support a different point of view
- reach a justified conclusion.

TIP
'To tell others about their faith' is the meaning of evangelism, which is part of a Christian's mission. Try to use these terms in your answer to show the depth of your understanding about this topic.

[12 marks]

Check your answers using the mark scheme on pages 159–160. How did you do? To feel more secure in the content you need to remember, re-read pages 30–43. To remind yourself of what the examiner is looking for, go to pages 7–13.

3 Judaism: beliefs and teachings

3.1 The nature of God: God as One

Essential information:

☐ Judaism is a monotheistic religion. This means that Jews believe there is only one God.

☐ The belief in God as One is expressed in the **Shema** – an important Jewish prayer.

God as One

The belief in one God forms the foundation of Judaism.

- This belief influences the way that Jews view the world.
- Jews believe that God is always present in people's lives. In addition, everything they see and experience is considered to be a meeting with God.

> **TIP**
> Remember that Christianity and Judaism are both monotheistic religions. This means they both believe in only one God. The difference is that Christians believe God is also three Persons.

God is a single, whole, indivisible being

God is the only being who should be praised and worshipped

God as One means ...

everything in the universe has been created and is sustained by this one God

God is the source of all Jewish morality, beliefs and values

The belief in one God is expressed in the Shema. This is an important Jewish prayer that is formed from passages in Deuteronomy and Numbers. It starts with the following words:

This phrase confirms the belief there is only one God.

> 66Hear, O Israel! The LORD is our God, the LORD alone. You shall love the LORD your God with all your heart and with all your soul and with all your might.99
> *Deuteronomy 6:4–5* [Tenakh]

This sentence shows how Jews should respond to this belief – by showing total loyalty, love and dedication towards God.

> **TIP**
> Some Jews write 'G–d' instead of 'God' as a sign of respect. Either spelling is acceptable in your exam.

Many Jews cover their eyes while reciting the first line of the Shema, to avoid distractions

A Write out Deuteronomy 6:4–5 (the start of the Shema), and explain what it means to Jews.

B 'For Jews, the belief in God as One simply means they should not worship any other gods.'
Give arguments against this statement.

3.2 The nature of God: God as creator

RECAP

Essential information:

☐ Jews believe God is the **creator** and sustainer. God created the universe out of nothing, exactly as he wanted it to be, and sustains the world so all species are able to live on it.

☐ Jews believe God gave humans free will (see page 57), and because of this, evil has to exist.

God as creator and sustainer

The Jewish scriptures are known as the Tenakh, and the first section of the Tenakh (the five books of Moses) is called the **Torah**. Genesis, which is the first book in the Torah, tells how God took six days to create the universe and everything in it:

| God took four days to make the universe fit to support life | → | God took two days to create all living creatures | → | God then rested and made the seventh day holy. When Jews celebrate Shabbat on this day (see page 66), they are reminded of God's importance and role as the creator |

- Many Orthodox and ultra-Orthodox Jews believe the events in Genesis literally happened about 6000 years ago. They reject scientific theories of evolution.
- Other Jews interpret the Genesis creation story less literally. They still believe God is the creator of everything, but accept the universe is much older and life has evolved over many years.

Jews believe that in addition to creating the universe, God also sustains it. He provides all the resources needed for life on earth to survive.

TIP
Orthodox Jews (and particularly ultra-Orthodox Jews) believe it is important to follow the laws and guidance in the Torah as strictly as possible (see page 64).

Evil and free will

In order for God to have the power and ability to create everything in the universe, Jews believe that God must be:

- **omnipotent** – all-powerful
- **omniscient** – all knowing
- **omnipresent** – everywhere at all times.

The belief that God created everything also means that God must have created evil. The existence of evil is considered to be a necessary consequence of free will:

| God gave people free will because he wants people to be able to choose to do good. This makes the act of doing good more significant | → | But in order to exercise free will, there must be a choice between good and bad | → | This means that evil has to exist |

The existence of free will explains why the world's resources are distributed unevenly. Jews who exercise free will to help to improve the balance of resources, by giving to those less fortunate, are helping to fulfil God's plan for his creation.

> **❝**I am the LORD and there is none else, I form light and create darkness, I make weal and create woe – I the LORD do all these things.**❞**
> *Isaiah 45:6–7* [Tenakh]

TIP
You can use this quote in your exam to show that Jews believe there is one God who created everything, including evil.

APPLY

(A) Explain **two** contrasting ways in which Jews interpret the Genesis creation story.

(B) 'Jews would have a better relationship with God if free will didn't exist.'

Evaluate this statement.

TIP
To 'evaluate' this statement, explain whether you think it is true or not and why. Consider how the existence of free will affects a Jew's relationship with God.

RECAP

Essential information:

- [ ] To help Jews use their free will correctly, God has given them many laws which he expects them to obey. This is why Jews view God as the lawgiver.
- [ ] God is also viewed as a judge, as he judges how well people follow his laws and rewards or punishes them as a result.
- [ ] Jews believe there are occasions in their history when God's presence has been experienced on earth. The divine presence of God on earth is called the **Shekhinah**.

God as lawgiver and judge

Jews believe God has given them many laws to follow. These laws help them to use their free will in a way that would be approved by God.

- There are **613 laws in the Torah** which teach people how they should behave. These are called **mitzvot**. They form the basis of the Halakah, which is the accepted code of conduct for Jewish life.
- The first ten mitzvot are the **Ten Commandments**. These are the ten laws that God gave to Moses after he rescued the Jewish slaves from Egypt. They are particularly important and form the foundation for all the other mitzvot.

Jews believe God judges them for how well they follow these laws, based on their actions, behaviour and beliefs. God's judgements are considered to be fair and tempered by his loving, merciful nature. For Jews there are two main times when God judges people:

1. **During the festival of Rosh Hashanah** (the Jewish new year). This is when God judges people for their actions over the past year and decides what the coming year will bring them (see page 74).
2. Many Jews also believe they will be **judged after death**, when God determines how they will spend the afterlife (see page 51).

Jewish children studying the mitzvot

The divine presence (Shekhinah)

The Shekhinah is the presence of God on earth. Jewish writings tell how the divine presence of God was experienced by the early Jews:

- In early Judaism, the **Tabernacle** was considered to house the divine presence of God. This was a portable temple, similar in structure to a tent, that the Jews carried with them on their journey through the wilderness to Canaan (see page 54).
- After Canaan was conquered, the Tabernacle was replaced with **Solomon's Temple** in Jerusalem. This Temple was the centre of Jewish worship at the time, and several of the prophets experienced the presence of God in the Temple.

For example, Isaiah 6:1–2 makes reference to the presence of God in the Temple:

> **"**In the year that King Uzziah died, I beheld my Lord seated on a high and lofty throne; and the skirts of His robe filled the Temple. Seraphs stood in attendance on Him.**"**
>
> *Isaiah 6:1–2* [Tenakh]

- The Tenakh describes how the Jews were led at times by **a pillar of fire or a cloud** on their journey to Canaan. These experiences were considered to be appearances from God that demonstrated his power and glory.

APPLY

A Give **two** examples of when Jews have experienced the divine presence of God on earth.

B 'It is more important for Jews to know about God's role as lawgiver and judge than it is to know about his role as creator and sustainer, as it has a greater impact on their lives today.'

Give arguments for and against this statement.

TIP

When giving arguments for or against a statement, it may first help to explain what parts of the statement mean. Here you could explain what it means to say that God is 'lawgiver and judge', or 'creator and sustainer'. Then explain how these beliefs impact upon the lives of Jews today.

3.4 Life after death, judgement and resurrection

Essential information:

☐ There is little agreement among Jews about the afterlife, and many do not think it is important to know what happens after death. They are more concerned with focusing on the present and living in a way that pleases God.

☐ Some Jews believe God will judge them after they die: some will go to heaven and others to Sheol (a place of waiting where souls are cleansed).

☐ Some Jews believe in **resurrection** (rising from the dead to live again). However, many Jews reject the idea of resurrection.

Life after death

The Jewish holy books do not contain much information about the afterlife, so beliefs about it have developed gradually over the centuries. This has led to differences among Jews about what happens after death.

One reason for the lack of agreement is that, in general, **Jews are not too concerned with the afterlife**. They think it is more important to focus on the present and to live in a way that is pleasing to God.

Heaven and Sheol

- Many Jews believe that if they follow their faith correctly, they will go to **heaven or paradise** (Gan Eden) when they die.
- There is no clear teaching about what heaven is like. It is considered to be where people are with God, but it is not known if this is a state of consciousness, or a physical or spiritual place.
- Some Jews believe that people who do not enter heaven go to **Sheol**, a place of waiting where souls are cleansed. Jews do not believe in a place of eternal punishment.

Judgement and resurrection

- Some Jews believe they will be judged by God **as soon as they die**. This belief is supported by Ecclesiastes 12:7.
- Others believe God will judge everyone **on the Day of Judgement**, after the coming of the Messiah (see page 52). This belief is supported by Daniel 12:2.
- Some Jews believe in the idea of physical or spiritual resurrection, but many do not.

Heaven or paradise (Gan Eden)?

Sheol?

Judgement immediately or later?

Resurrection?

> ❝And the dust returns to the ground
> As it was,
> And the lifebreath returns to God
> Who bestowed it.❞
> *Ecclesiastes 12:7* [Tenakh]

> ❝Many of those that sleep in the dust of the earth will awake, some to eternal life, others to reproaches, to everlasting abhorrence.❞
> *Daniel 12:2* [Tenakh]

(A) Explain **two** contrasting Jewish beliefs about judgement.
Refer to scripture or another source of Jewish belief and teaching in your answer.

(B) 'It does not matter if there are different beliefs about life after death within a religion.'

The start of two paragraphs have been written below, one against the statement and one in support of it. Finish the paragraphs by **developing the arguments further** and referring to Jewish beliefs.

"It matters if there are different beliefs about life after death within a religion because then believers don't know how to live their lives in a way that would guarantee them a good afterlife ..."

"It doesn't matter if there are different beliefs about life after death within a religion because it is more important to focus on the present ..."

TIP
When writing about a topic where there are different views on something (such as beliefs about the afterlife), start your sentences by saying 'Some/most/many people believe ...' to reflect this difference.

3.5 The nature and role of the Messiah

RECAP

Essential information:

- [ ] In Judaism, the **Messiah** ('the anointed one') is a future leader of the Jews who will rule over humanity with kindness and justice.
- [ ] The Messiah will rule during the **Messianic age**, which will be a time when the world is united in peace.

Origins of the Messiah

- The word 'Messiah' was originally used in the Tenakh to refer to the **kings of Israel**.
- The first king of Israel was **Saul**, who lived around the eleventh century BCE.
- Before Saul was made king, the prophet Samuel **anointed him with oil** to show he was chosen by God to rule over the Jews. (The word 'Messiah' means 'the anointed one'.)
- Today, the word 'Messiah' is used to refer to a **future leader of the Jews**.
- This leader is expected to be a future king of Israel – a descendent of Saul's successor, King David.

The nature of the Messiah

The Messiah is expected to lead the Jews during the Messianic age. This will be a time in the future of global peace and harmony, when everyone will want to become closer to God.

Orthodox Jews believe there is a descendent of King David in every generation who has the potential to become the Messiah. If the Jews are worthy of redemption, this person will be directed by God to become the Messiah.

> "Samuel took a flask of oil and poured some on Saul's head and kissed him, and said, 'The LORD herewith anoints you ruler over His own people."
>
> *1 Samuel 10:1* [Tenakh]

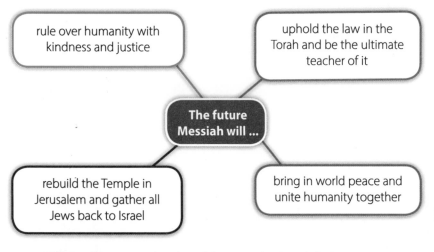

rule over humanity with kindness and justice

uphold the law in the Torah and be the ultimate teacher of it

The future Messiah will ...

rebuild the Temple in Jerusalem and gather all Jews back to Israel

bring in world peace and unite humanity together

Many **Reform Jews** reject the idea of the Messiah. They do believe in a future Messianic age, but believe this will be achieved by everyone working together to create world peace, rather than as the result of the leadership of one person.

Was Jesus the Messiah?

- **Christians** believe that Jesus was the Messiah. They believe this is because, through his death and resurrection, he saved humanity and established the Kingdom of God on earth (see pages 19–21). Some Christians believe that he will come at the end of the world to complete the Kingdom of God – a Messianic age.
- **Jews** do not believe that Jesus was the Messiah. This is because they believe that he did not fulfil the expectations that Jews have for the Messiah – he did not observe Torah law strictly enough or establish the Messianic age.

APPLY

(A) Explain **two** contrasting Jewish beliefs about the Messianic age.

(B) The idea of a Messianic age is not relevant in today's world.

Give arguments for and against this statement.

3.6 The Promised Land and the covenant with Abraham

RECAP

Essential information:

☐ The **Promised Land** is the land of Canaan, which God promised to Abraham and the Jews.

☐ After Abraham had travelled to Canaan, he made a **covenant** (agreement) with God. God promised Abraham he would be the father of many nations. In return, Abraham was required to live a life dedicated to God.

Abraham and the Promised Land

Abraham travelled to Canaan after he was promised this land by God, as a place where Abraham and his descendants could make 'a great nation'.

Abraham was born in the city of Ur, probably in the twentieth or nineteenth century BCE	→ At that time people worshipped idols (statues) of many different gods	→ From an early age, Abraham became convinced there was only one God who had created everything, and that worshipping idols was wrong

Before they reached Canaan, they settled on the way at Haran in Northern Mesopotamia ← Abraham and some of his family (including his wife Sarah) decided to leave Ur to travel to Canaan ← Abraham tried to convince the people in Ur to stop worshipping idols, but had little success

Many years later, God told Abraham to continue the journey to Canaan, promising to make a great nation through him →

❝ The LORD said to Abram [Abraham], 'Go forth from your native land and from your father's house to the land that I will show you. **I will make of you a great nation, And I will bless you** …' ❞
Genesis 12:1–2 [Tenakh]

Once Abraham and Sarah reached Canaan, God told Abraham, 'I give all the land that you see to you and your offspring forever' (Genesis 13:15 [Tenakh]). This became known as the Promised Land

The covenant with Abraham

- In Judaism, a covenant is an agreement between God and an individual person (made on behalf of the rest of the Jews).
- Various covenants have been made during the history of Judaism, and Jews believe these covenants are still binding today.
- After Abraham travelled to Canaan, God made a covenant with him.

What did God promise?	• To make Abraham the father of many nations
What was required of Abraham?	• To agree to 'Walk in My [God's] ways and be blameless.' (Genesis 17:1 [Tenakh])
How was the covenant sealed?	• Through the action of **circumcision** (the removal of the foreskin from the penis) • Abraham proved his acceptance of the covenant by being circumcised himself and by circumcising all the males in his household
How did God keep his side of the covenant?	• To make Abraham the father of many nations, God made it possible for Abraham's wife Sarah to conceive, despite the fact she was very old • Sarah gave birth to a son called Isaac. His birth is seen by some as a gift from God to mark the start of the covenant between Abraham and God

APPLY

(A) Write out a quote from the Torah which tells how God promised Abraham a land where he would make a 'great nation'.

(B) 'Abraham is a perfect role model for Jews because he showed complete dedication and obedience to God.'

Give arguments to support this statement.

TIP

Memorising short extracts from scripture will help you to gain marks in the 5 and 12 mark questions in your exam.

3.7 The covenant at Sinai and the Ten Commandments

RECAP

Essential information:

☐ The **covenant at Sinai** is the covenant between God and Moses, who represented the Jewish people. This requires Jews to follow God's laws (including the Ten Commandments) in return for his protection and blessing.

☐ The Ten Commandments are ten laws which were given to Moses by God after the Jews escaped from Egypt.

The escape from Egypt

The Ten Commandments were given to the Jews after they escaped from slavery in Egypt.

```
About 400 years after God     →    God chose Moses to lead their escape.    →    After God had sent a
made the covenant with             He told Moses to ask the Egyptian             number of plagues to
Abraham, the Jews were being       Pharaoh to release the Jews from             Egypt, the Pharaoh finally
forced to work as slaves in Egypt  slavery, so they could return to Canaan      agreed to release the Jews
                                                                                         ↓
This is where God gave Moses the   ←    When they arrived at Mount        ←    The Jews left Egypt and
Ten Commandments – these were           Sinai, Moses climbed the              wandered for many years in
carved on two tablets of stone that     mountain, leaving the rest of the     the desert in the Sinai region
Moses carried down the mountain         Jews at the base                       between Egypt and Canaan
```

The Ten Commandments

The Ten Commandments form the foundation of Jewish law. They give Jews important guidance on how to have a good relationship with God (the first four commandments), and how to have good relationships with each other to create a peaceful society (the last six commandments). They are recorded in Exodus 20:2–14.

The Ten Commandments form the basis of the **covenant at Sinai**. This is a covenant between God and the Jews, which was agreed at Mount Sinai under the following terms:

- God would protect the Jews from harm and be their God.
- In return, Jews would have to obey his laws (including the Ten Commandments and the other laws in the Torah).

This covenant is one of the main reasons why the Jews believe they are the chosen people of God.

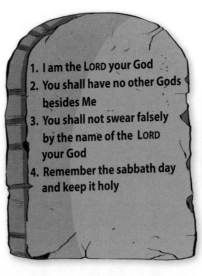

1. I am the LORD your God
2. You shall have no other Gods besides Me
3. You shall not swear falsely by the name of the LORD your God
4. Remember the sabbath day and keep it holy

5. Honour your father and your mother
6. You shall not murder
7. You shall not commit adultery
8. You shall not steal
9. You shall not bear false witness against your neighbour
10. You shall not covet

APPLY

 A Give **two** of the Ten Commandments.

 B 'The covenant at Sinai requires too much from the Jews for what they get in return.'

Write two paragraphs in response to this statement, **one arguing for it and one arguing against it**.

> **TIP**
> When writing arguments for or against a statement, make sure your arguments are backed up by evidence. Here you should refer to the terms of the covenant at Sinai.

3.8 Key moral principles in Judaism

Essential information:

☐ The concepts of justice, healing the world, and kindness to others are important moral principles in Judaism.

☐ These principles help Jews to live in a way that is pleasing to God. They involve helping to create a just world through showing love to others.

Justice

- **Justice** refers to bringing about what is right and fair, according to the law, or making up for a wrong that has been committed.
- Pursuing justice is a sacred duty for Jews. For example, in the Torah, the prophet Micah states that God requires people 'to do justice and to love goodness' (Micah 6:8 [Tenakh]).
- The laws in the Torah give guidance to Jews on how to treat the poor and vulnerable, to help achieve justice.
- Jews believe the Torah and the prophets were sent by God to help people understand how to bring about justice in a way that demonstrates mercy.

Healing the world

- **Healing the world** is an important concept in Judaism, which involves taking actions to help God's work in sustaining the world.
- Many Jews help to heal the world by contributing to social justice or helping to protect the environment. For example, they might volunteer for a charity such as World Jewish Relief, which helps those living in poverty.
- Some Jews believe healing the world involves more than just doing charity work or similar actions. They believe it should also include obeying the mitzvot and trying to become closer to God.

> **TIP**
> The concept of healing the world links to Jewish beliefs about God as the creator and sustainer. By helping to heal the world, Jews are helping to sustain the world that God created (see page 49).

Kindness to others

- Jews aim to show **kindness to others** by showing positive, caring actions towards all living things.
- Many of the laws in the Torah give guidance to Jews on how to be kind to others.
- The Torah teaches that Jews should love others as they love themselves. This instruction is given twice in Leviticus 19:

> ❝You shall not take vengeance or bear a grudge against your countrymen. Love your fellow as yourself❞
>
> *Leviticus 19:18 [Tenakh]*

> ❝The stranger who resides with you shall be to you as one of your citizens; you shall love him as yourself, for you were strangers in the land of Egypt❞
>
> *Leviticus 19:34 [Tenakh]*

Ⓐ Give **two** ways in which a belief in healing the world influences Jews today.

Ⓑ 'The moral principles of justice, healing the world, and kindness to others are all interlinked and equally important.'

Give arguments to support this statement.

3.9 Sanctity of life

Essential information:

- [ ] **Sanctity of life** refers to the idea that life is sacred and holy because it has been created by God.
- [ ] For Jews, belief in the sanctity of life means only God has the right to take life away. Jews are against practices such as murder and active euthanasia, as these quicken a person's natural death.
- [ ] Belief in the sanctity of life also means Jews have a duty to save a person's life if they can, even if this breaks Jewish law. This duty is called **pikuach nefesh**.

Sanctity of life

For Jews, belief in the sanctity of life stems from the creation story in Genesis.

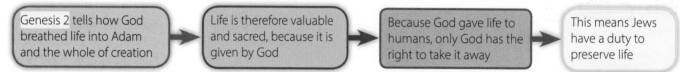

Genesis 2 tells how God breathed life into Adam and the whole of creation → Life is therefore valuable and sacred, because it is given by God → Because God gave life to humans, only God has the right to take it away → This means Jews have a duty to preserve life

For Jews, belief in the sanctity of life means they should **not do anything to quicken a person's natural death**. For example, this means active euthanasia and murder are wrong.

However, while Jewish law states that Jews have a duty to preserve life, there are different opinions about what this means in practice. For example, some Jews think a sick patient should be kept alive at all costs. Others think a patient's death shouldn't be prolonged if they are in great pain.

The importance of preserving life is expressed in Sanhedrin 4:5 in the Talmud:

> **❝** He who destroys one soul of a human being, the Scripture considers him as if he should destroy a whole world **❞**
>
> *Sanhedrin 4:5*

Saving a life (pikuach nefesh)

- A belief in the sanctity of life is behind the concept of pikuach nefesh. This is the obligation that Jews have to save a person's life if they can, even if doing so breaks Jewish laws.
- Pikuach nefesh emphasises how valuable human life is to Jews, as it puts human life above Jewish law.

Examples of laws that might be broken to save a life
- Jews are required to observe Shabbat, which means they are not allowed to do certain types of work from sunset on Friday to sunset on Saturday (see pages 66–67). But Jews are allowed to break Shabbat law in order to save a life.
- Examples in the Talmud of where it is possible to break Shabbat law include rescuing a child from the sea or putting out a fire. Examples today might include driving a sick person to hospital or performing a life-saving operation.

A Give an example of a Jewish law that could be broken to save a person's life.

B 'People shouldn't interfere with God's plan for each person, including his decision to take away their life.'

Write **two** paragraphs in response to this statement, one arguing against it and one arguing for it. **Refer to Jewish beliefs in each paragraph.**

TIP
One good way to start paragraphs like this is with the words 'Some Jews might agree/disagree with this statement because...'.

RECAP

Essential information:

☐ Jews believe God has given people **free will**: the ability to make their own decisions. Jews also believe their decisions have consequences, and will either bring them closer to God or lead them away from God.

☐ Mitzvot are the Jewish rules or commandments. Some of these teach Jews how to form a good relationship with God, while others teach Jews how to form good relationships with each other.

Free will

Jews believe God has given them the free will to make their own choices. But this does not mean people can do what they like without any consequences:

- Good actions lead to a life of fulfilment. They bring Jews closer to God and ensure they are judged favourably by him.
- Bad actions will not bring people closer to God, in life or after death.

In Genesis 3, Adam and Eve use their free will to disobey God and eat from the tree. They were banished from the garden of Eden as a result. This story shows God has given humans the choice of how to live their lives, but using free will to go against God has serious consequences.

Mitzvot

A mitzvah is a Jewish rule or commandment. There are 613 mitzvot in the Torah and others in the Talmud.

The mitzvot **give guidance to Jews on how to use their free will correctly**, to live in a way that pleases God. Jews believe that, as the mitzvot in the Torah came from God while the Jews were under the leadership of Moses, following them carefully makes it impossible to disobey God.

Mitzvot can be divided into two categories:

Mitzvot between man and God

- These are mitzvot that tell Jews how they can improve their relationship with God
- They cover areas such as worship, sacrifice, and the observance of festivals
- The most important are the first four of the Ten Commandments
- For example, the second commandment tells Jews to worship no other gods, and the fourth commandment tells Jews to remember God every Shabbat

Mitzvot between man and man

- These are mitzvot that tell Jews how to improve their relationship with other people
- This is important because the Torah teaches that Jews should show love towards other people and by doing this, Jews are showing their love for God
- They cover areas such as the treatment of workers and how to settle disputes
- They help Jews to live as members of their faith and community in a way that pleases God

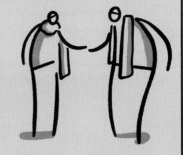

APPLY

(A) Explain **two** teachings that Genesis 3 gives Jews about free will.

Refer to scripture or another source of Jewish belief and teaching in your answer.

(B) 'Obeying the mitzvot between man and man should be more important to Jews than obeying the mitzvot between man and God.'

What is your opinion on this statement? **Explain your reasoning**.

Why might someone else have a different opinion?

3 Exam practice

Test the 1 mark question

1 Which **one** of the following is **not** one of the Ten Commandments?

  A Do not cause harm to anyone   B Do not steal

  C Do not worship any other God   D Honour your father and mother   **[1 mark]**

2 Which **one** of the following people sealed the covenant with God through the action of circumcision?

  A Abraham   B Moses   C King David   D The Messiah   **[1 mark]**

Test the 2 mark question

3 Give **two** different Jewish beliefs about the creation of the universe.   **[2 marks]**

1) _____

2) _____

4 Give **two** different occasions when Jews believe they will be judged by God.   **[2 marks]**

1) _____

2) _____

Test the 4 mark question

5 Explain **two** ways in which a belief in the sanctity of human life influences Jews today.   **[4 marks]**

● **Explain one way.**	One way a belief in the sanctity of life influences Jews today is that it means they shouldn't take any action that would quicken a person's natural death.
● Develop your explanation with more detail/an example/reference to a religious teaching or quotation.	For example, they shouldn't perform euthanasia because this makes a person die quicker than they would naturally.
● **Explain a second way.**	A second way a belief in the sanctity of life influences Jews today is that it means they should save someone's life even if this breaks Jewish law.
● Develop your explanation with more detail/an example/reference to a religious teaching or quotation.	For example, they're allowed to drive someone to the hospital during Shabbat, even though they're not supposed to do work on this day.

6 Explain **two** ways in which the covenant at Sinai influences Jews today.   **[4 marks]**

● **Explain one way.**	
● Develop your explanation with more detail/an example/reference to a religious teaching or quotation.	
● **Explain a second way.**	
● Develop your explanation with more detail/an example/reference to a religious teaching or quotation.	

7 Explain **two** Jewish beliefs about life after death.   **[4 marks]**

Test the 5 mark question

8 Explain **two** Jewish beliefs about the divine presence (Shekhinah).

Refer to scripture or another source of Jewish belief and teaching in your answer.

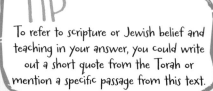

TIP

To refer to scripture or Jewish belief and teaching in your answer, you could write out a short quote from the Torah or mention a specific passage from this text.

● **Explain one belief.**	One belief about the divine presence is that God's divine presence was once housed in the Tabernacle.
● Develop your explanation with more detail/an example.	God manifested his glory to the Jews while they were travelling through the wilderness after escaping from Egypt. They carried a portable tent called the Tabernacle to represent God's constant presence with them throughout this journey.
● **Explain a second belief.**	Another belief about the divine presence is that God has sometimes made appearances on earth.
● Develop your explanation with more detail/an example.	God's presence on earth is sometimes very dramatic and changes lives.
● Add a reference to scripture or another source of Jewish belief and teaching. If you prefer, you can add this reference to your first belief instead.	For example, he once appeared to the prophet Isaiah in Solomon's Temple and called him to be a prophet. This story is given in Isaiah in the Tenakh.

9 Explain **two** moral principles that Jews can follow to live in a way that pleases God.

Refer to scripture or another source of Jewish belief and teaching in your answer.   **[5 marks]**

● **Explain one moral principle.**	
● Develop your explanation with more detail/an example.	
● **Explain a second moral principle.**	
● Develop your explanation with more detail/an example.	
● Add a reference to scripture or another source of Jewish belief and teaching. If you prefer, you can add this reference to your first belief instead.	

10 Explain **two** meanings of the Jewish belief that God is One.

Refer to scripture or another source of Jewish belief and teaching in your answer.   **[5 marks]**

3 Exam practice

Test the 12 mark question

11 'The mitzvot help Jews to use free will properly.'

Evaluate this statement. In your answer you should:

- give reasoned arguments to support this statement
- give reasoned arguments to support a different point of view
- refer to Jewish teaching
- reach a justified conclusion.

[12 marks]
[+3 SPaG marks

REASONED ARGUMENTS IN SUPPORT OF THE STATEMENT ● **Explain why some people would agree with the statement.** ● Develop your explanation with more detail and examples. ● Refer to religious teaching. Use a quote or paraphrase or refer to a religious authority. ● **Evaluate the arguments.** Is this a good argument or not? Explain why you think this.	Most Jews would agree with this statement because the mitzvot tell Jews how to behave in a way that is pleasing to God. There are 613 mitzvot in the Torah which give Jews rules for how to behave in all areas of life, from worship and the observance of festivals to settling disputes and treating workers fairly. They teach Jews how to have a good relationship with God and with each other. Jews believe these rules are necessary because God has also given them free will. This means they have the ability to make bad choices and decisions that would turn them away from God. But the mitzvot help Jews to make good choices and use their free will in a way that would be approved by God.

> **TIP**
> The answer begins well by explaining what the mitzvot are before saying how they help Jews. The student also addresses how free will might make it difficult to follow God if there were no mitzvot to help keep people on the right track. Always try to address all parts of the statement you are asked to evaluate.

REASONED ARGUMENTS SUPPORTING A DIFFERENT VIEW ● **Explain why some people would support a different view.** ● Develop your explanation with more detail and examples. ● Refer to religious teaching. Use a quote or paraphrase or refer to a religious authority. ● **Evaluate the arguments.** Is this a good argument or not? Explain why you think this.	Some Jews might argue that there are too many mitzvot to be helpful, and that trying to follow 613 separate rules is confusing and overwhelming. They might argue that general principles – such as showing kindness to others, and healing the world – are more useful in guiding Jews to use their free will properly. For example, the principle of showing kindness to others means that Jews should help and care for other people. This teaches Jews that a loving attitude is important. Some Jews might say that having a loving attitude towards everything will help them to use their free will better than trying to follow lots of specific mitzvot.

> **TIP**
> Rather than arguing that the mitzvot are unhelpful, the student argues that other moral principles might be more helpful in making wise choices. But it would also be acceptable to argue that keeping rigidly to rules may stop people growing up and being able to make mature choices of their own. A variety of different views will be credited as long as you provide reasons for them.

CONCLUSION ● **Give a justified conclusion.** ● Include your own opinion together with your own reasoning. ● **Include evaluation.** Explain why you think one viewpoint is stronger than the other or why you think they are equally strong. ● Do not just repeat arguments you have already used without explaining how they apply to your reasoned opinion/conclusion.	I believe that God gave the mitzvot to the Jews to help them live in a way he approves. Jews believe if they follow the mitzvot carefully, it is impossible to disobey God, so this means they must be using their free will properly. I think the detail in the 613 mitzvot gives helpful guidance to keep people close to God.

12 | 'Jews do not need to worry about trying to create a more peaceful society, because this will be achieved by the Messiah.'

Evaluate this statement. In your answer you should:

- give reasoned arguments to support this statement
- give reasoned arguments to support a different point of view
- refer to Jewish teaching
- reach a justified conclusion.

[12 marks]
[+3 SPaG marks]

REASONED ARGUMENTS IN SUPPORT OF THE STATEMENT ● **Explain why some people would agree with the statement.** ● Develop your explanation with more detail and examples. ● Refer to religious teaching. Use a quote or paraphrase or refer to a religious authority. ● **Evaluate the arguments.** Is this a good argument or not? Explain why you think this.	
REASONED ARGUMENTS SUPPORTING A DIFFERENT VIEW ● **Explain why some people would support a different view.** ● Develop your explanation with more detail and examples. ● Refer to religious teaching. Use a quote or paraphrase or refer to a religious authority. ● **Evaluate the arguments.** Is this a good argument or not? Explain why you think this.	
CONCLUSION ● **Give a justified conclusion.** ● Include your own opinion together with your own reasoning. ● **Include evaluation.** Explain why you think one viewpoint is stronger than the other or why you think they are equally strong. ● Do not just repeat arguments you have already used without explaining how they apply to your reasoned opinion/conclusion.	

13 | 'For Jews, it is more important to understand God as a judge than as anything else.'

Evaluate this statement. In your answer you should:

- give reasoned arguments to support this statement
- give reasoned arguments to support a different point of view
- refer to Jewish teaching
- reach a justified conclusion.

[12 marks]
[+3 SPaG marks]

Check your answers using the mark scheme on page 160. How did you do?
To feel more secure in the content you need to remember, re-read pages 48–57.
To remind yourself of what the examiner is looking for in your answers, go to pages 7–13.

4.1 The importance of the synagogue

RECAP

Essential information:

☐ The **synagogue** is a building where Jews meet for worship, study, social activities and charitable events. It is also where Jews celebrate festivals and rites of passage.

☐ The synagogue forms the centre of the Jewish religious community.

What is a synagogue?

- A synagogue provides a space for Jews to **meet and take part in a wide range of activities**, from worship and prayer to community meetings and social clubs.
- Synagogues are usually identified from their **use of Jewish symbols** on the outside of the building. For example, synagogues may display an image of a **menorah** (a many-branched candlestick) or the **Star of David** (a six-pointed star that represents King David, who ruled Israel in the tenth century BCE).
- Jews have a **number of different names** for the synagogue. It is sometimes called the 'house of prayer' or 'house of study'. Orthodox Jews often call it the 'shul', which means 'school'. Reform Jews sometimes call it the 'temple', in reference to the Temple in Jerusalem (an important centre of worship for early Jews).

The importance of the synagogue

The synagogue is important to Jews because it strengthens their community by providing a space for a variety of activities, including the following:

Worship and prayer
- The synagogue **provides a space for worship and communal prayer**
- Although Jews can pray anywhere, they believe it is good to pray together in a group: certain prayers can only be said in the presence of a **minyan** – a group of at least 10 adults
- Services are regularly held in the synagogue for Jews to pray and worship together

Education
- The synagogue helps to **educate Jews of all ages in their faith**
- Synagogues may provide classes in Hebrew for young Jews, to help them learn the language used in Jewish prayer
- Most synagogues have a library that helps older Jews to continue improving their understanding of the faith and its scriptures

Social activities
- Most synagogues **host a variety of activities for children, teenagers and adults in their social hall**
- Examples include youth clubs, music or drama groups, and groups for senior citizens
- The synagogue provides a place to discuss matters that are important to the community

Charitable events
- The synagogue **helps Jews to donate their time and money to charity**
- Synagogues often hold events to raise money for charity
- They also collect money or other items to be given to charity or distributed among the poor and needy

APPLY

(A) Give **two** ways in which someone might recognise a synagogue from the outside.

(B) 'The most important role of the synagogue is to provide a space for communal prayer.'

Evaluate this statement.

TIP

To 'evaluate' this statement, explain whether you think it is true or not and why. Consider why the activities held in a synagogue are important to Jews. For example, is it more important for Jews to be able to pray together, or to be educated in their faith?

RECAP

Essential information:

- [ ] The Ark (**Aron Hakodesh**) is the cabinet where the Torah scrolls are kept. It is the holiest place in the synagogue.
- [ ] The ever-burning light (**ner tamid**) is a light that is kept on at all times, and sits above the Ark. It symbolises God's presence.
- [ ] The reading platform (**bimah**) is the raised platform from where the Torah is read.

The prayer hall

- The prayer hall is the room in the synagogue where Jews come together for communal worship and prayer.
- It is usually rectangular in shape, with seats on three sides of the hall facing inwards towards the bimah, which is situated in the centre. The fourth side is where the Ark is kept, which is the focal point of the synagogue.
- The prayer hall might be decorated with patterns, Jewish symbols or extracts from scripture. Images of God, the prophets or other religious figures are not allowed, as this goes against the second commandment.

Important features of the prayer hall include the following:

Feature	Description	Significance
The Ark (Aron Hakodesh)	• An ornamental cabinet or container where the Torah scrolls are kept • Situated at the front of the synagogue, usually set into the wall facing Jerusalem • Usually reached by climbing up some steps • There are usually two stone tablets placed above the Ark, on which the start of each of the Ten Commandments is written	• The holiest place in the synagogue • Represents the original Ark of the Covenant. This first Ark was built to hold the stone tablets that contained the Ten Commandments, which God gave to Moses • The first Ark was taken to Jerusalem and placed in the Temple built by King Solomon. The Temple was the focal point of Jewish worship in early Judaism • Today, when Jews face the Ark in the synagogue, they face the city where the Temple once stood • By climbing up steps to reach the Ark, Jews are reminded that God is above his people and the sacred Torah is above humanity
The ever-burning light (ner tamid)	• A light that is placed in front of and slightly above the Ark • Traditionally an oil lamp, but most synagogues now use electric lights (with an emergency power source in case of a power cut)	• Symbolises God's presence, so it is never put out • A reminder of the menorah that was lit every night in the Temple in Jerusalem
The reading platform (bimah)	• A raised platform situated in most synagogues in the centre of the prayer hall • Where the Torah is read from during services	• Provides a focal point when the Torah is being read, making it easier for the congregation to see the reader and hear what is being said • To some Jews it is a reminder that the altar was the central feature of the courtyard in the Temple in Jerusalem

APPLY

(A) Write **three** sentences to describe what the Ark, the ner tamid and the bimah are.

(B) 'The prayer hall in a synagogue shows how important the Temple in Jerusalem was to Jews.'

List arguments in support of this statement.

TIP

Knowing the meaning of key Jewish words will be very useful for writing full answers in your exam.

4.3 Worship in Orthodox and Reform synagogues

RECAP

Essential information:

☐ In the UK today, there are two main groups within Judaism: **Orthodox** Judaism (which is more traditional) and **Reform** Judaism (which is more progressive).

☐ Jews are expected to pray three times a day. Orthodox synagogues hold daily services so Jews can pray together.

☐ Orthodox and Reform services differ in a number of ways.

Orthodox and Reform Judaism

Orthodox Judaism	Reform Judaism
· The traditional branch of Judaism	· A type of progressive Judaism
· Orthodox Jews emphasise the importance of **strictly following the laws in the Torah**	· Reform Jews emphasise the importance of **individual choice in deciding how to worship and practise the faith**
· They believe the Torah was given directly to Moses by God, so should be followed as closely as possible	· They believe the Torah was inspired by God but written by humans, so it can be adapted for modern times
· Orthodox Jews believe **men and women should have different roles**	· Reform Jews believe **men and women should be able to undertake the same roles**
· Currently all Orthodox rabbis are male, although there are women within the tradition who are working towards greater equality	· This means women in Reform Judaism can take on roles traditionally reserved for men, such as becoming a rabbi or being part of the minyan

Public worship

Services in the synagogue are led by either a rabbi (a Jewish religious leader and teacher), a cantor (a person who leads or chants prayers in the synagogue), or a member of the congregation. Orthodox and Reform services differ in the following ways:

Orthodox services	Reform services
Synagogues usually hold daily services	Synagogues often do not hold daily services; the focus instead is on celebrating Shabbat and festivals
The service is in Hebrew	The service is in Hebrew and the country's own language (English in the UK)
The person leading the service has his back to the congregation, so he is facing the Ark	The person leading the service faces the congregation most of the time
Men and women sit separately	Men and women sit together
Some of the congregation may arrive late and catch up at their own pace	Services are shorter than Orthodox ones but tend to be more rigidly structured; there is a set time and worshippers are usually present at the start
Men always cover their heads by wearing a skull cap and married women cover their heads by wearing a hat or scarf. This shows respect for God, and a recognition that God is above humanity	Most men wear a skull cap and some women do as well (or they might wear a hat instead)
The singing in the service is unaccompanied	The singing may be accompanied by musical instruments

APPLY

A **Explain** how Orthodox and Reform Judaism differ in their beliefs about the Torah. How does this influence their approach to worship?

B 'Reform services make it easier for people to understand what is happening than Orthodox services'.

What is your opinion about this statement? **Explain your reasoning**.

64

4.4 Daily services and prayer

RECAP

Essential information:

☐ Orthodox Jewish men (and some Reform Jews) often wear a **tallit** (a prayer shawl) and **tefillin** (small leather boxes containing extracts from the Torah) when they pray.

☐ Weekday services in the synagogue consist of a number of prayers, including the **Amidah** (the 'standing prayer'), which is the central prayer in Jewish worship.

Tallit and tefillin

During morning prayers, Orthodox Jewish men wear a tallit, and on weekdays they wear tefillin as well. Some Reform Jewish men and women wear them too.

	Description	Significance
Tallit	A prayer shawl made from wool or silk A long tassel is attached to each corner	The shawl reminds Jews they are obeying God's word whenever they wear it The tassels represent the mitzvot (see page 57)
Tefillin	A pair of small leather boxes containing extracts from the Torah, including some of the words of the Shema One is fastened with leather straps to the centre of the forehead, and the other is wound around the upper arm in line with the heart	Tefillin remind Jews that their mind should be concentrating fully on God when they pray, and their prayers should come from the heart

The format of Jewish services

On weekdays, prayer services are held in Orthodox synagogues in the morning, afternoon and evening. The service often consists of the following parts:

- **Opening prayers** are said. These might consist of prayers and psalms that praise and thank God.
- The **Shema** is recited, and accompanied by blessings.
- The **Amidah** ('standing prayer') is said. This is the central prayer of Jewish worship, and on a weekday it forms the core of all Jewish prayer services. It is prayed in silence while standing and facing Jerusalem.
  It consists of a series of blessings:
  - the first three blessings praise God and ask for his mercy
  - the middle thirteen blessings ask for God's help
  - the final three blessings thank God for the opportunity to serve him and pray for peace, goodness, kindness and compassion.
- The Amidah is sometimes followed by a **reading** from the Torah.
- **Final prayers** are said. These include the closing Aleinu prayer, which gives praise and thanks to God.

it is a way to communicate with God

communal prayer strengthens the Jewish community

Prayer is important to Jews because ...

it brings Jews closer to God

it helps Jews to remember what their faith is all about

APPLY

A Describe **two** parts of a prayer service in an Orthodox synagogue.

B 'Prayer is more important to Jews than helping to heal the world.'
Give arguments for and against this statement.

TIP
The concept of 'healing the world' is discussed on page 55.

RECAP

Essential information:

☐ **Shabbat** is the Jewish holy day of the week. It is a day of rest and renewal, starting just before sunset on Friday and continuing to sunset on Saturday.

☐ Services that are held in the synagogue for Shabbat include a brief service on Friday evening, the main service on Saturday morning, and sometimes an extra service especially for families with children.

What is Shabbat?

a gift from God of a day of rest and renewal

described in Jewish literature and poetry as a bride or queen

a day that God has commanded Jews to celebrate: the fourth commandment is 'Remember the sabbath day and keep it holy' (Exodus 20:8 [Tenakh])

Shabbat is ...

a time to relax and rest, worship God, and enjoy family life

a time to celebrate that God has kept his promises in the covenant between God and the Jews (see page 54)

a time to celebrate God's creation – Shabbat recalls the Genesis creation story, in which God created everything in six days and rested on the seventh day (see page 49)

Shabbat services

- On **Friday evening**, there is a brief service in the synagogue, during which Shabbat is welcomed like a bride coming to meet her husband (the Jewish people).
- Some synagogues hold a service during Shabbat for **families with children**, which includes storytelling, games and music.
- The main service is on **Saturday morning**. This service is longer than the weekday prayer services, as it includes a reading from the Torah and often a sermon, as well as prayers and blessings.

Before the reading is given, the following often happens:

Action	Significance
The congregation stands when the Ark is opened to reveal the Torah scrolls	This is a reminder of how the Jews stood at the bottom of Mount Sinai when Moses returned with the Ten Commandments
The Torah is taken from the Ark and dressed with a cover and various ornaments, such as a crown or belt	This is a reminder of the vestments worn by priests in early Judaism
The Torah is held in front of the congregation while verses from scripture are chanted; it is then paraded round the synagogue	This represents the march through the wilderness, when Jews carried the original Ark (containing the Ten Commandments) from Mount Sinai to Jerusalem
When the Torah passes through the synagogue, many Jews touch it with their prayer book or the tassels on their prayer shawl, and then touch their lips	This recalls Ezekiel 3:3, which tells Jews that God's words should be on their lips, and sweet like honey

- After the reading is finished, the Torah scrolls are dressed and paraded around the synagogue again, before being placed back in the Ark.
- The rabbi or visiting speaker then gives a sermon, which may be based on the reading or something important in the news.

APPLY

(A) Explain **two** actions that happen before the reading from the Torah is given in the main Shabbat service.

(B) 'Shabbat is a day for Jews to celebrate all that God has given them.'

Write a paragraph to explain why Jews would agree with this statement.

TIP

Here you could describe two actions and then explain their significance to Jews.

4.6 Shabbat in the home

RECAP

Essential information:

☐ To help make Shabbat a special occasion when no work is done, various preparations need to be made beforehand, such as cleaning the house and preparing the food.

☐ In the home, the start of Shabbat is marked through the lighting of the candles, and the end of Shabbat is marked through the havdalah service.

☐ The main celebration in the home is the Friday evening meal, which allows the family to relax and enjoy each other's company.

Shabbat preparations

Preparation	Significance
• All the work is done and the home is prepared before Shabbat begins on Friday evening • This involves cleaning the house, preparing the food, washing, and changing into smart clothes	• Most types of work are not allowed during Shabbat, as stated in the fourth commandment • Jews try to make their homes neat and presentable to welcome in Shabbat, which is seen as being like welcoming a special bride or queen into the home
• At least two candles are placed on the table	• The two candles represent the two commandments to 'remember' and 'observe' Shabbat
• Two loaves of challah bread are placed on the table	• These represent the food that God provided for the Jews on Shabbat while they were wandering in the wilderness
• Wine or grape juice is placed on the table (the wine is drunk from a special goblet called the Kiddush cup)	• Drinking Shabbat wine symbolises joy and celebration

Shabbat celebrations

Shabbat is welcomed through the **lighting of the candles**:

- A female member of the family (usually the wife) lights the two candles, shortly before sunset on Friday.
- She waves or beckons with her arms around the candles, then covers her eyes to say a blessing.
- She also says a prayer asking God to bless the family.

After the Friday evening service in the synagogue, the family **shares a special meal**:

- Before the meal, the parents bless their children, and the head of the household recites the Kiddush blessings while holding up the Kiddush cup.
- To begin the meal, the bread is blessed and passed round so everyone has a piece.
- The meal might last for a few hours, giving the family time to relax and enjoy each other's company. After each course,

religious stories might be told to the children or songs might be sung.

- The meal ends with a prayer of thanksgiving for the food.

After the Saturday morning service in the synagogue, the family **shares another special meal**. During the afternoon, parents may **spend time with their children** and **study the Torah**. The end of Shabbat is marked by the **havdalah service**:

- This is performed at home after the sun has set.
- Blessings are performed over a cup of wine, sweet smelling spices and a candle with several wicks.
- The spices and candle are believed to soothe and bring light to the house after Shabbat has ended.

> ❝ Blessed are You, Lord, our God, King of the Universe, who sanctifies us with the commandments, and commands us to light the candles of Shabbat. ❞
>
> *Shabbat Blessing*

APPLY

 A Give **two** preparations that are made in the home before Shabbat begins, and explain their significance.

B 'Shabbat is most important for Jews as a time to relax and enjoy being together as a family.'

Give arguments for and against this statement.

RECAP

Essential information:

- [ ] Jews may pray in the home instead of attending a synagogue. They are also reminded to focus on God in other ways in the home, such as through touching the mezuzah (a small box containing verses from the Torah).
- [ ] The **Tenakh** is the main Jewish sacred text and contains the written law. The **Talmud** is a commentary which helps Jews to put the laws in the Tenakh into practice.
- [ ] Studying the Tenakh and Talmud is very important to Orthodox Jews in particular.

Worship in the home and private prayer

- Jews are expected to **pray three times a day**, which they can do in the home or in the synagogue. They traditionally stand to pray, and if they are alone they pray silently.
- Jews are also reminded of God in the home in other ways. For example, many Jewish homes have one or more **mezuzot**. A mezuzah is a small box that contains a handwritten scroll of verses from the Torah, which is attached to a doorpost. Jews touch the mezuzah as a sign of respect to God and a reminder to obey his laws.
- In Jewish Orthodox homes, the layout of the kitchen will also remind Jews of God and the need to obey the dietary laws (see page 73).

Study of sacred writings

The Tenakh and the Talmud teach Jews how to obey God's laws in their everyday lives:

Writing	Overview	Contents
Tenakh (the written law)	• The Jewish sacred scriptures • A collection of 24 books (which can all be found in the Old Testament in the Christian Bible)	The Tenakh is in three main parts: 1 the **Torah**: the five books of Moses, which form the basis of Jewish law 2 the **Nevi'im** (the Prophets): eight books that continue to trace Jewish history and expand on the laws in the Torah 3 the **Ketuvim** (the Writings): eleven books that contain a collection of poetry, stories, advice, historical accounts and more

Talmud (the oral law)	• A commentary by the early rabbis on the Torah
	• Contains a collection of discussions and teachings about how to interpret the Torah and apply its laws to everyday life
		The Talmud is in two main parts:
		1 the **Mishnah**: a commentary on the Torah compiled by Rabbi Judah Ha'Nasi in 200 CE
		  • Ha'Nasi wrote down the oral law: the early teachings about how to interpret the Torah, which had been passed down from generation to generation by word of mouth
		  • there was a danger these teachings would be altered or misinterpreted without a written record of them, so Ha'Nasi compiled the Mishnah to stop this from happening
		2 the **Gemara**: a collection of discussions on the Mishnah, written down in 500 CE

- For Orthodox Jews, the Torah and Talmud are considered to be the source of all Jewish laws, legal teachings and decisions that affect their daily lives.
- For this reason they are studied extensively by Orthodox Jews, who may attend classes and lectures to develop their understanding.
- Reform Jews do not regard the Torah and Talmud with the same absolute authority and may not study them as much.

APPLY

A Give **two** ways in which Jews are reminded of God in the home.

B 'All Jews should carefully study the Talmud if they want to live in a way that pleases God.'

Evaluate this statement.

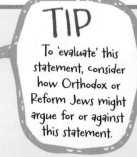

TIP
To 'evaluate' this statement, consider how Orthodox or Reform Jews might argue for or against this statement.

RECAP

Essential information:

☐ Family life is central to Jews, as it is where the Jewish faith is preserved and passed on to the next generation. Birth is an important rite of passage which the wider Jewish community helps to celebrate.

☐ Three Jewish ceremonies associated with birth are the **naming ceremony** (when the baby is formally named), **Brit Milah** (when a boy is circumcised), and the **redemption of the firstborn son** (when the firstborn son is 'redeemed' from Temple service).

Ceremonies for newborn Jews

In Judaism, there are three ceremonies which help a family to celebrate the birth of their child and welcome them into the Jewish community:

Ceremony	What it involves	Significance
Naming ceremony	• Boys and girls born into Orthodox families are **blessed in the synagogue on the first Shabbat after their birth** • The father recites the Torah blessing, and asks God for the good health of his wife and baby • **A baby girl's name will be announced at this point** • A boy will be named later at his circumcision • In Reform synagogues, both parents will take part in the naming ceremony, which may not necessarily be held on the first Shabbat after the child's birth	• The naming ceremony formally introduces the baby to the community and to God
Brit Milah	• **This ceremony happens when a baby boy is eight days old** • A close friend or relative places the baby on an empty chair that symbolises the presence of the prophet Elijah • A trained circumciser picks up the baby and places him on the knee of the person who has been given the honoured role of being 'the companion of the child' • The baby's father blesses his son • A blessing is said over wine and the baby is formally named • **The baby is circumcised in a simple operation** from which they can heal quite quickly • Family and guests then enjoy a festive meal to celebrate	• Brit Milah recalls the covenant God made with Abraham (see page 53), where God told Abraham that circumcision would 'be the sign of the covenant between Me and you' (Genesis 17:11 [Tenakh]) • It provides a lifelong reminder to a male Jew that they are one of God's chosen people
Redemption of the firstborn son	• Some Orthodox Jews give a small amount of money 31 days after the birth of their firstborn son, to 'redeem' him from Temple service (the Temple in Jerusalem no longer exists, but some Orthodox Jews maintain this tradition anyway) • **Five silver coins are given to a kohen**: a descendent of the priests who used to work in the Temple • Prayers are also said, asking that the child may 'enter into Torah, into marriage, and into good deeds'	• This tradition comes from the following command in Numbers 18 'but you shall have the first-born of man redeemed […] Take as their redemption price […] the money equivalent of five shekels' (Numbers 18:15–16 [Tenakh])

APPLY

 A Give **two** ways in which Orthodox and Reform Jews differ in their celebrations of a birth.

 B 'Jewish ceremonies associated with birth remind Jews of the importance of following God's laws.'

Give arguments to support this statement.

TIP
Even if you can't remember all the details of these ceremonies, try to remember why they are important to Jews.

RECAP

Essential information:

☐ When Jewish boys turn 13 and girls turn 12, they are considered to be old enough to take full responsibility for practising their faith.

☐ Boys celebrate coming of age at 13 with a **Bar Mitzvah** ceremony and become a 'son of the commandment'.

☐ In Reform Judaism, girls celebrate coming of age at 12 with a **Bat Mitzvah** ceremony and become a 'daughter of the commandment'.

The significance of Bar and Bat Mitzvah

it is when a Jew is seen to become an adult

preparing carefully for it brings Jews closer to God and the Jewish community

Bar or Bat Mitzvah is significant because …

it is when a Jew is expected to start strictly following Jewish law, and takes full responsibility for doing so

it is when a Jewish boy is allowed to become part of the minyan (see page 62)

Celebrating a Bar Mitzvah

- At the first opportunity after his thirteenth birthday (usually the first Shabbat), the boy reads from the Torah at the normal service in the synagogue. Many synagogues hold classes to prepare boys for this occasion.
- The boy wears a tallit for the first time, may lead part of the service – reading from the Torah or saying prayers – and makes a short speech.
- The boy's father thanks God for bringing his son to maturity, and declares he is now responsible for his own actions.
- After the service there is often a celebratory meal or party, where the boy receives gifts.

Celebrating a Bat Mitzvah

- Reform Jewish girls often have a Bat Mitzvah ceremony and celebrations that are very similar to a Bar Mitzvah.
- The girl reads from the Torah, gives a short speech, and may lead part of the service in the synagogue.
- This is often followed by a celebratory meal or party.
- Orthodox Jews sometimes mark a girl's Bat Mitzvah with a family meal and small religious gifts.

APPLY

A Give **two** ways in which a Jew might participate in a service as part of their Bar or Bat Mitzvah.

B 'The Bar or Bat Mitzvah ceremony is the most significant moment in a Jewish peson's life.'

The start of two paragraphs have been written below, one arguing against the statement and one in support of it. Finish the paragraphs by **developing the arguments further**.

"I agree with this statement because the Bar or Bat Mitzvah ceremony marks the point when a Jewish person has to take full responsibility for following Jewish law …"

"I disagree with this statement because there are other moments in a Jewish person's life that some might think are equally significant. For example, the Brit Milah ceremony …"

4.10 Marriage

RECAP

Essential information:

- [ ] In Judaism, **marriage** is a two-step process. A period of engagement called the **betrothal**, which typically lasts for a year, is then followed by the wedding itself.
- [ ] A Jewish wedding can be divided into three main parts: the betrothal ceremony, the signing and reading of the marriage contract, and the marriage of the couple.
- [ ] For Jews, marriage creates a spiritual bond between a couple and helps them to experience holiness in their everyday lives.

Betrothal

- Betrothal refers to the period of time before the wedding ceremony when the couple are engaged or promised to each other. This traditionally lasts for 12 months.
- Betrothal has legal status in Jewish law and can only be broken by death or divorce.
- During the year of betrothal the couple do not live together, but they do prepare for their future lives together.
- Traditionally a special betrothal ceremony was held a year before the wedding, but this ceremony is now held at the wedding itself.

The wedding

Jewish weddings take place in the synagogue or in a venue such as a hotel, on any day except Shabbat or a festival. A typical Jewish wedding includes the betrothal ceremony, the signing and reading of the marriage contract, and the marriage itself.

Before the wedding	• The couple may fast before the wedding to cleanse themselves of sin and come to the ceremony with the right attitude
The betrothal ceremony	• The bride joins the groom underneath the chuppah, which is a canopy that symbolises the couple's home • The bride and groom recite two blessings over wine, and in Orthodox weddings the groom places a plain ring on the bride's finger (Reform couples usually exchange rings)
The marriage contract	• The marriage contract is signed in the presence of witnesses, then read out and given to the bride • For Orthodox Jews this covers aspects such as the husband's duties to his wife, the conditions of inheritance upon his death, and how he will provide for his wife if they get divorced • For Reform Jews, the marriage contract usually focuses on spiritual aspirations rather than legal rights. It often describes mutual hopes for the marriage, which are the same for the husband and wife
The marriage itself	• The bride circles the groom seven times and seven blessings are recited • The rabbi makes a short speech and blesses the couple in front of the congregation • The groom breaks a glass under his heel to show regret for the destruction of the Temple in Jerusalem – this is a reminder that life involves hardship as well as joy • The congregation wishes the couple good luck
The wedding reception	• After the ceremony, the couple spend a short time together in a private room to symbolise their new status as a married couple • A wedding reception follows that includes music and dancing

For Jews, marriage is a way of experiencing holiness in everyday life. It creates a spiritual bond between a couple, where two souls are fused to become one. This is described in the Torah in Genesis 2.

> " Hence a man leaves his father and mother and clings to his wife, so that they become one flesh. "
>
> *Genesis 2:24* [Tenakh]

APPLY

(A) **Explain** what the term 'betrothal' means in Judaism.

(B) 'Jewish weddings show equality between men and women.'
Give arguments for and against this statement.

TIP
Don't forget that marks are added for spelling, so learn how to spell any key terms you may use in your answer.

4.11 Mourning for the dead

RECAP

Essential information:

- [ ] In Judaism there are set periods of mourning which decrease in intensity over the period of a year. These allow a family to grieve fully but also help them to get back to normal life.

- [ ] Most Jews are buried rather than cremated. A short funeral service is held at the cemetery, ideally within 24 hours after the person's death.

The periods of mourning

When the death is announced
- When Jews first hear of the death of a close family member, they make a small tear in their clothes, to follow the example of Jacob, as described in Genesis 37:34
- Jews also say a blessing that refers to God as the true judge, which shows they accept God's decision to take the person's life

The first period of mourning
- Most Jews are buried as soon after death as possible, usually within the first 24 hours
- Until then, Jews believe the deceased's soul should be comforted and supported by family members, because it does not fully leave the person until they are buried
- Close family are left to grieve without having to follow certain Jewish laws

The second period of mourning (shiva)
- Shiva is an intense period of mourning that lasts for seven days, starting on the day of the burial
- Mourners do not work but stay at home and hold prayer services three times a day
- One of the prayers said is the **kaddish**, which praises God and asks for peace
- Mourners do not wear make-up, shave or cut their hair: mirrors are covered over so mourners can't focus on their appearance

After the first year
- Formal mourning ends after a year
- Children continue to mark the anniversary of a parent's death by lighting a candle each year that burns for 24 hours
- Sons also recite the kaddish and, if possible, make a Torah blessing

The final period of mourning
- This lasts for eleven months
- Mourners do not attend parties
- Children continue to say the kaddish for a parent who has died

The third period of mourning
- This begins after shiva and lasts until 30 days after the person's death
- Normal life resumes but mourners do not listen to music, go to parties, shave or cut their hair
- Male mourners say the kaddish daily in the synagogue

The funeral

- Before the funeral, the body is carefully washed and wrapped in a plain linen cloth, as well as a tallit for men. It is placed in a simple coffin to show that everyone is equal in death.
- Funerals do not usually take place in the synagogue as this is considered to be a place for the living. Instead the body is taken straight to the cemetery.
- The funeral service includes prayers, psalms, readings from scripture, and a short speech by the rabbi.
- After the funeral, everyone washes their hands to show they are leaving death behind.
- Jewish law states a tombstone must be placed on the grave so the person is remembered.

APPLY

 A Describe **two** actions a Jewish person takes when they first hear of the death of a close family member, and **explain their significance**.

 B 'Jewish mourning customs help a family to accept and cope with a person's death.'

What is your opinion on this statement? **Explain your reasoning**.

TIP
Remember, even when you are writing about an emotional subject such as death, try to keep your answers as objective and balanced as possible.

4.12 Dietary laws

Essential information:

- [ ] Jews follow **dietary laws**: strict rules about what can and cannot be eaten, and how food should be prepared.
- [ ] Food that is acceptable to eat is called **kosher**, while food that is unacceptable to eat is called **trefah**.
- [ ] Milk and meat cannot be mixed, so many Jewish kitchens have two food preparation areas to keep these separate.

Jewish dietary laws

The dietary laws **originate from passages in the Torah**, particularly Leviticus 11 and Deuteronomy 14. Some Jews think the laws were originally for hygiene or health reasons.

The laws categorise food as being **acceptable (kosher)** or **unacceptable (trefah)**.

- Kosher food includes: certain types of meat (such as cows and sheep), fish that has scales and fins (such as salmon and tuna), cheese that has been officially declared kosher, and any fruit and vegetables that are free of insects.
- Trefah food includes: pork, camel, reptiles, rodents, seafood without scales (such as crab and prawns), cheese that is not kosher, insects and amphibians (such as frogs).
- **Orthodox Jews** follow the dietary laws strictly. They believe the laws have come from God to test their obedience and help develop their self-control. The laws remind people daily of their faith, and mark out Jewish people as different from others.
- Many **Reform Jews** think the laws are outdated in modern British society, and it is up to an individual whether to follow them or not.

Preparing food

Kosher animals must be **killed in a certain way**. For example:

- the animal must be slaughtered with a very sharp knife by a trained Jew
- the animal has to be conscious when it is killed
- blood is drained from the animal as Jews are not permitted to consume food containing blood.

> **"** But make sure that you do not partake of the blood; for the blood is the life, and you must not consume the life with the flesh. **"**
>
> *Deuteronomy 12:23 [Tenakh]*

Jews must also be careful to **keep milk and meat separate**. Dairy products and meat are not allowed to be eaten at the same time. In addition, several hours must pass between eating meat and anything containing milk. Most Jews believe the reason for this comes from an instruction in Exodus: 'You shall not boil a kid in its mother's milk' (Exodus 23:19 [Tenakh]).

For this reason:

- many Orthodox homes have kitchens with two sinks and two food preparation areas, to keep milk and meat separate
- Jews may also colour-code their utensils, cutlery and crockery, so one set is used for meat dishes and another for dairy products
- most synagogues have kosher kitchens, so they can prepare food for events without breaking dietary laws
- Jews who live in non-Jewish communities often find it difficult to eat out and make sure their food is prepared correctly.

 A Write out a passage from the Torah which deals with the dietary laws, and explain what it means for Jews today.

B 'The Jewish dietary laws should be relaxed because they are too difficult to follow.'

Evaluate this statement.

TIP

To 'evaluate' this statement, consider whether you think Jews would agree with it or not. Think about the different arguments that Orthodox and Reform Jews might have in response to the statement.

RECAP

Essential information:

☐ **Rosh Hashanah** is a festival that marks the start of the Jewish new year. Many Jews believe that during Rosh Hashanah, God judges their actions over the past year and decides their fortune for the coming year.

☐ **Yom Kippur** is the holiest and most important day in the year, when God's judgement from Rosh Hashanah is finalised.

☐ During the ten days between the start of Rosh Hashanah and Yom Kippur, Jews try to make up for their wrongdoings over the past year and seek forgiveness from God.

Rosh Hashanah

Origins and meaning	• Rosh Hashanah **remembers God's creation of the world,** and is also a **day of judgement**
	• It is considered to be the anniversary of the day on which God created humans, as described in Genesis 1. Some Jews believe that on this day, God weighs up and judges a person's actions over the past year, deciding what their fortune will be like in the year to come
Observance	**Improving God's judgement:**
	• Jews believe God's judgement can be influenced by their behaviour during the festival, so they try to **take actions that will improve God's judgement**
	• This might include praying, doing charity work, and atoning or making up for any harm they have caused over the past year
	Celebrating at home:
	• The day before Rosh Hashanah, preparations are made similar to those made for Shabbat
	• The evening Rosh Hashanah starts, families **share a festive meal** with symbolic foods. For example, apples dipped in honey symbolise hope for a sweet new year
	Attending services in the synagogue:
	• At the evening service in the synagogue, prayers are said asking God to continue to be the king of the world for the coming year
	• Next morning at the synagogue a ram's horn is blown 100 times
	• This is followed by a service which is longer than usual, with special prayers

Yom Kippur

Origins and meaning	• Yom Kippur, which is known as the **Day of Atonement**, is the holiest day in the Jewish calendar
	• Its origins stem from Leviticus 16:30, which tells Jews that on Yom Kippur, 'atonement shall be made for you to cleanse you of all your sins' [Tenakh]
	• Jews believe God's judgement is finalised on this day, so it is the last chance to repent for any sins
Observance	**Attending services in the synagogue:**
	• Many Jews spend much of Yom Kippur in the synagogue
	• They focus on **asking God to forgive their sins**, to help restore their relationship with him
	• Jews take part in a general confession of sins as a community
	• During the final service, Jews are given one last chance to confess their sins. The doors of the Ark are then closed, showing that God's judgement is now sealed
	Observing other rituals:
	• During Yom Kippur, Jews fast for 25 hours and do no work
	• They wear white as a symbol of purity
	• Bathing, wearing leather shoes, and having sex are also forbidden

APPLY

(A) Give **two** differences between the ways in which Rosh Hashanah and Yom Kippur are observed.

(B) 'It is more important to show kindness to others during Rosh Hashanah than at any other time in the year.'

Do you think Jews would agree with this statement? **Explain your reasoning.**

RECAP

Essential information:

☐ **Pesach** (also called Passover) is a festival that lasts for seven or eight days. It celebrates the Jews' escape from slavery in Egypt.

☐ One of the most important parts of the festival is the Passover Seder, which is a meal with special foods that families share on the first evening of Pesach.

Origins of, importance of and preparations for Pesach

- Pesach **celebrates the Jews' escape from slavery in Egypt**, after which they spent many years wandering in the desert before reaching the land of Canaan (see page 54).
- In particular, Pesach remembers the **final plague** that God sent to Egypt to persuade the Pharaoh to release the Jews. This killed the firstborn children of the Egyptians but 'passed over' the houses of the Jewish slaves.
- Pesach is important for Jews as it celebrates their escape from slavery to create the birth of the Jewish nation, when they were given the law that made them God's chosen people. It is a time for Jews to gives thanks to God for their redemption, and to feel empathy with those who still live under oppression.
- The most important preparation is to **remove leaven (yeast) from the home**. Removing leaven recalls how the Jews did not have time to let their bread rise when they escaped from Egypt.
- After cleaning the house, some parents or children hide bread crumbs to find and burn, to show all leaven has been removed.
- Some firstborn males fast before Pesach starts, in thanksgiving for their ancestors' escape from death.

The Passover Seder

- On the first evening of Pesach, families **celebrate with a special meal** (called the Passover Seder).
- During the meal, the youngest member of the family asks four questions about the meaning of Pesach rituals. In reply, the story of the escape from Egypt is told from a book called the Haggadah.

During the meal, the following are served:

Item	Significance
Red wine	• A reminder of the lambs' blood the Jews smeared on their doorposts to save their children from the final plague • During the meal, four glasses of wine are blessed and shared to represent the four freedoms God promised in Exodus 6:6–7
Unleavened bread	• This fulfils God's command to celebrate the escape from Egypt by eating unleavened bread for seven days each year (Exodus 12:15) • Some of the bread is hidden for children to hunt for later – the finder receives a small prize
On the Seder plate: • a green vegetable, often parsley, to dip in salt water • two bitter herbs such as horseradish and romaine lettuce • charoset (a sweet paste) • an egg and a lamb bone	• The green vegetable symbolises new life in the Promised Land • The salt water represents the tears shed in slavery • The bitter herbs represent the bitterness of slavery • The sweet charoset symbolises the mortar Jews had to use when slaves, and reminds Jews that life is now sweeter • The egg and lamb bone are reminders of sacrifices made in the Temple of Jerusalem

APPLY

(A) Explain **two** ways in which Pesach celebrations remember the Jews' escape from Egypt.

(B) 'Pesach rituals are important because they teach Jewish children about the history of Judaism.'

Write a paragraph that supports this statement. Then write a paragraph which supports a different point of view.

TIP
Think about why Pesach rituals might be important for other reasons.

4 Exam practice

Test the 1 mark question

1 Which **one** of the following is a light that is kept on at all times in the synagogue?

   A Aron Hakodesh   B Bimah   C Ner tamid   D Tefillin   **[1 mark]**

2 Which **one** of the following is the name of the 'standing prayer', which forms the core of all Jewish prayer services?

   A Aleinu   B Amidah   C Havdalah   D Shema   **[1 mark]**

Test the 2 mark question

3 Give **two** ways in which Jews celebrate when a boy becomes 13 years old.   **[2 marks]**

1) _____

2) _____

4 Give **two** ways in which Orthodox and Reform prayer services differ from each other.   **[2 marks]**

1) _____

2) _____

Test the 4 mark question

5 Explain **two** ways in which the synagogue is used.   **[4 marks]**

● **Explain one way.**	One way the synagogue is used is to provide education for young Jews.
● Develop your explanation with more detail/an example/ reference to a religious teaching or quotation.	For example, young Jews might take classes in Hebrew in preparation for their Bar or Bat Mitzvah.
● **Explain a second way.**	Another way the synagogue is used is for communal prayer.
● Develop your explanation with more detail/an example/ reference to a religious teaching or quotation.	For example, Orthodox synagogues hold daily services in the prayer hall so Jews can pray together.

6 Explain **two** reasons why Jews study the Tenakh and the Talmud.   **[4 marks]**

● **Explain one reason.**	
● Develop your explanation with more detail/an example/ reference to a religious teaching or quotation.	
● **Explain a second reason.**	
● Develop your explanation with more detail/an example/ reference to a religious teaching or quotation.	

7 Explain **two** ways in which Jews celebrate Rosh Hashanah.   **[4 marks]**

4 Exam practice

Test the 5 mark question

8 Explain **two** ways in which Shabbat is celebrated in the home.

Refer to scripture or another source of Jewish belief and teaching in your answer.

[5 marks]

● **Explain one way.**	*One way in which Shabbat is celebrated in the home is with a special meal on the Friday evening.*
● Develop your explanation with more detail/an example.	*The meal is relaxed and might last for a few hours, with religious stories or songs between the courses.*
● **Explain a second way.**	*Another way Shabbat is celebrated in the home is through the lighting of two candles.*
● Develop your explanation with more detail/an example.	*The candles are lit just before sunset on Friday to mark the start of Shabbat.*
● Add a reference to scripture or another source of Jewish belief and teaching. If you prefer, you can add this reference to your first belief instead.	*Judaism teaches that Shabbat is like a bride or queen, and the candles are lit to welcome her into the home.*

9 Explain **two** ceremonies that take place after a Jewish baby is born.

Refer to scripture or another source of Jewish belief and teaching in your answer.

[5 marks]

TIP

Remember that the reference to scripture or Jewish belief and teaching needs to be relevant to the point you are making. This means it should back up the point, instead of being about something else.

● **Explain one ceremony.**	
● Develop your explanation with more detail/an example.	
● **Explain a second ceremony.**	
● Develop your explanation with more detail/an example.	
● Add a reference to scripture or another source of Jewish belief and teaching. If you prefer, you can add this reference to your first belief instead.	

10 Explain **two** dietary laws that are followed by Orthodox Jews.

Refer to scripture or another source of Jewish belief and teaching in your answer.

[5 marks]

4 Exam practice

Test the 12 mark question

11 'The most important duty of Jews is to attend the synagogue.'

Evaluate this statement. In your answer you should:

- give reasoned arguments to support this statement
- give reasoned arguments to support a different point of view
- refer to Jewish teaching
- reach a justified conclusion.

[12 marks]

REASONED ARGUMENTS IN SUPPORT OF THE STATEMENT ● **Explain why some people would agree with the statement.** ● Develop your explanation with more detail and examples. ● Refer to religious teaching. Use a quote or paraphrase or refer to a religious authority. ● **Evaluate the arguments.** Is this a good argument or not? Explain why you think this.	*Some Jews might agree with this statement because the synagogue is the centre of the Jewish community. It is where Jews can worship, celebrate festivals and rites of passage, and meet other Jews. Attending the synagogue helps to strengthen the Jewish community.* *Jews believe it is good to pray together, and some prayers can only be said in the presence of a minyan (10 or more adults). The synagogue provides a space for prayer, which is very important to Jews because it is how they develop their relationship with God.* *Many synagogues also provide classes for Jews and have a library so Jews can learn more about their faith. This also helps them to become closer to God.*
REASONED ARGUMENTS SUPPORTING A DIFFERENT VIEW ● **Explain why some people would support a different view.** ● Develop your explanation with more detail and examples. ● Refer to religious teaching. Use a quote or paraphrase or refer to a religious authority. ● **Evaluate the arguments.** Is this a good argument or not? Explain why you think this.	*Some Jews might argue that there are more important duties for Jews. For example, they might say the most important duty is to obey the mitzvot. God expects Jews to follow his laws in return for his blessing and protection. This was made official in the covenant at Sinai so it is a duty that Jews are expected to follow.* *Other Jews might say the most important duty is simply to worship God. But they don't have to attend a synagogue to do this. For example, Jews are allowed to pray at home, and they can study the Torah at home. They can also take part in Jewish celebrations at home like the Passover Seder and the havdalah service.*
CONCLUSION ● **Give a justified conclusion.** ● Include your own opinion together with your own reasoning. ● **Include evaluation.** Explain why you think one viewpoint is stronger than the other or why you think they are equally strong. ● Do not just repeat arguments you have already used without explaining how they apply to your reasoned opinion/conclusion.	*I think most Jews would say that their most important duty is to worship God and obey his laws. Attending a synagogue, for example to pray and study, probably makes this a lot easier. But I think most Jews would say it isn't necessary, whereas obeying the mitzvot and worshipping God is.*

TIP
This is a well balanced answer, providing good support and argument for the opinions expressed, and a justified conclusion.

12 'Men and women are treated equally in Jewish practices.'

Evaluate this statement. In your answer you should:

- give reasoned arguments to support this statement
- give reasoned arguments to support a different point of view
- refer to Jewish teaching
- reach a justified conclusion.

TIP

Remember, some questions in the exam will require you to combine your knowledge of different topics. Try to consider links and connections between different topics when you revise.

[12 marks]

REASONED ARGUMENTS IN SUPPORT OF THE STATEMENT ● **Explain why some people would agree with the statement.** ● Develop your explanation with more detail and examples. ● Refer to religious teaching. Use a quote or paraphrase or refer to a religious authority. ● **Evaluate the arguments.** Is this a good argument or not? Explain why you think this.	
REASONED ARGUMENTS SUPPORTING A DIFFERENT VIEW ● **Explain why some people would support a different view.** ● Develop your explanation with more detail and examples. ● Refer to religious teaching. Use a quote or paraphrase or refer to a religious authority. ● **Evaluate the arguments.** Is this a good argument or not? Explain why you think this.	
CONCLUSION ● **Give a justified conclusion.** ● Include your own opinion together with your own reasoning. ● **Include evaluation.** Explain why you think one viewpoint is stronger than the other or why you think they are equally strong. ● Do not just repeat arguments you have already used without explaining how they apply to your reasoned opinion/conclusion.	

13 'Jewish mourning rituals are helpful for a person who is mourning the death of someone they love.'

Evaluate this statement. In your answer you should:

- give reasoned arguments to support this statement
- give reasoned arguments to support a different point of view
- refer to Jewish teaching
- reach a justified conclusion.

[12 marks]

Check your answers using the mark scheme on pages 160–161. How did you do?

To feel more secure in the content you need to remember, re-read pages 62–75.

To remind yourself of what the examiner is looking for in your answers, go to pages 7–13.

5.1 Religious teachings about human sexuality

RECAP

Essential information:

- [ ] **Human sexuality** refers to how people express themselves as sexual beings.
- [ ] **Heterosexual** relationships are between a man and a woman, whereas **homosexual** relationships are between members of the same sex.
- [ ] The Christian Church and Orthodox Judaism teach that heterosexual relationships within marriage are the ideal, and part of God's plan for humanity.
- [ ] Some Christians, and Liberal and Reform Jews, accept homosexual relationships that are loving and committed.
- [ ] Many people in Britain today believe homosexuals should have the same rights as heterosexuals. This is reflected in the fact that same-sex marriage is now legal in the UK.

You might be asked to compare beliefs on homosexual relationships between Christianity (the main religious tradition in Great Britain) and another religious tradition.

Attitudes towards sexual relationships

	Christian views	**Jewish views**

General attitudes towards sexual relationships 	• The Christian Church teaches that sex expresses a deep, loving, life-long union that first requires the **commitment of marriage**.
	• Not all Christians agree with this, but all are against unfaithfulness.
	• The Bible teaches that heterosexual relationships are part of **God's plan** for humans.
	• Genesis 1:28 and 2:24 say that a man and woman should be united together and 'increase in number'.
		• In Judaism, sex is seen as a wonderful creation of God, not just for having children but for **expressing love and companionship within marriage**.
		• In the Torah, God created Eve as a companion for Adam.
		
		   ❝ The Lord God said, 'It is not good for man to be alone; I will make a fitting helper for him.' ❞
		   Genesis 2:18 [Tenakh]
		
		• Sex is only permissible within marriage.
		• Jewish law recognises the rights of both women and men to have sexual fulfilment in marriage.

Views on homosexual relationships	• Some Christians oppose homosexual relationships because they believe this goes against God's plan. • The Catholic Church teaches that homosexual relationships are unacceptable because sex should have the possibility of creating new life. • The Church of England welcomes homosexuals living in committed relationships, but does not allow same-sex marriage in church. Some other Churches do. • Some Christians think loving, faithful homosexual relationships are just as holy as heterosexual ones.	• The Torah is clear that sex between men is forbidden: 'Do not lie with a male as one lies with a woman; it is an abhorrence' (Leviticus 18:22 [Tenakh]). • Orthodox Judaism considers homosexual relationships to be wrong. • Reform and Liberal Judaism teach that loving, committed homosexual relationships are as valid as heterosexual ones.

APPLY

(A) Explain **two** contrasting religious beliefs about homosexual relationships.

(B) 'Sex has been devalued in British society.'

Evaluate this statement, referring to **two** religious arguments, and **two** non-religious arguments.

TIP
Contrasting religious beliefs may come from <u>within</u> religions as well as <u>between</u> religions. Make sure you write about religious beliefs and not just about commonly held opinions.

5.2 Sexual relationships before and outside marriage

Essential information:

- [ ] The Anglican and Catholic Churches and Judaism teach that **sex before marriage** (sex between two single unmarried people) is wrong.

- [ ] All religions teach that **sex outside marriage** or **adultery** (voluntary sexual intercourse between a married person and someone who is not their husband or wife) is wrong.

You might be asked to compare beliefs on sex before marriage between Christianity (the main religious tradition in Great Britain) and another religious tradition.

Sexual relationships before marriage

Sex before marriage is now widely accepted in British society, although it is against the beliefs of many religious people.

Christian views	Jewish views
• For many Christians, sex expresses a deep, lifelong union that requires the commitment of marriage. It should not be a casual, temporary pleasure. • Anglican and Catholic Churches teach that sex before marriage is wrong. • Some liberal Christians think sex before marriage can be a valid expression of love, particularly if the couple are intending to get married or have a life-long commitment. • Christians believe it is wrong to use people for sex, to spread sexually transmitted infections or to risk pregnancy outside of marriage. ❝Flee from sexual immorality.❞ *1 Corinthians 6:18 [NIV]*	• Judaism traditionally considers sex before marriage as immoral and irresponsible, as it undermines the importance of creating a family through which Jewish religion and culture is passed down. • The Torah warns against promiscuity and sexual conduct that harms others, who are all created in God's image (Genesis 1:27). • Orthodox Jews, following laws in Leviticus and guidance in the Talmud, believe that premarital sex is forbidden. • In Haredi Jewish families, a chaperone accompanies an engaged couple when they meet.

Sexual relationships outside marriage

All religions generally teach that adultery is wrong as it involves lies, secrecy and the betrayal of trust. Most non-religious people are against adultery for similar reasons.

Christian views	Jewish views
• Christians are against adultery as it breaks the marriage vows they make before God, and threatens the stable relationship needed for their children's security. • Adultery is against one of the Ten Commandments (Exodus 20:14). • Jesus once forgave a woman caught committing adultery, but ordered her to leave her life of sin (John 8:1–11).	• Judaism emphasises the importance of faithfulness in marriage. • Adultery is considered a serious sin, along with murder and worshipping false gods. It goes against one of the Ten Commandments (Exodus 20:14). • Adultery breaks the spiritual bond of marriage and risks the happiness and security of the whole family.

A Here are two religious beliefs about sexual relationships outside of marriage (adultery). Develop **one** of the points by referring to a relevant religious teaching or quotation.

"Christians think sex outside marriage (adultery) is wrong because it breaks the vows couples make at their wedding."

"Jews believe having an affair is wrong because it goes against God's Commandments."

B Give **two** points in support and **two** points against the statement, 'It is not always wrong to have sex before marriage.'

Develop one of them by adding more detail or an example.

TIP
For an evaluation question it is important to develop the reasons that you give.

5.3 Contraception and family planning

RECAP

Essential information:

☐ There are three types of **contraception** (methods used to prevent pregnancy): artificial (e.g. condoms, the pill), natural (e.g. the rhythm method) and permanent (sterilisation).

☐ In Britain, there is widespread acceptance of contraception to help family planning, prevent unwanted pregnancies, reduce global overpopulation and prevent the spread of sexually transmitted infections.

☐ Most Christians and Jews accept **family planning** (controlling how many children a couple has and when they have them) in certain circumstances, but not to prevent having children altogether.

You might be asked to compare beliefs on contraception between Christianity (the main religious tradition in Great Britain) and another religious tradition.

Religious and non-religious attitudes

Group	Beliefs	Favoured methods
Catholics	• Artificial contraception goes against natural law and the purpose of marriage. • Sex should always be open to creating new life. • Family planning should only involve natural methods of contraception.	The rhythm method (avoiding sex at fertile times of the month).
Anglicans and Non-conformists	• Contraception is allowed for couples to develop their relationship before having children, to space out pregnancies, to avoid harming the mother's health, or to limit the number of children in a family so they can all be cared for. • In 1930 the Church of England approved artificial contraception used 'in the light of Christian principles'. • Christians who believe life begins at the moment of conception are against methods that prevent the fertilised egg from developing, as this is seen as causing an abortion and a form of murder.	A preference for contraception that prevents conception from taking place. 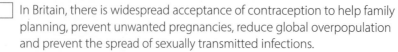
Orthodox Jews	• Orthodox Judaism accepts the use of contraception by married couples to prevent risk to the mother's health, to delay or space children out for financial reasons, or to limit the number of children if this is thought to benefit the family. • Sterilisation is forbidden as it damages the body which God created.	A preference for the contraceptive pill as it does not interfere with the sexual act or destroy semen.
Reform Jews	• Reform Jews allow contraception for many reasons, including social and financial reasons. • They accept that some couples may choose to use contraception before marriage.	Any type of contraception, although the 'morning after' pill should only be used if the mother's health is at risk.
Non-religious people in British society	• There is widespread acceptance of artificial contraception to help family planning. • Many people think it is responsible to use contraception to prevent unwanted pregnancies, control population growth, and prevent the spread of sexually transmitted diseases.	Any type of contraception.

APPLY

A   Give **two** religious beliefs about the use of contraception.

B   'Religious authorities should not preach about family planning.'

Evaluate this statement. Refer to religious arguments in your answer.

5.4 Religious teachings about marriage

RECAP

Essential information:

☐ **Marriage** is a legal union between a man and a woman (or, in some countries, including the UK, two people of the same sex) as partners in a relationship.

☐ Different religious and non-religious groups vary in their views about the purpose and nature of marriage, and whether **same-sex marriage** is acceptable.

☐ **Cohabitation** refers to a couple living together and having a sexual relationship without being married.

What is the nature and purpose of marriage?

Christian views

- A gift from God and part of the natural law.
- A covenant (agreement) before God in which the couple promises to live faithfully together till death.
- A unique relationship between a man and woman that allows for the possibility of creating new life.

> " God blessed them and said to them, 'Be fruitful and increase in number.' "
>
> *Genesis 1:28 [NIV]*

- A spiritual bond of trust that reflects the love of Christ for the Church.
- The proper place to enjoy sex, raise children in a religious faith, and provide a secure, stable environment for family life.

> " The Church sees marriage between a man and woman, as central to the stability and health of human society. "
>
> *House of Bishops of the General Synod of the Church of England*

Jewish views

- A binding contract (ketubah) that protects the woman's financial security.
- The spiritual binding together of a man and woman in love, making a lifelong commitment to each other.
- Part of God's plan at creation: 'Hence a man leaves his father and mother and clings to his wife, so that they become one flesh' (Genesis 2:24 [Tenakh]).
- Provides a secure foundation to raise a family, pass on the Jewish faith to the next generation, express sexual intimacy, provide companionship, and grow spiritually.

Non-religious views

- A legal union between two people in a relationship.
- A serious, lifelong commitment made in public to another person.
- Provides legal and financial benefits.

Cohabitation and same-sex marriage

- **The Catholic Church** and **Orthodox Judaism** oppose cohabitation as they believe sex should only take place within marriage.
- Many **Anglican and Protestant Christians** and **Reform Jews** accept that although marriage is best, people may cohabit in a faithful, loving and committed way without being married.
- **Orthodox Judaism** forbids homosexual relationships. Many Orthodox Jews were opposed to the changes in law that made same-sex marriages legal.
- Many Christians were also opposed to legalising same-sex marriage, because it seemed to be changing the nature of marriage. The law protects Churches that oppose homosexual marriage and they are not forced to conduct same-sex marriages against their beliefs.
- **Liberal and Reform Jews**, like some **liberal Christians**, accept same-sex marriages; some groups are willing to bless or conduct same-sex marriages in a religious ceremony.

TIP
Show you understand that there are contrasting perspectives on cohabitation within Christianity and Judaism.

APPLY

A Give **two** religious beliefs about the nature of marriage.

B 'Marriage gives more stability to society than cohabitation.'

Develop an argument to support this statement.

TIP
Simply write down two different beliefs. 'Give' indicates that there is no need to go into detail.

5.5 Divorce and remarriage

RECAP

Essential information:

☐ In the UK, **divorce** (legal ending of a marriage) is allowed after one year if a marriage cannot be saved.

☐ **Remarriage** is when someone marries again while their former husband or wife is still alive.

☐ Religions try to balance ethical arguments between the sanctity of marriage vows made before God and compassion for people whose marriage has broken down.

Reasons for divorce

- addiction
- lack of communication
- people changing and growing apart
- inability to have children
- domestic violence
- **Reasons for divorce**
- adultery
- illness or disability
- immaturity
- work and money pressures

Christian and Jewish views on divorce and remarriage

Christian views	Jewish views
• Some Christians believe the **sanctity of the marriage vows** means they must be kept no matter what. • The Catholic Church teaches that **marriage is a sacrament** that is permanent, lifelong and cannot be dissolved by civil divorce. Catholics can separate but not remarry while their partner is still alive. • Other Christians believe that sometimes divorce is the **lesser of two evils** and should be allowed for compassionate reasons. • Protestant Churches (e.g. Methodists) accept civil divorce and allow remarriage in church under certain conditions. Divorced Anglicans can remarry in church with the bishop's permission. • These Christians think the Church should **reflect God's forgiveness** and allow couples a second chance for happiness. • Jesus taught that anyone who divorced and remarried was **committing adultery** (Mark 10:11–12). • But Matthew 5:32 says, 'If a man divorces his wife for any cause other than unchastity [unfaithfulness] he involves her in adultery' [NIV].	• Marriage is a voluntary contract, so divorce is allowed if both people agree. • The Torah says a man can divorce his wife for shameful conduct (Deuteronomy 24:1), but in practice it is not necessary for the couple to give reasons for wanting a divorce. • Couples should try reconciliation first, but can divorce if they no longer love each other as 'one flesh'. • Jewish law states that couples must get a religious divorce ('get'), as well as a civil divorce. The husband, with his wife's consent, must apply to the Jewish court (**Bet Din**) for a religious divorce to break the marriage contract (**ketubah**). • After divorce, Jews are encouraged to remarry. • For Orthodox and Reform Jews, a woman cannot remarry without a get. Liberal Jews do not require a get.

TIP

Note that Mark 10:11–12 suggests divorce is always wrong, but Matthew 5:32 suggests it is acceptable in cases of unfaithfulness.

Christian and Jewish responses to couples having marriage problems

- Christian churches may offer counselling, prayer and sacraments to support the couple.
- They may refer the couple to outside agencies such as Relate and ACCORD.
- Christians may be encouraged to bring forgiveness and reconciliation into their marriage.
- Jewish couples are encouraged to try reconciliation and many will seek the advice of their rabbi.

APPLY

(A) Explain **two** contrasting religious views about remarriage.

(B) 'Divorce is never right.'

Evaluate this statement, supporting your answer with arguments from **two** different views, and evaluating them.

TIP

The contrast can come from <u>within</u> the same religion or from <u>between</u> religions.

RECAP

Essential information:

☐ There are different types of **families** (people related by blood, marriage or adoption) in Britain, including nuclear families, extended families, and families with same-sex parents.

☐ In most families, parents and children are expected to fulfil certain roles and obligations to each other. For example, parents are expected to care for their children, and children are expected to obey their parents.

Types of families

Nuclear family

- A mother, father and children.
- The most common family type in the West.
- For Christians and Jews, it fulfils God's plan for a man and woman to be united together and increase in number (Genesis 1:28 and 2:24).

Extended family

- Includes grandparents and other relatives as well.
- In Biblical times, many people lived in extended families for extra support.
- The Jewish people view themselves as an extended family, descending from Abraham, Isaac and Jacob.

Families with same-sex parents

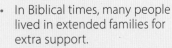

- When a homosexual couple raise children together.
- Some Christians and Orthodox Jews disapprove of same-sex parents as they believe children should grow up with a male and female role model as parents.
- Other Christians, and Reform and Liberal Jews, think it is more important for children to be in a secure and loving family regardless of the gender of the parents.

Polygamous families

- When a man has more than one wife.
- Illegal in the UK.
- For Christians and Jews, it goes against God's plan for marriage to be between one woman and one man (Genesis 2:24).
- For Christians, it can also lead to sexual immorality (1 Corinthians 7:2).

Role of parents and children

In Christianity and Judaism, parents and children are expected to fulfil certain roles or duties.

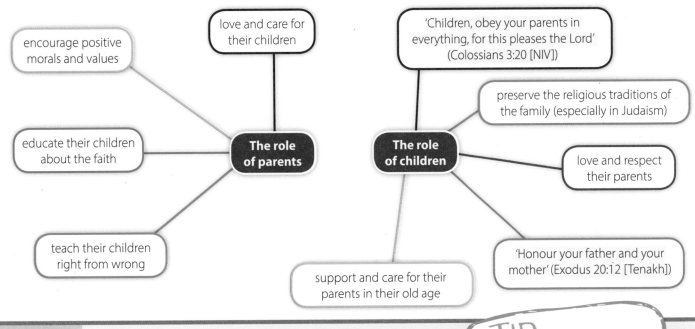

encourage positive morals and values

love and care for their children

'Children, obey your parents in everything, for this pleases the Lord' (Colossians 3:20 [NIV])

preserve the religious traditions of the family (especially in Judaism)

educate their children about the faith

The role of parents

The role of children

love and respect their parents

teach their children right from wrong

support and care for their parents in their old age

'Honour your father and your mother' (Exodus 20:12 [Tenakh])

APPLY

A Give **two** religious beliefs about the nature of the family.

B 'Children should grow up in a loving, secure family whatever the gender of their parents.'

List arguments for and against the statement. **Include religious views.**

> **TIP**
> The 'nature' of families can mean the different types of families that exist nowadays, or it may also refer to what a family should ideally be like.

5.7 The purpose of families

Essential information:

☐ The family is the main building block of society where **procreation** (bringing babies into the world) takes place.

☐ Happy, healthy families create **stability** for their members and society, helping to **protect children** and keep them safe from harm.

☐ For Christians and Jews, another purpose of the family is to **educate children in their faith** (bringing up children according to the religious beliefs of the parents).

The purpose of families

Procreation

- Mainly takes place within the family.
- For Christians, and particularly Catholics, procreation is an important purpose of the family.
- Jews consider a large family a blessing from God.

Stability and the protection of children

- Families provide secure, stable environments for children to grow up in.
- Families offer mutual support and protection for their members.

> **"** Children thrive, grow and develop within the love and safeguarding of a family. Within the family we care for the young, the old and those with caring needs. **"**
>
> *The Church of England website*

The purpose of families

Educating children in a faith

- Christian parents are expected to be good role models and teach their children Christian values.
- They should teach children about the faith and nurture their spiritual lives, which they may do through daily prayer.
- Some parents send their children to faith schools or groups run by their church for religious education.
- For Jews, bringing up their children in the Jewish faith is a duty placed on them by God.
- The Shema instructs parents to teach children God's laws: 'Take to heart these instructions […] Impress them upon your children' (Deuteronomy 6:6–7 [Tenakh]).
- A child learns how to be a Jew from family life, through stories of Jewish scripture and traditions, and through observing the Sabbath, festivals, and dietary laws.
- Parents encourage children to take part in classes and activities provided by the synagogue.

TIP
The 'purpose of families' means what families are for, or why families are needed in society.

 A Develop **both** these points by explaining in more detail, adding an example, and referring to a relevant quotation from sacred writings.

"Christian parents teach their children moral values."

"Jewish parents bring their children up in their faith."

 B 'Families should do more for their elderly relatives in Britain today.'
Evaluate this statement, giving **two** points of view.

5.8 Religious attitudes to gender equality

RECAP

Essential information:

☐ **Gender equality** means that men and women should be given the same rights and opportunities as each other.

☐ Issues standing in the way of gender equality include **gender prejudice** (holding biased opinions about people based on their gender), **sexual stereotyping** (having a fixed idea or image of how men and women will behave), and **gender discrimination** (acting against someone on the basis of their gender).

Gender discrimination and prejudice

The Sex Discrimination Act of 1975 made gender discrimination illegal in the UK. Despite this, it still occurs today.

Catholic women are not allowed to be ordained as priests and Orthodox Jewish women cannot become rabbis

In the UK, some women are paid less than men for doing the same jobs

Examples of gender prejudice and discrimination

In Judaism, only a man can initiate divorce and can refuse to grant a get to his wife

In the UK, women make up roughly half the workforce, but men hold a higher proportion of senior positions

Views on gender prejudice and discrimination, and the roles of men and women, vary between people based on their religious and personal beliefs.

In the UK	Christian views	Jewish views
• In the past, men had more power and rights than women. • Traditional roles involved men working to support the family, and women caring for the home and raising children. • Today, most people in the UK are against gender prejudice and discrimination, but it still occurs. • The roles of men and women have become more flexible, and childcare is often shared more equally between parents. • Who takes on what role in a family may be decided by financial considerations or the different skills of the parents. 	• Christians believe all people are created equal in the image of God (Genesis 1:27). ❝There is neither Jew nor Gentile, neither slave nor free, nor is there male and female, for you are all one in Christ Jesus.❞ *Galatians 3:28* [NIV] • The command to love one's neighbour means discrimination is wrong. • Jesus treated women with respect and welcomed them as disciples. • Some traditional Christians think husbands should rule over their wives, based on a literal interpretation of Genesis 3:16. • Most Christians today see marriage as an equal partnership.	• Jews believe all people are created equal in the image of God (Genesis 1:27). • The Tenakh tells stories of well-respected women prophets, e.g. Deborah, Abigail and Huldah. • In Orthodox Judaism, roles are 'separate but equal': men support the family and women care for the children and home. Women can have careers outside the home but always try to fulfil their role as wife and mother. • In Reform and Liberal Judaism, women can become rabbis, sit with men in the synagogue, and handle the Torah scrolls. They have equality of opportunity in all other areas of life, sharing duties within religion and the home.

APPLY

(A) **Explain the difference** between prejudice and discrimination.

(B) **Develop an argument** in support of the statement, 'Men and women do not have equal rights' by explaining in more detail, adding an example and referring to a religious teaching or quotation.

TIP You can also use information from the theme 'Human rights and social justice' in your answers.

5 Exam practice

Test the 1 mark question

1 Which **one** of the following is **not** a reason why some marriages fail?

A ☐ Domestic violence   B ☐ Adultery   C ☐ Addiction   D ☐ Stability   **[1 mark]**

2 Which **one** of the following describes a nuclear family?

A ☐ A couple, children and grandparents   B ☐ A couple and their children

C ☐ A couple, children, aunts and uncles   D ☐ A couple without children   **[1 mark]**

Test the 2 mark question

3 Give **two** religious beliefs about gender equality.   **[2 marks]**

1) _____

2) _____

4 Give **two** religious beliefs about cohabitation.   **[2 marks]**

1) _____

2) _____

Test the 4 mark question

5 Explain **two** contrasting beliefs in contemporary British society about sex before marriage.

In your answer you should refer to the main religious tradition of Great Britain and one or more other religious traditions.   **[4 marks]**

● **Explain one belief.**	*Some Christians believe that sex before marriage is all right if the couple has a committed, loving relationship.*
● Develop your explanation with more detail/an example/ reference to a religious teaching or quotation.	*Although they think that it is better to get married, they accept that people can be faithful to each other and committed to the relationship even if they have not been officially married.*
● **Explain a second belief.**	*Orthodox Jews do not agree with sex before marriage because it undermines the importance of creating a family through which Jewish religion and traditions are passed down.*
● Develop your explanation with more detail/an example/ reference to a religious teaching or quotation.	*They think that children have a right to be born into a secure family and that sex before marriage can lower the dignity of the people involved.*

TIP

It is important to say 'some' here, as many Christians, including the Orthodox and Catholic Churches, disapprove of sex before marriage.

6 Explain **two** contrasting religious beliefs about divorce.

In your answer you must refer to one or more religious traditions.   **[4 marks]**

● **Explain one belief.**	
● Develop your explanation with more detail/an example/ reference to a religious teaching or quotation.	
● **Explain a second belief.**	
● Develop your explanation with more detail/an example/ reference to a religious teaching or quotation.	

TIP

You can answer this question from the perspective of two denominations or from two religions.

7 Explain **two** contrasting religious beliefs about human sexuality.

In your answer you must refer to one or more religious traditions.   **[4 marks]**

5 Exam practice

Test the 5 mark question

8   Explain **two** religious beliefs about the nature of marriage.

Refer to sacred writings or another source of religious belief and teaching in your answer.   **[5 marks]**

● **Explain one belief.**	*Jews believe that marriage was intended by God for the sharing of love and companionship between a man and a woman.*
● Develop your explanation with more detail/an example.	*The Torah explains that Eve was created to be a companion for Adam (Genesis 2:18).*
● **Explain a second belief.**	*A Christian belief about the nature of marriage is that marriage is a sacrament.*
● Develop your explanation with more detail/an example.	*This means that marriage is a lifelong union blessed by God, because the couple makes promises before God that they will be faithful to each other 'till death us do part'.*
● Add a reference to sacred writings or another source of religious belief and teaching. If you prefer, you can add this reference to your first belief instead.	*The Bible reflects this idea when it says, 'That is why a man leaves his father and mother and is united to his wife, and they become one flesh.'*

TIP
There is no need to put the Bible reference in your answer as long as you quote or paraphrase the passage.

9   Explain **two** religious beliefs about the purpose of families.

Refer to sacred writings or another source of religious belief and teaching in your answer.

[5 marks]

● **Explain one belief.**	
● Develop your explanation with more detail/an example.	
● **Explain a second belief.**	
● Develop your explanation with more detail/an example.	
● Add a reference to sacred writings or another source of religious belief and teaching. If you prefer, you can add this reference to your first belief instead.	

10   Explain **two** religious beliefs about the role of children in a religious family.

Refer to sacred writings or another source of religious belief and teaching in your answer.

[5 marks]

Test the 12 mark question

11 'The love and care parents show in bringing up their children is all that matters; the sex of the parents is unimportant.'

Evaluate this statement. In your answer you:

- should give reasoned arguments in support of this statement
- should give reasoned arguments to support a different point of view
- should refer to religious arguments
- may refer to non-religious arguments
- should reach a justified conclusion.

[12 marks]

[+3 SPaG mark

REASONED ARGUMENTS SUPPORTING A DIFFERENT VIEW ● **Explain why some people would support a different view.** ● Develop your explanation with more detail and examples. ● Refer to religious teaching. Use a quote or paraphrase or refer to a religious authority. ● **Evaluate the arguments.** Is this a good argument or not? Explain why you think this.	*It is true that the love and care parents show in bringing up their children is the most important thing for a good family life. Without love and care, children would grow up deprived of stability and security. But the statement says 'the sex of the parents is unimportant' and that is where people may have different views.* *Some Christians disapprove of same-sex parents because they think God made people male and female so that they would 'be fruitful and increase in number' (Genesis 1:28). Same-sex couples cannot do this naturally. Some also think the ideal for children is to grow up with a male and female role model as parents. Orthodox Jews believe that homosexual relationships are morally wrong so do not approve of such couples raising children. An important role of religious parents is to bring up their children in their faith. If their religion disagrees with homosexual relationships, then it is difficult for same-sex parents to bring their children up within the religion that disapproves of their behaviour.*
REASONED ARGUMENTS IN SUPPORT OF THE STATEMENT ● **Explain why some people would agree with the statement.** ● Develop your explanation with more detail and examples. ● Refer to religious teaching. Use a quote or paraphrase or refer to a religious authority. ● **Evaluate the arguments.** Is this a good argument or not? Explain why you think this.	*On the other hand, many liberal Christians and Reform Jews think that it is more important that children are raised in a secure and loving family regardless of the gender of their parents. There is nothing to say same-sex parents are not religious even if particular faiths disapprove of their relationships. Many can still bring their children up to love God or live spiritual and morally good lives.*
CONCLUSION ● **Give a justified conclusion.** ● Include your own opinion together with your own reasoning. ● **Include evaluation**. Explain why you think one viewpoint is stronger than the other or why they are equally strong. ● Do not just repeat arguments you have already used without explaining how they apply to your reasoned opinion/conclusion.	*In conclusion, I think that whether parents are good at bringing up children depends on the individuals and not on their gender. Some heterosexual couples spoil their children or even abuse them, which does not show good parenting. Many children live in single-parent families so do not have the benefit of a male and female role model anyway. The most important thing any family should have is love, and this is at the heart of all religions.*

TIP
In this answer the student begins presenting a different point of view followed by arguments supporting the statement. It doesn't matter which order the arguments appear in, as long as you remember to include both sides.

TIP
Religious attitudes to some issues vary <u>within</u> religions as well as <u>between</u> religions, so it helps to say 'some Christians' or 'liberal Christians' to show you understand that not all Christians share the same views.

TIP
This is a top level answer which uses logical chains of reasoning and well supported arguments with reference to religion. The justified conclusion does not merely repeat what was said but offers a personal viewpoint supported by examples.

12 'Marriage is the proper place to enjoy a sexual relationship.'

Evaluate this statement. In your answer you:

- should give reasoned arguments in support of this statement
- should give reasoned arguments to support a different point of view
- should refer to religious arguments
- may refer to non-religious arguments
- should reach a justified conclusion.

[12 marks]
[+3 SPaG marks]

REASONED ARGUMENTS IN SUPPORT OF THE STATEMENT ● **Explain why some people would agree with the statement.** ● Develop your explanation with more detail and examples. ● Refer to religious teaching. Use a quote or paraphrase or refer to a religious authority. ● **Evaluate the arguments.** Is this a good argument or not? Explain why you think this.	
REASONED ARGUMENTS SUPPORTING A DIFFERENT VIEW ● **Explain why some people would support a different view.** ● Develop your explanation with more detail and examples. ● Refer to religious teaching. Use a quote or paraphrase or refer to a religious authority. ● **Evaluate the arguments.** Is this a good argument or not? Explain why you think this.	
CONCLUSION ● **Give a justified conclusion.** ● Include your own opinion together with your own reasoning. ● **Include evaluation.** Explain why you think one viewpoint is stronger than the other or why they are equally strong. ● Do not just repeat arguments you have already used without explaining how they apply to your reasoned opinion/conclusion.	

TIP

When evaluating a statement like this one, do not simply list what different people think about the issue, for example 'Christians would agree that the best place to enjoy sex is in marriage. Jews also think...' Remember to explain the reasons why they hold these opinions and to add an evaluation of how convincing you find these views to be.

13 'It is wrong for religious couples to use artificial contraception within marriage.'

Evaluate this statement. In your answer you:

- should give reasoned arguments in support of this statement
- should give reasoned arguments to support a different point of view
- should refer to religious arguments
- may refer to non-religious arguments
- should reach a justified conclusion.

[12 marks]
[+3 SPaG marks]

Check your answers using the mark scheme on pages 161–162. How did you do?
To feel more secure in the content you need to remember, re-read pages 80–87.
To remind yourself of what the examiner is looking for, go to pages 7–13.

6.1 The origins of the universe

Essential information:

☐ The **Big Bang theory** suggests there was a massive expansion of space that set the creation of the universe in motion. This theory is accepted by most Christians and Jews.

☐ Christians and Jews also use the Genesis creation stories to explain the origins of the universe, which they believe was created by God.

Christian and Jewish beliefs about the creation of the universe

Christians and Jews believe the universe was designed and made by God out of nothing. The creation story in Genesis 1 says that God made the universe and all life in it in six days, resting on the seventh.

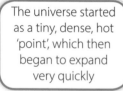

Day 1 – Light and darkness
Day 2 – The sky
Day 3 – Land, sea, vegetation and plants
Day 4 – The sun, moon and stars
Day 5 – Fish and sea creatures, birds
Day 6 – Animals and humans
Day 7 – God was pleased and rested

- **Some Fundamentalist Christians** believe the creation story describes exactly how the universe was created. Others believe that the seven days describe seven longer periods of time.
- **Liberal Christians** believe the creation story is symbolic, where the main message is that God created the universe. They might look to science to understand *how* God did this.
- Some **Orthodox Jews** believe the creation story should be taken literally, and that it describes the exact way the world was created.

- **Reform Jews** understand the creation story as a way of emphasising the special place that humans have in God's creation. They are made in the image of God and have a responsibility for the world.
- Many Jews believe the days referred to in the story are not days as we now understand them, but indications of the different stages of creation, each of which may represent millions of years.

> ❝In the beginning God created the heavens and the earth❞
>
> *Genesis 1:1–2* [NIV]

> ❝And God created man in His image, in the image of God He created him; male and female He created them.❞
>
> *Genesis 1:27* [Tenakh]

The Big Bang theory

| The universe started as a tiny, dense, hot 'point', which then began to expand very quickly | → | As the universe expanded and cooled, matter became separated by great distances | → | Gravity grouped the matter into stars and galaxies | → | The universe has continued to expand over billions of years to form the cosmos as we know it today |

- Many Christians and Jews accept the Big Bang theory, but unlike atheists they believe the Big Bang was caused by God and that the universe came about by design, not by accident.
- It is possible to accept the Big Bang theory and the Genesis creation story if the story is not interpreted literally, and each 'day' in the story is taken to mean a much longer period of time.

Ⓐ Give **two** contrasting ways in which people interpret the Genesis creation story.

Ⓑ Can the Big Bang theory be a way of explaining how God created the earth? Give at least **one** reason for agreeing and **one** for disagreeing.

RECAP

Essential information:

☐ Christians and Jews believe the earth to be valuable because God created it.

☐ Christians and Jews believe that people have a duty to protect and care for the earth and its environment; this is known as **stewardship**.

How valuable is the world?

- For Christians and Jews, the beauty of the world can give a sense of **awe** (devout respect for God's power of creation) and **wonder** (marvelling at the complexity of the universe).
- They believe the earth and nature are so amazing because they provide everything humans and other living things need to survive.
- It is a duty in both religions to respect, nurture and care for the environment.

> **❝** When I consider your heavens [...] what is mankind that you are mindful of them, human beings that you care for them? **❞**
>
> *Psalm 8:3–4* [NIV]

Stewardship and dominion

- The Tenakh and the Bible make it clear that humans were given responsibility to look after the earth for God.

Christian beliefs	Jewish beliefs
• Genesis 2 says that Adam, the first man on earth, was given the role of stewardship over the earth, looking after it for God. > **❝** The Lord God took the man (Adam) and put him in the Garden of Eden to work it and take care of it. **❞** > *Genesis 2:15* [NIV] • This responsibility has been passed down to humankind, which means it is the role of all humans to look after the earth for God. If they use it wrongly, they are destroying what belongs to God. • In return for looking after the earth, humans are allowed to use it to sustain life.	• In return for the God-given privilege of living on earth, humans have a duty to manage the earth to ensure it is not damaged or destroyed. • Failing to look after the environment is neglecting what God has given to humans to protect. • The Jewish concept of bal tashchit ('do not destroy') forbids any unnecessary destruction. > **❝** See to it that you do not spoil and destroy My world; for if you do, there will be no one else to repair it. **❞** > *Ecclesiastes Rabbah 7:13* [Tenakh]

- Christianity and Judaism teach that God gave humans power and authority to take charge of the earth. This is called **dominion**.
- A minority interpret this as meaning that humans can do whatever they want because they are in charge.
- Most Christians and Jews believe that doing whatever they want is selfish, destructive and against what God requires from humans.

> **❝** [...] fill the earth and subdue it. Rule over the fish in the sea and the birds in the sky and over every living creature that moves on the ground. **❞**
>
> *Genesis 1:28* [NIV]

The use of natural resources

- Population growth is having a great impact on the environment and natural world. For example, forests are being destroyed. **Non-renewable resources** such as oil, coal and gas are being used up and will eventually run out.
- It is increasingly important to encourage **sustainable development** (progress that tries to reduce the impact on the natural world for future generations). Scientists are developing **renewable energies** from sources that won't run out, such as wind or solar energy.
- Christians and Jews believe they should avoid waste and conserve energy, for example by turning off unused electrical appliances, reusing bags when shopping, and recycling waste.

TIP

Stewardship has a specific religious meaning. The examiner will be impressed if you can use it properly.

APPLY

A What does stewardship mean?

B 'God's earth is a wonderful and valuable place.'

Give **two** reasons to agree with this and **develop each one**.

6.3 The use and abuse of the environment, and pollution

Essential information:

☐ Air, land and water **pollution** (making something dirty and contaminated, especially the environment) are a major threat to life on earth.

☐ Christians and Jews show their concern by taking action to help to protect the earth against **abuse** – misuse of the world and the environment.

The main types of pollution

Pollution has increased with the growing population.

Pollution type	Cause	Possible problems caused
Air	Fumes from factories and transport	Global warming, climate change, acid rain, diseases such as asthma and lung cancer
Land	Poor disposal of waste	Chemicals pollute the earth causing poisoned wildlife, inefficient farming and poisoned food
Water	Dumping waste into rivers and seas	Oil spills and plastic waste kill birds and marine life

Christian and Jewish beliefs

Christians and Jews want to prevent misuse of the environment. They might base their views on the following teachings:

Christian teachings	Jewish teachings
• The world is on loan to humans, who have been given the responsibility by God to look after it (Genesis 1:28). • The parable of the Talents (Matthew 25:14–30) warns that God will be the final judge about how responsible humans have been in looking after the earth. • Pollution is not loving towards others – Jesus teaches Christians to 'love your neighbour' (Luke 10:27 [NIV]).	• Humans are accountable to God for how they look after the earth. ❝You have made him master over Your handiwork, laying the world at his feet❞ *Psalm 8:7* [Tenakh] • The Torah instructed Jews to rest the land every seven years to help protect it and allow it to regain its fertility (Leviticus 25:4–5). • Jews are instructed not to destroy trees in Deuteronomy 20:19.

What do Christians and Jews do about the environment?

- In **1986**, religious leaders met at **Assisi** in Italy to discuss how religious people everywhere could help to care for the environment.
- As part of their statement in The Assisi Declarations on Nature, Christians wrote: 'Every human act of irresponsibility towards creatures is an abomination [disgrace]' (Alliance of Religions and Conservation).
- Religious leaders met again at **Ohito** in Japan in **1995**, where they stressed that being in charge of creation does not give people the right to abuse, spoil, waste or destroy the earth.
- Some Christians and Jews support organisations that aim to protect the environment on a global scale, such as Greenpeace, Friends of the Earth, or the Coalition on the Environment and Jewish Life.
- Some Christian and Jewish groups work in their local communities to clean up the environment, for example by litter-picking.

 Explain **two** religious beliefs about why polluting the earth is wrong.

 'Religious believers are not doing enough to help the environment'.

Evaluate this statement.

RECAP

Essential information:

☐ Christians and Jews believe that God made all living creatures and that they should be treated well.

☐ There are different Christian and Jewish views about animal experimentation and using animals for food.

You might be asked to compare beliefs on animal experimentation between Christianity (the main religious tradition in Great Britain) and another religious tradition.

The use of animals for food

Vegetarians do not eat meat or fish, while **vegans** do not eat animals or food produced by animals (such as eggs). Vegans also try not to use products that have caused harm to animals (such as leather).

Christian views	Jewish views
• Christianity has no rules about eating meat. • Romans 14:3 says Christians should be sensitive to the beliefs of others about what they wish to eat. • Most Christians eat meat. They believe God gave humans animals to use for food. ❝Everything that lives and moves about will be food for you.❞ *Genesis 9:3* [NIV] • Some Christian vegetarians and vegans point out that if crops were grown on land currently used to raise animals for meat, there would be much more food to go round and this would please God.	• The Torah describes how God gave Noah permission to eat meat after the flood (Genesis 9:3). Many Jews today eat meat, although some choose to be vegetarians or vegans. • Jewish dietary laws give strict rules about how animals must be slaughtered to keep their suffering to a minimum. • They also forbid eating meat from certain animals (such as pigs), and do not allow meat and dairy products to be mixed. • Food that Jews are allowed to eat is called kosher.

❝The one who eats everything (including meat) must not treat with contempt the one who does not, and the one who does not eat everything must not judge the one who does, for God has accepted them.❞

Romans 14:3 [NIV]

Christian and Jewish beliefs about animal experimentation

• Scientists use animals to test new products such as cosmetics, medicines and food, to make sure they are safe for humans to use.
• Causing animals unnecessary harm and stress is against Christian and Jewish teachings.
• Most Christians and Jews believe that if testing is proved to be necessary, and the welfare of the animals is considered, it is justified to ensure human safety (e.g. to develop new medicines).
• Most Christians and Jews believe that testing cosmetics on animals is wrong. This is banned in the UK and Israel.
• Many Christians and Jews believe that stewardship involves treating all life with care as it is given by God. However, some Christians and Jews would also use the principle of dominion to support using animals to benefit humans.

APPLY

A Explain **two** contrasting beliefs in contemporary British society about animal experimentation. You should refer to the main religious tradition in Great Britain and one or more other religious traditions.

B 'Experimenting on animals is wrong because it is cruel.'

Develop this statement and elaborate it with religious teachings, explaining how the teachings are relevant to the argument.

TIP
You could use the Christian idea of dominion and one other religious teaching in order to have contrasting beliefs.

RECAP

Essential information:

☐ Religion and science both attempt to explain the origins of human life.

☐ Many Christians and Jews think it is possible to believe both the creation story and the theory of **evolution** (how organisms are thought to have developed from earlier forms of life).

The origins of human life in the Bible and the Torah

Genesis 1 says that God created all life, with human life being created last: 'So God created mankind in his own image, in the image of God he created him; male and female he created them' (Genesis 1:27 [NIV]).

Genesis 2 describes how God created the first man, Adam, from the soil and breathed life into him.

> **❝** the LORD God formed man from the dust of the Earth. He blew into his nostrils the breath of life, and man became a living being. **❞**
>
> *Genesis 2:7* [Tenakh]

- Adam was given responsibility to look after his environment – the Garden of Eden.
- Some time later, while Adam was asleep, God took one of his ribs and used it to create a woman, Eve. God intended

for Eve to help Adam, and that they would live in a close relationship with each other and with him.

- Adam and Eve disobeyed God by eating fruit from the forbidden tree when tempted by a serpent to do so.
- God punished Adam and Eve for their disobedience. They were removed from the Garden of Eden, Adam was told that men must work hard because the ground would produce thorns and thistles, and Eve was told that women would endure pain in childbirth.
- Adam and Eve regretted their disobedience. Being aware of this regret is an essential part of following and serving God.
- God created everything necessary for Adam and Eve to live on earth and to be the start of the human race.
- The story shows that humans are very special to God because they were created in his image.

The theory of evolution

In 1859, in a book called *On the Origin of Species by Means of Natural Selection*, Charles Darwin put forward the theory of evolution. He suggested that as the earth cooled, conditions became right to support life. Simple organisms then evolved over many years into other species:

| Life started with single-celled creatures in the sea | → | Over a long period of time they evolved (changed) into creatures capable of living on land | → | Humans started evolving around 2.5 million years ago | → | They developed into humans with the same anatomy as us about 200,000 years ago |

Over time, creatures needed to change or **adapt** to their surroundings. The ones that did this best thrived. This is called survival of the fittest.

Religious debate on evolution

- Some Christians and Jews are creationists who believe that the origin of human life is exactly as recorded in scripture, and who reject the theory of evolution.
- Many Christians and Jews accept the mainstream scientific view of evolution and do not believe it should cause conflict with their faith. They believe God created the beginnings of life and set everything in motion to develop over the course of history.
- Some Jews argue that the theory of evolution may be correct as the days in Genesis are not meant to be taken as 24 hour days, but as much longer periods of time.

APPLY

(A) Explain **two** religious responses to the theory of evolution.

(B) 'The story of Adam and Eve is more important than the theory of evolution.'

Write **two chains of reasoning**, one that agrees with this view and one that disagrees with it. A chain of reasoning includes an opinion, a reason, development of your reasoning and religious beliefs and teaching.

TIP

Chains of reasoning are important in 12 mark questions.

RECAP

Essential information:

- ☐ Abortion is legal in the UK provided doctors agree it meets certain criteria.
- ☐ Christians and Jews believe in the **sanctity of life**: that life is holy and given by God, therefore only God can take it away.
- ☐ However, when considering the issue of abortion, many people will also consider **quality of life** (the general well-being of a person, in relation to their health and happiness).

 You might be asked to compare beliefs on abortion between Christianity (the main religious tradition in Great Britain) and another religious tradition.

Abortion in the UK

- **Abortion** is the deliberate removal of a foetus from the womb in order to end a pregnancy.
- In the UK, an abortion can take place in a licensed clinic if two doctors agree there is a risk to the physical or mental health of the mother, the baby, or existing children in the family.
- Abortion can only happen during the first 24 weeks of pregnancy unless the mother's life is in danger or the foetus is severely deformed. In these cases there is no time limit.

Christian and Jewish beliefs about abortion

Christian beliefs	Jewish beliefs

• Christians believe in the sanctity of life. This means that human life is sacred as it is made in the image of God. All human life should be valued and respected.
 	
• Psalm 139:13 suggests to Christians that abortion is wrong as it is taking away what God has created.
 	
   ❝For you created my inmost being; you knit me together in my mother's womb.❞
   Psalm 139:13 [NIV]
 	
• Some Christians may agree with abortion if the baby is likely to have a very poor quality of life, for example if they will be born with a severe disability.
 	
• Other Christians may support abortion if it appears to be the kindest option in the circumstance, for example in instances of rape.
 	
• The Catholic Church, along with many evangelical Christians, believes that abortion is wrong because life begins at conception, so abortion is taking away life given by God.
	• Jews believe in the sanctity of life. Humans are made in the image of God, which makes life precious.
	
	• Jews have a duty to save and preserve life wherever possible (pikuach nefesh).
	
	• Judaism teaches that a foetus does not become a person until it is halfway down the birth canal, so abortion is not considered to be murder.
	
	• However, the foetus should be protected because it is growing towards being a person, and should not be harmed without a very good reason.
	
	• This means most Jews are against abortion unless there are serious reasons to consider it.
	
	• For example, if the pregnancy is the result of rape or incest, if the baby will be born disabled or have a poor quality of life, or if the mother's health is at risk if the pregnancy continues. (The mother's life is considered to be more important than the life of the foetus.)
	
	• A rabbi may be consulted by a Jew considering an abortion, as there are different views in Judaism about when it should be allowed.

APPLY

A Give **two** religious teachings that may be used to argue against abortion.

B 'If the child's quality of life is not going to be good, abortion is the best option.'

Write and fully develop an argument to support this statement, then write a second developed argument to support a different point of view. Include religious arguments in your answer.

TIP
It may be a good idea to define terms such as 'quality of life' in your answer.

RECAP

Essential information:

- [ ] **Euthanasia** means 'a good or gentle death', and involves painlessly ending the life of someone who is dying.
- [ ] Christians and Jews generally oppose euthanasia, although some may agree with it when it seems to be the most loving action to take.

 You might be asked to compare beliefs on euthanasia between Christianity (the main religious tradition in Great Britain) and another religious tradition.

What is euthanasia?

Active euthanasia involves taking deliberate steps to end a person's life, for example by giving them a lethal injection. This is illegal in the UK. There are three main types of euthanasia:

Voluntary:	**Involuntary:**	**Non-voluntary:**
the ill person asks for their life to be ended because they don't want to live any more.	the person is capable of expressing a choice but is not given the opportunity to do so.	the person is unable to express a choice, for example a baby or a person in a coma.

- Doctors can decide to withhold treatment if it is in the patient's best interests, for example by not resuscitating a person after a heart attack or by withdrawing food. This would not be considered euthanasia as it is allowing death to take place rather than actively ending a life.
- Some countries in Europe allow euthanasia under certain strict criteria.

Christian beliefs

Some Christians believe that euthanasia may be acceptable in some cases to end a person's suffering, but many believe it is never right to take a life.

Arguments in favour	**Arguments against**
• God gives people free will to end their own life.	• Euthanasia is a form of murder.
• Euthanasia may be the most loving and compassionate thing to do, following Jesus' teaching to 'love your neighbour' (Luke 10:27 [NIV]).	• It is open to abuse and may be against the will of the ill person.
• Euthanasia allows a good and gentle death, which may not be the case if natural death occurs.	• Only God should take life at the time of his choosing.
• Euthanasia allows a dignified death.	• It goes against the sanctity of life.
• Drugs to end life are God-given so can be used.	• If euthanasia were legal, the very old could feel pressure to end their lives in order not to burden their family.
	• The Salvation Army has said that euthanasia and assisted suicide 'undermine human dignity and are morally wrong'.

Jewish beliefs

- Judaism teaches that euthanasia is murder, regardless of whether the person wants to die.
- All human life is sacred and of great value. People are still fully human during the final stages of their life, and should receive good medical care and attention.

> **"** A season is set for everything, a time for every experience under heaven: A time for being born and a time for dying. **"**
>
> *Ecclesiastes 3:1–2* [Tenakh]

- Judaism teaches that doctors have a duty to save and preserve life.
- This does not mean that doctors should extend the suffering of the dying. For example, doctors can turn off life-support machines if they are preventing a natural death, and pain relief can be given even if it may make death happen sooner.

APPLY

A **Explain** an argument in favour of euthanasia and show how religious beliefs may disagree with this.

B 'Active euthanasia should never be allowed.'

Write an argument to support this statement **and develop your reasoning**. Add and explain some religious teaching to elaborate your answer.

TIP
If you include love and compassion in your answer, make sure you explain who it is loving and compassionate towards.

6.8 Death and the afterlife

RECAP

Essential information:

☐ Both Christians and Jews believe that death is not the end but the beginning of an afterlife.

☐ Both believe that God will judge everyone (both believers and non-believers) on how they have lived their lives on earth.

☐ God's judgement will determine what happens to people after death.

Is death the end?

For both Christians and Jews, belief in an afterlife and God's judgement has an effect on how they live their lives.

Christian beliefs	Jewish beliefs
• Christians believe that death is the beginning of an eternal life that depends on faith in God. • It begins at death or on the Day of Judgement, when God judges people's behaviour as well as their faith in following Jesus. • God's judgement results in the person spending **eternity** (a state that comes after death and never ends) either with God in heaven or without God in hell.	• Jews believe that life is more of an immediate concern than death. • There are different opinions between Jews about what happens after death. • There are references in the Torah to death being a time to re-join one's ancestors, and in the Tenakh to a place of silence and darkness called Sheol. • Orthodox Jews believe in resurrection – a time when the soul will reunite with the body. Some attach this belief to the coming of the Messiah. • Reform and Liberal Jews do not believe in such a resurrection. • Orthodox Jews believe in heaven (Gan Eden) once a temporary soul-cleansing process has taken place. They do not believe in eternal punishment.

TIP

See pages 21–23 and 51 for more on Christian and Jewish beliefs about life after death and God's judgement.

The value of human life

- All religions emphasise that everyone is accountable for their actions on earth and all actions have consequences, good or bad. Both Christians and Jews believe that God gives guidance about how to live their lives, but God also gives humans free will to choose between doing right and doing wrong.
- Doing the right thing involves resisting temptation to stray from God's path.
- These decisions have important consequences for eternal life after death. Making the right choices, resisting temptation and following their faith in the way God requires will ensure an eternal afterlife with God.

Everybody can choose how to live their one life	→	Being given free will shows that God considers human life to be of great value	→	Human life should be respected in the way people behave towards each other	→	How people decide to act has eternal consequences	→	This encourages believers to follow God and obey his laws

APPLY

A **Explain** what Christians believe will happen on the Day of Judgement.

B 'The fear of eternal punishment is the only thing that makes religious people value human life.'

Develop an idea that agrees with this statement and one that does not. Include religious teaching.

6 Exam practice

Test the 1 mark question

1 Which **one** of the following gives the meaning of the term euthanasia?

A ☐ A type of abortion

B ☐ A method of animal testing

C ☐ A good or gentle death

D ☐ A scientific view about the origin of the earth

[1 mark]

2 Which **one** of the following gives the meaning of the term sanctity of life?

A ☐ Life never ends

B ☐ Life is sacred

C ☐ Life is of high quality

D ☐ Life has an end

[1 mark]

Test the 2 mark question

3 Give **two** religious reasons for reducing pollution.

1) _____

2) _____

[2 marks]

4 Give **two** religious beliefs about heaven.

1) _____

2) _____

[2 marks]

Test the 4 mark question

5 Explain **two** contrasting beliefs in contemporary British society about abortion.

In your answer you should refer to the main religious tradition of Great Britain and one or more other religious traditions.

[4 marks]

● **Explain one belief.**	Christians believe that life is God-given.
● Develop your explanation with more detail/an example/ reference to a religious teaching or quotation.	For some Christians, ending life prematurely is not allowed because it is against God's plan for that person, even if they haven't yet been born.
● **Explain a second belief.**	Many Jews believe that in certain circumstances abortion is the best option.
● Develop your explanation with more detail/an example/ reference to a religious teaching or quotation.	If the child is unlikely to survive or if the life of the mother is in danger then abortion is the loving thing to do.

TIP

This question says that 'you should refer to the main religious tradition of Great Britain' so you need to make at least one reference to Christianity.

6 Explain **two** similar religious beliefs about animal experimentation.

In your answer, you must refer to one or more religious traditions.

[4 marks]

● **Explain one belief.**	
● Develop your explanation with more detail/an example/ reference to a religious teaching or quotation.	
● **Explain a second belief.**	
● Develop your explanation with more detail/an example/ reference to a religious teaching or quotation.	

TIP

This question asks for 'two similar religious beliefs'. You could refer to a similar belief from two different religions, such as Christianity and Judaism, or from two different traditions within the same religion, such as Catholicism and Protestantism. But remember that the beliefs must be **similar**.

7 Explain **two** contrasting religious beliefs about the use of natural resources.

In your answer, you must refer to one or more religious traditions.

[4 marks]

6 Exam practice

Test the 5 mark question

8 Explain **two** religious beliefs about what happens when a person dies.

Refer to sacred writings or another source of religious belief and teaching in your answer.   **[5 marks]**

● **Explain one belief.**	*Orthodox Jews believe in the resurrection of the dead.*
● Develop your explanation with more detail/an example.	*This is a time when the soul will reunite with the body, and is often connected to the coming of the Messiah.*
● Add a reference to sacred writings or another source of religious belief and teaching. If you prefer, you can add this reference to your second belief instead.	*This view is supported by the book of Daniel: 'Many of those who sleep in the dust of the earth will awake, some to eternal life.'*
● **Explain a second belief.**	*Christians believe the faithful will be granted a place in heaven by God.*
● Develop your explanation with more detail/an example.	*Heaven is seen as existence in the presence of God, which lasts for eternity.*

> **TIP**
> In this answer, the reference to sacred writing has been added here to the first belief.

> **TIP**
> These beliefs come from separate religions. Separate beliefs from the same religion can also be used.

9 Explain **two** religious beliefs about the duty of human beings to protect the earth.

Refer to sacred writings or another source of religious belief and teaching in your answer.   **[5 marks]**

● **Explain one belief.**	
● Develop your explanation with more detail/an example.	
● **Explain a second belief.**	
● Develop your explanation with more detail/an example.	
● Add a reference to sacred writings or another source of religious belief and teaching. If you prefer, you can add this reference to your first belief instead.	

10 Explain **two** religious beliefs about the origins of the universe.

Refer to sacred writings or another source of religious belief and teaching in your answer.   **[5 marks]**

Test the 12 mark question

11 'Religious believers should not eat meat.'

Evaluate this statement. In your answer you:

- should give reasoned arguments in support of this statement
- should give reasoned arguments to support a different point of view
- should refer to religious arguments
- may refer to non-religious arguments
- should reach a justified conclusion.

[12 marks]

[+3 SPaG mark

REASONED ARGUMENTS IN SUPPORT OF THE STATEMENT ● **Explain why some people would agree with the statement.** ● Develop your explanation with more detail and examples. ● Refer to religious teaching. Use a quote or paraphrase or refer to a religious authority. ● **Evaluate the arguments.** Is this a good argument or not? Explain why you think this.	*Eating meat involves the killing of animals to provide the meat. This is seen by many religious believers as cruel and unnecessary and they are quite happy to be vegetarians. For others, it is not just the killing of the animals that is the problem – the way they are treated throughout their short lives is much worse. Their death, so they can be used as meat, is often merciful because it ends their inhumane treatment. Some of the worst abuse happens to chickens who live their lives in cages in barns and never see daylight or breathe fresh air because they never leave their cage. This completely ignores the stewardship role humans have which means they should care for all living creatures. All living beings are valuable to God: 'not one of them is forgotten by God'.*
REASONED ARGUMENTS SUPPORTING A DIFFERENT VIEW ● **Explain why some people would support a different view.** ● Develop your explanation with more detail and examples. ● Refer to religious teaching. Use a quote or paraphrase or refer to a religious authority. ● **Evaluate the arguments.** Is this a good argument or not? Explain why you think this.	*Most Christians and Jews do eat meat because they believe it is a good source of protein or they like the taste of it. Although they believe that animals should not be treated cruelly, they believe that animals were created by God for human use, which includes killing them for food. As far as we know Jesus ate meat, and the fact that food laws are important in Judaism, and include rules about how to kill animals for meat, means that Judaism is not against the eating of meat.*
CONCLUSION ● **Give a justified conclusion.** ● Include your own opinion together with your own reasoning. ● **Include evaluation**. Explain why you think one viewpoint is stronger than the other or why they are equally strong. ● Do not just repeat arguments you have already used without explaining how they apply to your reasoned opinion/conclusion.	*So there is a difference of opinion concerning whether it is right to eat meat. Although I can see why some people prefer not to kill animals, I believe that meat is important for a balanced diet. Also many farmers would lose their livelihoods if people stopped eating meat. In my opinion it would be unfair on religious believers if they were prevented from enjoying meat. I can see that if your religion opposes meat eating then you would need to keep the rules of your faith. However, neither Christianity nor Judaism does this, although some Christians and Jews choose to become vegetarians anyway.*

TIP

This section about the treatment of animals shows an excellent chain of reasoning. It starts with an introductory statement, followed by development that refers to religious teaching.

TIP

Although there is good content in here, greater development about food laws in Judaism would improve it, e.g further explanation about how animals are killed humanely.

TIP

This is a good conclusion because it includes reference to the arguments already made and supports them with more reasoning, not just the same as before.

12 'The law on abortion should be changed in the UK.'

Evaluate this statement. In your answer you:

- should give reasoned arguments in support of this statement
- should give reasoned arguments to support a different point of view
- should refer to religious arguments
- may refer to non-religious arguments
- should reach a justified conclusion.

[12 marks]
[+3 SPaG marks]

REASONED ARGUMENTS IN SUPPORT OF THE STATEMENT ● **Explain why some people would agree with the statement.** ● Develop your explanation with more detail and examples. ● Refer to religious teaching. Use a quote or paraphrase or refer to a religious authority. ● **Evaluate the arguments.** Is this a good argument or not? Explain why you think this.	
REASONED ARGUMENTS SUPPORTING A DIFFERENT VIEW ● **Explain why some people would support a different view.** ● Develop your explanation with more detail and examples. ● Refer to religious teaching. Use a quote or paraphrase or refer to a religious authority. ● **Evaluate the arguments.** Is this a good argument or not? Explain why you think this.	
CONCLUSION ● **Give a justified conclusion.** ● Include your own opinion together with your own reasoning. ● **Include evaluation**. Explain why you think one viewpoint is stronger than the other or why they are equally strong. ● Do not just repeat arguments you have already used without explaining how they apply to your reasoned opinion/conclusion.	

13 'Humans should use the earth's resources however they wish.'

Evaluate this statement. In your answer you:

- should give reasoned arguments in support of this statement
- should give reasoned arguments to support a different point of view
- should refer to religious arguments
- may refer to non-religious arguments
- should reach a justified conclusion.

[12 marks]
[+3 SPaG marks]

Check your answers using the mark scheme on pages 162–163. How did you do?
To feel more secure in the content you need to remember, re-read pages 92–99.
To remind yourself of what the examiner is looking for, go to pages 7–13.

7.1 The Design argument

RECAP

Essential information:

☐ The **Design argument** says that because everything in the universe is so intricately made, it must have been created by God. Therefore God exists.

☐ Christians and Jews are **theists** (people who believe in God). They believe that God planned and created the earth. **Atheists**, who don't believe in God, believe the universe was not created but evolved naturally. **Agnostics** believe there is not enough evidence that God exists or that God created the universe.

Different versions of the Design argument

Christian and Jewish argument	God's creation is perfect and good. God created order in the world and put humans in charge of it. Because the earth is well-ordered, balanced, complex and beautiful, it must have been designed. The only one powerful enough to design the universe is God. Therefore he must exist.
William Paley	Paley (1743–1805) argued that the workings of a watch are so intricate they must have been designed and made by a watchmaker. Something so complex cannot be produced by chance. Similarly, the universe is so complex and intricate that it must have been designed and made, and the only possibility is that it was the work of God.
Isaac Newton	Newton (1642–1726) used the existence of the human thumb as evidence that God designed the universe. The thumb allows precise and delicate movement, with which humans can do such things as tie a shoelace or write a letter. This is sufficient evidence of design which can only have been achieved by God.
Thomas Aquinas	In the thirteenth century, Aquinas stated that only an intelligent being could keep everything in the universe in regular order. The fact the planets rotate in the solar system without colliding is because of God.
F. R. Tennant	In the 1930s, Tennant said that since everything was just right for humans to develop, the world must have been designed by God. He referred to the strength of gravity being absolutely right, and said that if the force and speed of the explosion caused by the Big Bang had been slightly different, life could not have developed on earth.

Objections to the Design arguments

- Natural selection happens by chance. Species 'design' themselves through the process of evolution, not through a designer God.
- The amount of suffering in the world proves there is no designer God, because a good God would not have designed and allowed bad things, such as natural disasters and evil.
- The order in the universe, which is necessary to support life, makes it look as though it is designed. In reality, the order and structure in nature is imposed by humans to help explain it.

TIP

You should learn strengths and weaknesses of the Design argument and be prepared to argue the case for each, regardless of what you believe.

APPLY

(A) Summarise the main points of **two** of the Design arguments.

(B) 'The Design argument proves that God exists.'

Write **two** developed arguments in response to this statement, one in agreement and one against.

Essential information:

☐ The **First Cause argument** (or cosmological argument) states that there has to be an uncaused cause that made everything else happen.

> **TIP**
> This five-point chain of reasoning gives a simple overview of the First Cause argument. Try to remember it so you can use it to explain the First Cause argument in your exam.

The First Cause argument

The logical chain of reasoning for the First Cause argument runs like this:

Everything that exists or begins to exist must have a cause → As the universe exists and had a beginning, it too must have a cause → There must be something existing with no cause, which is **eternal** (has no beginning or end), to cause everything else to exist → The eternal first cause can only be God → This means God must exist

The key assumption in the First Cause argument is that the universe had a starting point or cause, like all other things that exist. Christians and Jews say the starting point was God, who set a chain of events into motion that created the universe. As God is eternal, he has no starting point.

Many scientists believe the universe started with the Big Bang. Theists ask what existed before the Big Bang. They believe the answer is God and that he was the cause of it.

Thomas Aquinas' First Cause argument

In the thirteenth century, Thomas Aquinas argued that everything in the universe is caused to exist. Nothing can become something by itself. According to Thomas Aquinas, as everything we see is caused to exist, including the universe, it must have a creator. This uncaused cause of creation can only be God, who is eternal.

Jewish First Cause arguments

In the eleventh century, Rabbi Bachya ben Joseph ibn Paquda argued that as nothing creates itself, there must be a self-existent, eternal first cause which brought the universe into being.

In the twelfth century, Maimonides, a Jewish philosopher and scholar, stated that as the world must have been created 'in time', it must have had a creator to create it in time.

Objections to the First Cause argument

- If everything that exists has a cause, who or what caused God?
- If God is eternal then the universe could be eternal as well.
- The idea that everything has a cause does not necessarily mean the universe has to have a cause as well (or that the cause must be God).
- The Big Bang was a random event and had nothing to do with God.
- Religious creation stories, about how God brought the universe into being, are myths. The truth they tell is spiritual, not actual.

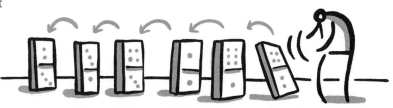

(A) Explain carefully **two** of the objections to the First Cause argument.

(B) 'The First Cause argument proves that God exists.'

Write **two** developed arguments in response to this statement, one in agreement and one against.

RECAP

Essential information:

☐ **Miracles** are seemingly impossible events that cannot be explained by natural or scientific laws.

☐ Theists believe miracles are the action of God and prove his existence. They show God's love and help to strengthen a believer's faith.

 You might be asked to compare beliefs on miracles between Christianity (the main religious tradition in Great Britain) and another religious tradition.

The argument from miracles and objections to it

Theists argue that:
- If there is no scientific explanation for an event, it must be caused by something outside nature.
- God is the only thing that exists outside nature.
- These events must be the result of God's intervention in the world.
- **Therefore God must exist.**

Atheists and agnostics may argue that:
- Miracles are no more than lucky coincidences.
- They may have scientific explanations we don't yet know about.
- Miracle healings could be the result of mind over matter or misdiagnosis.
- Some miracles are deliberately made up for fame or money.
- **Therefore what appear to be miracles have nothing to do with God, so they cannot prove God exists.**

David Hume, a philosopher in the eighteenth century, gave the following arguments against miracles:

- Miracles deny the laws of nature but there can never be enough evidence to prove this can happen.
- Witnesses to miracles are unreliable, as most of them are uneducated, primitive people.
- Religions depend on miracles to prove they are true but all religions cannot be right.

Even some theists object to miracles because they make God seem unfair. They ask why God would choose someone to benefit from a miracle over millions who are not so fortunate. An all-just and all-loving God wouldn't do that.

Christian and Jewish responses to miracles

Christian responses	Jewish responses
• Christians view miracles as evidence of God's existence and work in the world. The fact that some people convert to Christianity after experiencing a miracle is seen as proof of God's existence. • Jesus worked many miracles, such as healing the sick or bringing the dead back to life. • Jesus' incarnation and resurrection are considered the most important miracles in Christian teaching. • Lourdes is recognised by the Church as a place where miracles have occurred – the Catholic Church has recorded 69 miracles there.	• Miracles are wonders that show God's loving power. • The Tenakh refers to 'signs' and 'wonders' to describe extraordinary events that are clear signs of God's power. • One example is when God provided fire to burn Elijah's offering to him (1 Kings 18:38–39). • A traditional Jewish saying states that a person is a fool if they believe every miracle claim is actually true, but they are a non-believer if they do not believe such miracles could have happened at all.

APPLY

 A Explain carefully **one** example of a miracle.

 B Finish this sentence with a **detailed explanation**, then write a detailed explanation that gives a different point of view.

"When David Hume argued against miracles I believe he was right because..."

RECAP

Essential information:

☐ Some people use science and the existence of **suffering** (living with unpleasant conditions) and **evil** (the opposite of good) to challenge the existence of God.

☐ Christians and Jews respond by saying there does not have to be a conflict between religion and science, and that evil and suffering exist because of free will.

How science is used to challenge belief in God

Arguments against the existence of God	Christian and Jewish responses
 • Some atheists think religious beliefs, especially about God, were invented by people to answer questions about the universe that in the past could not be explained. • Science can now answer many questions that in the past couldn't be answered without the idea of God. • In the future, science will be able to answer all questions, so the idea of God is no longer necessary or helpful. • The fact that science is getting closer to creating human life provides further evidence that God does not exist.	• Many Christians and Jews see no conflict between science and religion, as they believe the Genesis creation stories should not be interpreted literally. • They believe science reveals the laws by which God created the universe. • Science cannot disprove God. God himself created science along with everything else. • As God gave humans intelligence to learn more about God's creation, it is important to do so because it gives a clearer understanding of God. • Some Christians and Jews reject the theory of evolution because they take the Genesis creation stories literally. ❝ The big bang […] does not contradict the divine act of creation; rather, it requires it. ❞ *Pope Francis*

Evil and suffering as an argument against the existence of God

Atheists argue that the existence of evil and suffering proves God does not exist:

God is believed to be all-knowing, all-powerful and all-loving → If this is true, God should be aware of evil → If God is aware of evil, he should want to use his powers to prevent the effects of it → God doesn't do this, so he doesn't exist

Christian responses	Jewish responses
• Suffering and evil are the result of free will. They were brought into God's perfect world by Adam and Eve, who used their free will to disobey God. • If God constantly intervened against evil, humans would have less freedom. • If there was no good and evil, people would not be able to demonstrate qualities such as compassion and generosity. • Allowing suffering means people can make mistakes and learn from them.	• Evil arises because humans have freedom of choice in moral issues. • Suffering tests people's faith and character. • God allows evil but does not will it. God's reasons for allowing evil cannot be known by humans. • If God constantly intervened to prevent evil, humans would not be free.

TIP
Remember that a logical chain of reasoning can express an opinion, give a reason to support the opinion and further develop the reason, possibly using religious arguments to elaborate it.

APPLY

 A Explain **two** reasons why atheists might believe that evil and suffering prove God doesn't exist.

 B Write **two** logical chains of reasoning, one to agree that science is correct in challenging the existence of God and the other to disagree.

7.5 Special revelation and enlightenment

Essential information:

☐ Most religions believe there is supreme, final, fundamental power in all reality, an **ultimate reality**. This ultimate reality could be a God or gods, which are referred to as being **divine**.

☐ **Special revelation** is God making himself known through direct personal experience.

☐ Special revelation and enlightenment are both sources of knowledge about the divine.

How may God be known?

- Some theists argue that God cannot be known because he is pure mystery and beyond human understanding.
- Human language limits God and so he cannot be adequately described.
- Others believe that two ways in which God can be known is if he chooses to reveal himself through either special or general **revelation** – an enlightening, divine or supernatural experience in which God shows himself.

Special revelation

- Special revelation is when a person experiences God directly in a particular event. It usually has a profound effect on those involved and can be life changing.
- Theists consider special revelations to be rare and many believe in God all their lives without experiencing such events.
- In the Bible, Mary received a special revelation from the angel Gabriel that she would become the mother of Jesus (Luke 1:26-38).
- Jewish scriptures describe God's special revelation to Jews through the law, the prophets and the covenant.
- There are many stories of prophets in the Tenakh (such as Isaiah and Amos) hearing God's call and giving God's message to the people.
- Moses experienced God's special revelation in events such as God appearing and communicating with him through the burning bush (Exodus 3:1–17).

Visions

- **Visions** are a type of special revelation. They usually involve seeing an image of a person or spiritual being, who reveals something about the nature of God.
- In Christianity and Judaism, this is interpreted as being a spiritual experience and holds great meaning for the person receiving it.
- However, both religions study reports of visions carefully and reject them if they are against the Bible or Tenakh.
- Christians believe there are several examples of visions in the Bible, including Saul's vision on the Damascus Road in Acts 9:1–19. He experienced a blinding light and was spoken to by Jesus. Afterwards he changed his name to Paul, was baptised as a Christian and committed himself to the Christian faith – a faith whose followers he had previously persecuted.
- An example in Judaism is when the prophet Isaiah had a vision of God in heaven, which persuaded him to pass God's message on to the people (Isaiah 6:1–6).
- Some atheists believe visions can be explained by sleep deprivation or drug use.

 You might be asked to compare beliefs on visions between Christianity (the main religious tradition in Great Britain) and another religious tradition.

Enlightenment

Buddhists do not believe in God. However, they use meditation and other spiritual practices to discover the meaning of ultimate reality by gaining true knowledge (**enlightenment**). In striving for enlightenment, they aim to discover how to end suffering and achieve happiness.

 A   Using **one** detailed example, explain the meaning of special revelation.

B   'Those who see visions are only hallucinating.'

Write a detailed argument that shows what you think about this statement.

RECAP

Essential information:

☐ Some seek to understand the divine by using **general revelation** – God making himself known through ordinary experiences. These ordinary experiences could be through **nature** (the physical world or environment) or **scripture** (the sacred writings of a religion).

What is general revelation?

Below are some forms of general revelation. Such experiences may not convince an atheist that God is real, but can help theists to strengthen their faith.

| Seeing God's presence in nature | Learning about God through studying the lives of religious leaders close to God | Coming to understand God through reason, conscience or morality | Experiencing God through worship and scripture |

Nature as a way of understanding the divine

- Many Christians and Jews believe that God is revealed to them through the beauty of the world he created.
- This may lead to awe and wonder at God's power, which may result in stronger faith.
- Atheists and humanists might argue that observing nature can give them a greater understanding of the world but not of God.

 You might be asked to compare beliefs on nature as a general revelation between Christianity (the main religious tradition in Great Britain) and another religious tradition.

> "The heavens declare the glory of God; the skies proclaim the work of his hands [...] night after night they reveal knowledge."
> *Psalm 19:1–2 [NIV]*

> "How many are the things You have made, O LORD; You have made them all with wisdom; the earth is full of Your creations."
> *Psalm 104:24 [Tenakh]*

Scripture as a way of understanding the divine

- **Fundamentalist Christians** believe the Bible contains God's actual words, which must not be changed or questioned. **Orthodox Jews** believe the same about the Torah, as the word of God revealed through Moses.
- **Liberal Christians** believe the Bible was inspired by God, but the words must be seen in their original context and may be understood differently in today's world. **Reform and Liberal Jews** have similar views about the Torah.
- When Christians and Jews read or listen to words of scripture, they hope to gain a better understanding of their faith and to receive spiritual strength from God's words.
- Jews believe the Tenakh reveals God's commands to them and his saving actions on behalf of all Jews.
- Readers of scripture can feel God's presence in the words they are reading because the words have hidden depths.

The power of the words is so strong that people come to believe in the faith just by reading or hearing them.
- For **atheists**, scripture does not prove God is real or reveal anything about God.
The writings are merely the authors' opinions rather than the word of God.

TIP
Including your personal view may improve your answer, but don't forget to develop your point with reasons to support it.

 APPLY

A Explain **two** forms of general revelation.

B **Develop this point** about whether scripture can help people to believe in God.

"It is easy to believe that an ancient book can help people to believe in God even though it was written so long ago."

7.7 Different ideas about the divine

RECAP

Essential information:

☐ Religions have different ideas about the divine.

☐ Christianity and Judaism see God as omnipotent, omniscient, benevolent, personal, impersonal, immanent and transcendent.

Descriptions of God's nature

The limitations of language make describing a God without limits very difficult. However, certain terms can be used to help describe God's nature, including the following:

Omnipotent
- Almighty and all-powerful
- Capable of doing anything (including creating the universe)

Omniscient
- All-knowing
- Aware of everything that has happened in the past, present or future

Personal
- Has human characteristics, e.g. being merciful and compassionate
- People can have a relationship with God through prayer

Transcendent
- Is beyond and outside life on earth
- Not limited by the world, time or space
- Does not act within the world or intervene in people's lives

Immanent
- Is present in the universe and involved with life on earth
- Acts in history and influences events
- People can experience God in their lives

Impersonal
- Has no human characteristics
- Is unknowable and mysterious
- Is more like an idea or a force than a person

TIP
You could be examined about any of these terms, so make sure you understand all of them.

Can God be immanent and transcendent, personal and impersonal?

For Christians and Jews, God can be both immanent and transcendent, and personal and impersonal.

- Even though God is the eternal, unlimited creator of the universe (transcendent and impersonal), theists can have a personal relationship with him (immanent and personal).
- Christians believe God is personal because he allows followers to join in a relationship with him. God is described as a Father who loves and cares for his children. This relationship is enabled by prayer.
- Jews believe they have a special relationship with God because of the covenant made with him through Abraham and Moses. They believe God will protect them if they obey his laws.
- For Christians, God's immanence is revealed both in Jesus, who they believe is God made man, and also in the work of the Holy Spirit.
- But God is also the transcendent creator of the universe and can be seen as an impersonal force of power. Christians and Jews believe God is beyond human understanding.

> "You have searched me, LORD, and you know me. You know when I sit and when I rise; you perceive my thoughts from afar."
> *Psalm 139:1–2* [NIV]

> "For God so loved the world that he gave his one and only Son, that whoever believes in him shall not perish but have eternal life."
> *John 3:16* [NIV]

> "I am the LORD and there is none else, I form light and create darkness, I make weal and create woe – I the LORD do all these things."
> *Isaiah 45:6–7* [Tenakh]

APPLY

(A) Give **two** terms to describe God's nature and explain what they mean.

(B) 'It is not possible to fully express God's nature in words.'

Write **two** developed points of view about this statement, one in favour and one that expresses a different opinion.

TIP
Even though a quote such as this has a specific religious theme, don't forget to include specific religious content in your answer.

7.8 The value of revelation and enlightenment

Essential information:

- [ ] Theists believe that revelation and enlightenment are valuable sources of knowledge about the divine.
- [ ] Revelations are difficult to prove because they are subjective, personal experiences. What some theists may regard as revelations, non-theists may understand in other ways.

The value of revelation

For theists, revelation can:

- provide proof of God's existence
- help to start a religion
- enable believers to have a relationship with God
- help people to know how God wants them to live.

Individual revelations have a great impact on the lives of those who receive them, even to the extent that they change their religious thinking completely.

Revelation: reality or illusion?

Revelation cannot be proved, so how do believers know it is real? They may ask themselves these questions.

Question	Religious responses
Does their revelation match the real world?	The more the revelation aligns with what actually happens, the more likely it is to be real. For example, a revelation that claims people can fly is unlikely to be believed. A revelation that claims the water in a holy place can cure, and it then does, is more likely to be real.
Does it fit with other revelations accepted by a religion?	If it contradicts a long-held belief of a religion, it is less likely to be a true revelation. However, beliefs may change over time (e.g. about slavery or homosexual relationships) so this is not always the case.
Does it change the faith or the life of a person?	God's revelation to Abraham caused him to abandon his belief in idols, follow the one God and travel to Canaan to establish the Jewish nation. Such revelations are more likely to be accepted as true because they have such a powerful influence on a person's life.
How is it that different religions have different revelations? They can't all be correct.	Different religions offer different paths to the divine. Within a faith there are different interpretations of sacred texts and how these apply to moral issues. If a particular interpretation disagrees with another verse in the Bible/Tenakh, the interpretation may be questionable.

Alternative explanations for the experiences

Atheists and others who do not believe in revelations might give the following explanations for them.

| Drug or alcohol use | Wishful thinking | Genuine error | Physical or mental illness | Deliberate lying for fame/money |

  APPLY

A Develop **three** of the alternative explanations for revelations.

B 'Revelation proves that God exists.'

Write a reasoned answer to express the atheist point of view to this statement.

TIP
You can develop each of these alternative explanations by providing an example. For instance, there have been cases in the news of people who have claimed to have had revelations from God and later their claims were found to be fraudulent.

111

Test the 1 mark question

1 | Which **one** of the following describes a person who believes in God?

    A | Atheist   B | Agnostic   C | Theist   D | Humanist   **[1 mark]**

2 | Which **one** of the following is not an attribute of God?

    A | Compassionate   B | Mortal   C | Transcendent   D | Eternal   **[1 mark]**

Test the 2 mark question

3 | Give **two** weaknesses of the First Cause argument.   **[2 marks]**

1) _____

2) _____

4 | Give **two** possible causes of suffering.   **[2 marks]**

1) _____

2) _____

Test the 4 mark question

5 | Explain **two** contrasting beliefs in contemporary British society about the Design argument for God's existence.

In your answer you must refer to one or more religious traditions. You may refer to a non-religious belief.   **[4 marks]**

● **Explain one belief.**	*Christians believe that the beauty and intricacy of nature proves that God created the world.*
● Develop your explanation with more detail/an example/ reference to a religious teaching or quotation.	*William Paley said that just as a watch's intricate workings show evidence of design, so does the universe, which is more complex than a watch.*
● **Explain a second belief.**	*Atheists disagree with the Design argument because they do not believe there is a God.*
● Develop your explanation with more detail/an example/ reference to a religious teaching or quotation.	*They think that the natural world evolved after the Big Bang, a random event, and through natural selection creatures designed themselves without a need for God.*

> **TIP**
> Remember 'contrasting' means different. Here the answer refers to Christianity and contrasts it with an atheist view.

6 | Explain **two** contrasting beliefs about miracles.

In your answer you must refer to one or more religious traditions. You may refer to a non-religious belief.   **[4 marks]**

● **Explain one belief.**	
● Develop your explanation with more detail/an example/ reference to a religious teaching or quotation.	
● **Explain a second belief.**	
● Develop your explanation with more detail/an example/ reference to a religious teaching or quotation.	

7 | Explain **two** similar beliefs about general revelation.

In your answer you must refer to one or more religious traditions. You may refer to a non-religious belief.   **[4 marks]**

Test the 5 mark question

8   Explain **two** religious beliefs about visions.

Refer to sacred writings or another source of religious belief and teaching in your answer.   **[5 marks]**

● **Explain one belief.**	*Jews believe that God can be revealed to people in a special, direct way through visions.*
● Develop your explanation with more detail/an example.	*For example, Moses had a vision of God through a burning bush, which persuaded him that God had a special task for him.*
● **Explain a second belief.**	*A Christian belief about visions is that they reveal a message to a person that makes them want to spread the word of God to other people.*
● Develop your explanation with more detail/an example.	*Since they believe the vision was given for a specific purpose, they often begin a life of preaching or sharing their experiences with others.*
● Add a reference to sacred writings or another source of religious belief and teaching. If you prefer, you can add this reference to your first belief instead.	*An example of a vision in the Bible is in Acts, where it says Saul (who later became Paul) received a vision of Jesus on the Damascus Road. Saul was temporarily blinded and when he regained his sight he changed from persecuting Christians to preaching the gospel of Jesus to everyone.*

TIP
When questions ask for two religious beliefs, it is fine to answer from different religions, as here. Visions is one of the three topics in this chapter about which you may be asked (in a differently worded question) to give a view from Christianity (the main religious tradition of Great Britain) and one or more other religious traditions.

9   Explain **two** religious beliefs about special revelation.

Refer to sacred writings or another source of religious belief and teaching in your answer.   **[5 marks]**

● **Explain one belief.**	
● Develop your explanation with more detail/an example.	
● **Explain a second belief.**	
● Develop your explanation with more detail/an example.	
● Add a reference to sacred writings or another source of religious belief and teaching. If you prefer, you can add this reference to your first belief instead.	

TIP
Make sure you write about special revelation, **not** general revelation.

TIP
This question is not an evaluation, so do **not** give your opinion or write arguments against revelation. Don't forget to include a source of religious teaching in the answer.

10   Explain **two** religious ideas about God.

Refer to sacred writings or another source of religious belief and teaching in your answer.   **[5 marks]**

Test the 12 mark question

11 'The First Cause argument proves that God exists.'

Evaluate this statement. In your answer you:

- should give reasoned arguments in support of this statement
- should give reasoned arguments to support a different point of view
- should refer to religious arguments
- may refer to non-religious arguments
- should reach a justified conclusion.

[12 marks]

[+3 SPaG marks]

REASONED ARGUMENTS IN SUPPORT OF THE STATEMENT ● **Explain why some people would agree with the statement.** ● Develop your explanation with more detail and examples. ● Refer to religious teaching. Use a quote or paraphrase or refer to a religious authority. ● **Evaluate the arguments.** Is this a good argument or not? Explain why you think this.	The First Cause argument says that everything that exists has a cause. It is obvious to everyone that the universe exists because we live in it! Therefore the universe too must have a cause – something must have started it. But that something had to be eternal and not caused by something else, otherwise that other thing would be the cause, and so on. Christians and Jews believe that God is the eternal, almighty cause that began the process of creation of everything we know. Everything except God has a beginning in time. God was the eternal being that set off the Big Bang in time, which led to evolution and the world as we know it today.
REASONED ARGUMENTS SUPPORTING A DIFFERENT VIEW ● **Explain why some people would support a different view.** ● Develop your explanation with more detail and examples. ● Refer to religious teaching. Use a quote or paraphrase or refer to a religious authority. ● **Evaluate the arguments.** Is this a good argument or not? Explain why you think this.	Atheists are people who do not believe there is a God. They would argue that the First Cause argument does not prove there is a God because there are flaws in the logic – the argument contradicts itself. For example, if everything has a cause, what caused God? They also point out that saying God is eternal so nobody made him is just a convenient excuse. If God is eternal, why cannot the universe be eternal? Of course, if the universe is eternal, it doesn't need a first cause and was never created. This then removes the need for a God to cause the universe to exist. They also point out that the Big Bang just happened and there was no cause for it.
CONCLUSION ● **Give a justified conclusion.** ● Include your own opinion together with your own reasoning. ● **Include evaluation.** Explain why you think one viewpoint is stronger than the other or why they are equally strong. ● Do not just repeat arguments you have already used without explaining how they apply to your reasoned opinion/conclusion.	In conclusion, I think that although the First Cause argument may seem convincing because it depends on something everyone can observe – that everything that happens has a cause – in the end it fails to convince me that a God is the First Cause of the universe. The argument relies on the universe having a beginning and a cause, but just because things in our world have causes does not necessarily mean the universe itself had one. Christians and Jews may use the Genesis creation story to support their arguments in favour of the statement, but as I am an atheist, I am not persuaded by myths.

TIP It is good to mention the Big Bang here, and it links well to the previous argument. This point could be developed further, perhaps with a brief explanation of the Big Bang theory, and some evaluation as to how convincing it is.

TIP This conclusion is good because it doesn't just repeat points already made to justify the opinion. It is also clearly linked to the quote in the question.

12 'Miracles prove that God exists.'

Evaluate this statement. In your answer you:

- should give reasoned arguments in support of this statement
- should give reasoned arguments to support a different point of view
- should refer to religious arguments
- may refer to non-religious arguments
- should reach a justified conclusion.

[12 marks]

[+3 SPaG marks]

REASONED ARGUMENTS IN SUPPORT OF THE STATEMENT ● **Explain why some people would agree with the statement.** ● Develop your explanation with more detail and examples. ● Refer to religious teaching. Use a quote or paraphrase or refer to a religious authority. ● **Evaluate the arguments.** Is this a good argument or not? Explain why you think this.	
REASONED ARGUMENTS SUPPORTING A DIFFERENT VIEW ● **Explain why some people would support a different view.** ● Develop your explanation with more detail and examples. ● Refer to religious teaching. Use a quote or paraphrase or refer to a religious authority. ● **Evaluate the arguments.** Is this a good argument or not? Explain why you think this.	
CONCLUSION ● **Give a justified conclusion.** ● Include your own opinion together with your own reasoning. ● **Include evaluation.** Explain why you think one viewpoint is stronger than the other or why they are equally strong. ● Do not just repeat arguments you have already used without explaining how they apply to your reasoned opinion/conclusion.	

> **TIP**
> Make sure your focus is on both miracles and the existence of God.

13 'The existence of evil and suffering proves that God does not exist.'

Evaluate this statement. In your answer you:

- should give reasoned arguments in support of this statement
- should give reasoned arguments to support a different point of view
- should refer to religious arguments
- may refer to non-religious arguments
- should reach a justified conclusion.

[12 marks]

[+3 SPaG marks]

Check your answers using the mark scheme on page 163. How did you do?
To feel more secure in the content you need to remember, re-read pages 104–111.
To remind yourself of what the examiner is looking for, go to pages 7–13.

8 Religion, peace and conflict

8.1 Introduction to religion, peace and conflict

RECAP

Essential information:

☐ Some Christians (such as Quakers) believe war is always wrong, while others believe war is acceptable under certain conditions.

☐ Most Jews are prepared to fight for their country and their faith; the Promised Land was conquered and protected through fighting.

☐ The concepts of peace, justice, forgiveness and reconciliation are important both in the aftermath of conflict and as tools to prevent war from happening in the first place.

Key concepts of peace, justice, forgiveness and reconciliation

Peace	Justice
• **Peace** is the absence of conflict and war, which leads to happiness and harmony. • The aim of war may be to create peace, but this can be hard to achieve because of the instability and resentment left after a war ends. • Peace is also a feeling of happiness and tranquillity that can come through prayer and meditation, which helps people to avoid conflict. • Both Christians and Jews believe God will bring peace to the world at some time in the future. <blockquote>" He will judge between the nations and will settle disputes for many peoples […] Nation will not take up sword against nation, nor will they train for war any more. " *Isaiah 2:4 [NIV]*</blockquote>	• **Justice** is bringing about what is right and fair, according to the law, or making up for a wrong that has been committed. • Justice is linked to equality, and the idea that it is just and fair to give everyone the same opportunities. • If certain governments or parts of the world are seen to be the cause of inequality and injustice, conflict may result. • Both Christians and Jews believe that God, as the ultimate judge, will establish justice at some point in the future (Isaiah 2:4). • The Jewish prophets taught the importance of justice, particularly for the poor and vulnerable (Micah 6:8). 
Forgiveness	**Reconciliation**
• **Forgiveness** is showing compassion and mercy, and pardoning someone for what they have done wrong. • Forgiveness does not necessarily mean no action should be taken to right a wrong, but when conflict is over forgiveness should follow. • Christians are taught to forgive others if they wish to be forgiven (the Lord's Prayer). • Both Christians and Jews believe God offers forgiveness to all who ask in faith. • For Jews, Yom Kippur offers an opportunity to express sorrow for sin and seek God's forgiveness.	• **Reconciliation** means restoring friendly relationships after conflict. • It requires a conscious effort (and sometimes much work) to rebuild the relationship. • Reconciliation doesn't mean ignoring the past but focuses on building a constructive relationship for the future. • Many Christians and Jews work for peace and reconciliation in conflict situations. 

APPLY

(A) Explain **two** religious beliefs about forgiveness.

(B) Make a list of **three** arguments for and **three** arguments against the statement, 'Religious believers should not take part in wars.'

8.2 Violent protest and terrorism

RECAP

Essential information:

☐ In the UK, the right to **protest** (express disapproval, often in a public group) is a fundamental democratic freedom, but it is illegal to protest violently.

☐ **Terrorism** (the unlawful use of violence, usually against innocent civilians, to achieve a political goal) is a much more serious form of violent protest.

☐ Christianity and Judaism are against violent protest and terrorism.

 You might be asked to compare beliefs on violence between Christianity (the main religious tradition in Great Britain) and another religious tradition.

Violence and protest

- All religions generally agree that conflict should be avoided if possible, but they have different views about when violence may be justified.
- Protests allow people to express their objection to something in public, but protests can sometimes turn violent.
- Many Christians and Jews believe that protesting to achieve what is right is acceptable as long as violence is not used.

Here are two examples of peaceful protests organised by religious people:

- In the 1950s and 1960s, the Christian pastor Dr Martin Luther King Jr organised peaceful protests against unjust racial laws in the USA.
- These succeeded in changing US law and bringing civil rights to all its citizens of any race.

- In October 2015, a group of pro-Israel supporters protested peacefully outside the Palestinian Mission in London.
- They held a minute's silence to pay respect to the victims on both sides of the conflict between Israel and Palestine, and chanted slogans such as 'Yes to peace, no to terror'.

Terrorism

- Some individuals or groups use terrorism to further their cause by killing innocent people.
- Suicide bombers, gunmen shooting into crowds, and using vehicles to injure pedestrians are all examples of terrorism.
- Terrorists aim to make society aware of their cause, frighten people and push the authorities into giving way to their demands.
- Terrorists may link their cause with a religion, but **no religion promotes terrorism**.
- Most Christians and Jews believe terrorism is wrong as it targets innocent people. They prefer more peaceful ways of resolving issues.

> **❝**Do not repay anyone evil for evil […] If it is possible, as far as it depends on you, live at peace with everyone.**❞**
> *Romans 12:17–18* [NIV]

> **❝**We must always take sides. Neutrality helps the oppressor, never the victim. Silence encourages the tormentor, never the tormented. Sometimes we must interfere.**❞**
> *Elie Wiesel, Nobel Peace Prize winner*

APPLY

(A) Give **two** reasons why some religious people may wish to protest.

(B) **Develop this argument** to support the statement, 'Terrorism is never justified' by explaining in more detail, adding an example, or referring to a relevant religious teaching or quotation.

"Terrorism kills innocent people. It uses violence to frighten and intimidate ordinary citizens who are just going about their daily lives. It can never be justified no matter what the cause."

RECAP

Essential information:

☐ Some reasons for war include **greed** (selfish desire for something), **self-defence** (acting to prevent harm to yourself or others), and **retaliation** (deliberately harming someone as a response to them harming you).

☐ Christianity and Judaism teach that war should never be motivated by greed or retaliation, but most Christians and Jews believe that fighting in self-defence is morally acceptable.

☐ Judaism teaches that war should not be motivated by greed, but that retaliation for an unprovoked attack or in self-defence may be justifiable.

> **TIP**
> Other reasons for war such as political disputes, regime change, clash of cultures or disputes between ethnic groups within a nation can be included in your answers on this topic.

Greed, self-defence and retaliation as reasons for war

Greed

- Wars may be fought out of greed to gain more land or control of important resources (such as oil).
- **Christianity** teaches that greed is wrong.

> ❝For the love of money is a root of all kinds of evil. ❞
> *1 Timothy 6:10 [NIV]*

- **Judaism** teaches that greed goes against the commandment 'You shall not covet' (Exodus 14:17 [Tenakh]).
- The Jewish prophets criticised people for cheating the poor in order to increase their own wealth and power (Amos 2:6–7 and 4:1).

Retaliation

- Wars are sometimes fought in retaliation against a country that has done something very wrong.
- **Christians** try to follow the advice of Jesus, who taught that retaliation is wrong.

> ❝But I tell you, do not resist an evil person. If anyone slaps you on the right cheek, turn to them the other cheek also. ❞
> *Matthew 5:39 [NIV]*

- **Judaism** condemns vengeance: 'You shall not take vengeance or bear a grudge against your countrymen. Love your fellow as yourself' (Leviticus 19:18 [Tenakh]).
- In his code of Jewish Law, Maimonides referred to revenge as an unworthy action in everyday life, but some Jews find this advice difficult to follow in situations of war.

Reasons for war

Self-defence

- People might fight in self-defence when their country is under attack, or to help defend other nations who are under threat. For example, during the Second World War the UK fought to defend itself against Nazi invasion, and also to defeat what it saw as an evil threat to the whole of Europe.
- Many **Christians** believe fighting in self-defence is morally acceptable, providing all peaceful ways of solving the conflict have been tried first.

> ❝Do not repay anyone evil for evil […] If it is possible, as far as it depends on you, live at peace with everyone. ❞
> *Romans 12:17 [NIV]*

- **Jews** believe self-defence is an acceptable reason for war, particularly to defend the nation of Israel from attack.

> **TIP**
> Retaliation is different from self-defence. It may sometimes be justifiable to defend your country in self-defence, but retaliation is a spiteful action to punish an enemy for something they have done.

APPLY

A Which **one** of the following is **not** a reason for war?

a) Self-defence   b) Greed
c) Retaliation   d) Forgiveness

B 'Retaliation is a justifiable reason for war.'

Write a paragraph to **explain whether you agree or disagree** with the statement. Include religious teachings and explain how the teachings are relevant to the argument.

RECAP

Essential information:

- [ ] **Nuclear weapons** are weapons that work by a nuclear reaction. They devastate huge areas and kill large numbers of people.

- [ ] Other types of **weapons of mass destruction** (weapons that kill large numbers of people and/or cause great damage) include chemical weapons and biological weapons.

- [ ] No religion supports the use of these weapons, although some religious believers do support nuclear deterrence (stockpiling nuclear weapons to deter or prevent an enemy attack).

The use of nuclear weapons

- US forces used atom (nuclear) bombs on the Japanese cities of Hiroshima and Nagasaki during the Second World War, causing 140,000 people to die in Hiroshima alone.
- Japan surrendered, ending the war, so some people say the use of these weapons was justified.
- Since then many countries have developed powerful nuclear weapons as a deterrent (to prevent an enemy attack).

Weapons of mass destruction

- In addition to nuclear weapons, other weapons of mass destruction are **biological weapons** (using living organisms to cause disease or death) and **chemical weapons** (using chemicals to harm humans and destroy the natural environment).
- The production, stockpiling and use of these weapons is illegal worldwide.
- Despite this, many countries still possess them.

> You might be asked to compare beliefs on weapons of mass destruction between Christianity (the main religious tradition in Great Britain) and another religious tradition.

Religious views

- Both Christians and Jews believe that only God has the right to end life.
- One of the Ten Commandments is 'You shall not murder' (Exodus 20:13 [Tenakh]).
- Weapons of mass destruction kill huge numbers of innocent civilians, so many Christians and Jews believe their use can never be justified.
- Some Christians and Jews believe that although killing in war is not usually considered to be murder, the use of nuclear weapons, which would kill huge numbers of innocent civilians, can never be justified.
- Many Christians believe the use of these weapons goes against the teachings of Jesus.
- Some Christians see the stockpiling of nuclear weapons as a useful deterrent to maintain peace and prevent attack.

> **❝** [we] call on the world to recognise that violence begets violence; that nuclear proliferation [the spread of nuclear weapons and technology] benefits no one **❞**
> *Rabbi David Saperstein*

> **❝** [...] any use of nuclear weapons would violate the sanctity of life and the principle of dignity core to our faith traditions **❞**
> *Steve Hucklesby*

APPLY

A Explain **two** contrasting beliefs in contemporary British society about weapons of mass destruction. In your answer you should refer to the main religious tradition of Great Britain and one or more other religious traditions.

B **Develop this argument** to support the statement, 'There are no good reasons for countries to possess nuclear weapons' by referring to a relevant religious teaching or quotation.

"Nuclear weapons could kill huge numbers of people and destroy much of the earth. They have a long lasting impact on the earth because of radiation that will poison the ground."

TIP

Make sure you choose contrasting viewpoints.

RECAP

Essential information:

☐ A **just war** is a war which meets internationally accepted criteria for fairness.

☐ The just war theory gives the conditions that must apply to make a war justifiable, and the rules on how the war must be fought to make sure it is ethical.

☐ The just war theory was developed by Christians and is accepted by many Christians and Jews today, although most think it is much better to prevent war from happening at all.

☐ Some Christians, such as Quakers, disagree with the just war theory because it defends the concept of war.

Conditions of a just war

For a war to be just it must:
• be fought for a **just cause** (e.g. in self-defence or to defend others, not to gain territory or resources or in retaliation)
• be declared by a **proper legal authority**
• have a **just intention** (fought to promote good or defeat wrongdoing; justice and peace must be restored afterwards)
• be a **last resort** (other ways of solving the problem must be tried first)
• have a reasonable **chance of success** (the good gained by winning should outweigh the evil which led to the war)
• be **proportional** (excessive force should not be used and innocent civilians must not be killed)

> **TIP**
> The mnemonic 'CLIPS' will help you remember some conditions for a just war:
> C – just CAUSE
> L – LAST resort
> I – Right INTENTION
> P – PROPORTIONALITY
> S – reasonable chance of SUCCESS
> But don't forget proper legal authority!

Rules about how a war must be fought
• The war should be fought by **just means** (innocent civilians should not be targeted or harmed).
• Only **appropriate force should be** used (including type of force and how much force).
• **Internationally agreed conventions** must be obeyed (Geneva Convention rules).

> **TIP**
> It will be helpful if you know some examples of wars so that you can support your opinion about whether war can be justified according to the just war theory.

Jewish teachings about war

Judaism recognises three types of war:

- **Obligatory wars** that God commanded Jews to fight (e.g. the conquest of Canaan under Joshua).
- **Defensive wars**, including pre-emptive strikes against a potential enemy. Jews are obliged to defend themselves if attacked.
- **Optional wars** fought for a good reason when all peaceful ways to prevent conflict have been tried first.

Jews have rules about how a war must be fought. For example, civilians and the landscape must be protected (Deuteronomy 20:19), and prisoners must be treated with dignity.

Wars should not be fought to build an empire, destroy another nation, steal resources or take revenge.

> ❝If your enemy is hungry, give him bread to eat; if he is thirsty, give him water to drink. ❞
> *Proverbs 25:21* [Tenakh]

APPLY

(A) Give **two** reasons why some religious people believe it is right to fight in a war.

(B) **Develop** this argument against the statement, 'The just war theory is the best religious response to whether it is right to fight' by explaining in more detail, adding an example, or referring to a relevant religious teaching or quotation.

"The just war theory is not the best religious response because it accepts that sometimes war is right, when in fact it is never right."

8.6 Holy war and religion as a cause of violence

RECAP

Essential information:

☐ A **holy war** is fighting for a religious cause or God, controlled by a religious leader.

☐ Although all religions generally promote peace and harmony, religion is sometimes seen as a cause of violence in the contemporary world.

What is a holy war?

- A holy war is fought for a religious cause, such as to defend the faith from attack.
- It must be authorised by a religious leader.
- It is believed those who take part gain spiritual rewards.
- The Crusades are examples of holy war. These were battles between Christians and Muslims in the eleventh to fourteenth centuries. Both believed God was on their side.
- Most Christians and Jews today believe it is better to defend the faith through words rather than violence.
- The Tenakh refers to God helping the Jews to win battles to settle in the Promised Land (obligatory wars), but for most Jews, the concept of holy war no longer applies.

TIP
Although some conflicts may seem to be about two religious groups fighting each other, the reasons for conflict may be more political or economic than religious.

Religion as a cause of violence

Christian views	Jewish views
• Most Christians today do not respond violently to an attack on their faith. • Most Christians accept Jesus' teaching that not only violence, but the anger that leads to violence, is wrong (Matthew 5:21–22). • Jesus said, 'Put your sword back in its place, for all who draw the sword die by the sword' (Matthew 26:52 [NIV]).	• Jews were subjected to violence during the Second World War when six million Jews died at the hands of the Nazis, not because they threatened violence or war, but just because they were Jews. • Most Jews in the UK do not respond violently to an attack on their faith, but may protest peacefully against anti-Semitism. • Most Jews do not believe that the teachings of their faith encourage a violent response. They believe they should keep within the law and rely on the police to take appropriate action.

Although all religions generally promote peace and harmony, there are examples of recent conflicts that have had a religious aspect to them, or examples of violence that have been justified as helping to defend the faith. For example:

> During 'the Troubles' in Northern Ireland (1968–1998), conflict between Catholics and Protestants led to acts of discrimination and violence. However, many consider this to have been a political conflict rather than a religious one.

> A small minority of Orthodox Jews living in the West Bank region believe there is a divine obligation to reclaim the whole of the land of Israel by removing Palestinian settlers. They believe that the conquest and settlement of Israel is an obligatory war, or 'war by commandment', but the Israeli government and most Israeli Jews reject this interpretation.

APPLY

A Give **two** features of holy wars.

B **Evaluate** this argument to support the statement, 'There is no place for a holy war in contemporary Britain.'

"People have religious freedom. No one has to fight for the right to worship God in the way they wish."

8.7 Pacifism and peacemaking

Essential information:

☐ **Pacifism** is the belief of people who refuse to take part in war and any other form of violence.

☐ **Peacemaking** is the action of trying to establish peace, and a **peacemaker** is someone who works to establish peace in the world or a certain part of it.

 You might be asked to compare beliefs on pacifism between Christianity (the main religious tradition in Great Britain) and another religious tradition.

What is pacifism?

Pacifists believe that:

- war and violence can rarely or never be justified
- it is best to prevent war from becoming a possibility by promoting justice and peace
- prayer and meditation can help people to be at peace with themselves and others.

Christian views	Jewish views
• The Religious Society of Friends (Quakers) is a Christian denomination that strongly supports pacifism. • During the First World War some people called conscientious objectors refused to fight and faced punishment. Many conscientious objectors took non-fighting roles as cooks, doctors, nurses or mechanics instead, e.g. volunteering for the Friends' Ambulance Unit. • Christian pacifists follow Jesus' example and teaching: 'Blessed are the peacemakers, for they shall be called children of God' (Matthew 5:9 [NIV]). • Many Christians are not pacifists because they believe war can be justified under certain criteria (see page 120).	• Judaism teaches that peace is an ideal, but that war is sometimes a necessary evil and a duty of the faith. • The Tenakh advises people to 'Shun evil and do good, seek peace and pursue it' (Psalm 34:15 [Tenakh]). • The prophet Micah said that when God's kingdom of justice was established war would not be necessary to settle disputes (Micah 4:3). • The prophet Isaiah spoke of 'peace without limit' when the Messiah would reign on David's throne 'in justice and in equity' (Isaiah 9:6–7 [Tenakh]).

Modern-day peacemakers

Many pacifists and peacemakers believe it is important to resist oppression and injustice in non-violent ways, to help create a just and equal world where conflict is not necessary. Christian and Jewish pacifists believe that peace comes through religious faith, supported by prayer and following God's law, and by actively working to promote human rights.

> **TIP**
> You need to be able to talk about individuals involved in peacemaking and the work they have done.

Three examples of modern-day peacemakers are Mairead Corrigan, Betty Williams and Dr Marshall Rosenberg.

Mairead Corrigan and Betty Williams

- A Catholic and a Protestant from Northern Ireland who formed the 'Peace People' organisation in 1976.
- Organised peace marches and other events throughout the UK to bring Catholics and Protestants together, and to call for peace between the two sides in Northern Ireland.
- Awarded the 1976 Nobel Peace Prize.

Dr Marshall Rosenberg

- A Jewish psychologist who founded the Centre for Nonviolent Communication.
- The Centre grew out of work he was doing with those in the USA who, in the 1960s, were campaigning for equal rights for all. He tried to make peace between rioting students and college administrators.
- Offered courses on non-violent communication in over 60 countries to help people such as teachers, healthcare providers, police officers, faith leaders and individual families to resolve conflict in a peaceful way.

 A Explain **two** contrasting beliefs in contemporary British society about pacifism.

 B Write down **two** arguments in support of the statement, 'Promoting justice and human rights is the best way of preventing conflict.'

Now **develop each argument** by explaining in more detail or by giving examples.

RECAP

Essential information:

☐ Victims of war include those directly involved in the fighting, their families and dependents, and refugees whose homes and societies have been destroyed.

☐ There are many organisations that offer help and care for victims of war (such as Caritas and Magen David Adom UK). Christians and Jews support organisations such as these.

Providing help to victims of war

There are many organisations that help the victims of war, from those providing shelter and supplies for refugees to those providing medical and psychological care for members of the military.

Christian views	Jewish views
• Christians support such organisations because Jesus taught people to 'love your neighbour as yourself' (Mark 12:31 [NIV]). • In the parable of the Good Samaritan (Luke 10:25–37), Jesus taught that everyone is everybody else's neighbour, regardless of race, age, gender, religion or political beliefs.	Jewish organisations that help victims of war base their work on two Jewish beliefs: • Saving a life (**pikuach nefesh**) – the obligation to save a life even if it means breaking Jewish law (see page 56). • Healing the world (**tikkun olam**) – being involved in God's work to sustain the world (see page 55). ❝ He who destroys one soul of a human being, the Scripture considers him as if he should destroy a whole world, and him who saves one soul of Israel, the Scripture considers him as if he should save a whole world. ❞ *Sanhedrin 4.5*

Organisations that help victims of war

Two examples of religious organisations that help victims of war are Caritas and Magen David Adom UK.

Caritas	Magen David Adom UK
• A Catholic organisation that helps the poor and promotes justice worldwide. • Inspired by the teachings of Jesus and the Catholic Church. • Aims to provide practical help to those suffering through conflict. • In 2015, provided food and shelter to refugees fleeing the civil war in Syria. • Also provided translators and legal services so the refugees could make informed decisions about their futures.	• A Jewish charity based in the UK that raised nearly £7 million in 2013. • Funds an emergency medical and ambulance service in Israel. • Provides medical care and treatment for anyone regardless of nationality, race, religion, political affiliation, etc. • This includes victims of conflict throughout the world. • Provides first aid training in Israel.

APPLY

 A Give **two** ways in which religious believers help victims of war.

B 'The point of war is to kill the enemy, not help them to survive.'

Give **two** reasons to agree with this statement and **two** reasons to oppose it.
Develop one of them by adding religious teaching to your answer.

8 Exam practice

Test the 1 mark question

1. Which **one** of the following best expresses the religious ideal of bringing about what is right and fair?

A | Peace   B | Forgiveness   C | Justice   D | Defence   **[1 mark]**

2. Which **one** of the following are **not** weapons of mass destruction?

A | Chemical weapons   B | Nuclear weapons   C | Biological weapons   D | Conventional weapons   **[1 mark]**

Test the 2 mark question

3. Give **two** conditions of a just war.   **[2 marks]**

1) _____

2) _____

4. Give **two** reasons why many religious people do **not** support violent protest.   **[2 marks]**

1) _____

2) _____

Test the 4 mark question

5. Explain **two** contrasting beliefs in contemporary British society about whether countries should possess weapons of mass destruction.

In your answer you should refer to the main religious tradition of Great Britain and one or more other religious traditions.   **[4 marks]**

● **Explain one belief.**	The Religious Society of Friends (Quakers) are a Christian denomination who believe that no country should possess weapons of mass destruction, because they can kill large numbers of innocent civilians.
● Develop your explanation with more detail/an example/ reference to a religious teaching or quotation.	Countries who possess these weapons have to be prepared to use them, and if they did, it would go against Jesus' teaching to 'turn the other cheek' and 'love your enemies'.
● **Explain a second belief.**	The Jewish state of Israel is thought to have nuclear weapons, therefore some Jews would argue that possessing these weapons is necessary in order to prevent war and to help keep the peace.
● Develop your explanation with more detail/an example/ reference to a religious teaching or quotation.	Although Jews believe their use is against God's law not to murder, they may still wish to have such weapons as a deterrent to others.

TIP

It is good practice to include a religious teaching to support your explanation of religious beliefs.

6. Explain **two** contrasting beliefs in contemporary British society about pacifism.

In your answer you should refer to the main religious tradition of Great Britain and one or more other religious traditions.   **[4 marks]**

● **Explain one belief.**	
● Develop your explanation with more detail/an example/ reference to a religious teaching or quotation.	
● **Explain a second belief.**	
● Develop your explanation with more detail/an example/ reference to a religious teaching or quotation.	

7. Explain **two** similar religious beliefs about forgiveness.

In your answer you must refer to one or more religious traditions.   **[4 marks]**

Test the 5 mark question

8   Explain **two** religious beliefs about helping victims of war.

Refer to sacred writings or another source of religious belief and teaching in your answer.

● **Explain one belief.**	*One Christian belief about helping victims of war is that Christians should treat everyone as if they were a neighbour to them, as Jesus commanded.*
● Develop your explanation with more detail/an example.	*Victims of war may be suffering because they have lost everything including people they love, so even if Christians do not know them, they should not ignore their suffering but offer to help them in whatever way they can.*
● **Explain a second belief.**	*Jews support organisations that help victims of war because they believe in pikuach nefesh, that saving a life is a duty that is even more important than following Jewish law.*
● Develop your explanation with more detail/an example.	*Jews appreciate what it is like to be victims of oppression and war so they try to help others in that situation.*
● Add a reference to sacred writings or another source of religious belief and teaching. If you prefer, you can add this reference to your first belief instead.	*They believe in healing or repairing the world (tikkun olam) by volunteering for charities that help those in need such as victims of violence and conflict.*

TIP
If you cannot remember an exact quotation from sacred writings, you may express it in your own words.

TIP
The Jewish moral principle of healing the world comes from Jewish tradition, so is accepted as 'a source of religious belief and teaching' for your answer.

9   Explain **two** reasons why some religious people believe it is right to fight in a war.

Refer to sacred writings or another source of religious belief and teaching in your answer.

● **Explain one reason.**	
● Develop your explanation with more detail/an example.	
● **Explain a second reason.**	
● Develop your explanation with more detail/an example.	
● Add a reference to sacred writings or another source of religious belief and teaching. If you prefer, you can add this reference to your first belief instead.	

10   Explain **two** religious beliefs about reconciliation.

Refer to sacred writings or another source of religious belief and teaching in your answer.

[5 marks]

Test the 12 mark question

11 'The just war theory is the best religious response to whether it is right to fight.'

Evaluate this statement. In your answer you:

- should give reasoned arguments in support of this statement
- should give reasoned arguments to support a different point of view
- should refer to religious arguments
- may refer to non-religious arguments
- should reach a justified conclusion.

[12 marks]

[+3 SPaG mark

REASONED ARGUMENTS IN SUPPORT OF THE STATEMENT ● **Explain why some people would agree with the statement.** ● Develop your explanation with more detail and examples. ● Refer to religious teaching. Use a quote or paraphrase or refer to a religious authority. ● **Evaluate the arguments.** Is this a good argument or not? Explain why you think this.	*Although religious people think it is better to avoid war and violence, if faced with a decision about whether or not it is right to fight, the just war theory gives them some guidance. The theory has several criteria including that the war must be declared by a leader of a state, it should be proportional in the amount of force that is used and civilians should be protected. Although the theory was originally developed by Christians (Augustine and Aquinas), its principles are accepted by Jews too.* *The theory is a good response because it makes sure wars are not fought about something unimportant or in a way which breaks internationally agreed rules. This is important because God wants people to protect innocent civilians rather than killing them. Jews have rules about how a war should be fought, including allowing civilians to get out of harm's way and not destroying the landscape that is a source of food.*
REASONED ARGUMENTS SUPPORTING A DIFFERENT VIEW ● **Explain why some people would support a different view.** ● Develop your explanation with more detail and examples. ● Refer to religious teaching. Use a quote or paraphrase or refer to a religious authority. ● **Evaluate the arguments.** Is this a good argument or not? Explain why you think this.	*Some Christians do not agree with the just war theory. These Christians may be pacifists like the Quakers who think that all war is wrong whether it is considered 'just' or not. The best religious response to whether it is right to fight is to follow the teaching of Jesus, who said 'Blessed are the peacemakers'. Jesus taught people to 'turn the other cheek' and he forgave his persecutors on the cross.*
CONCLUSION ● **Give a justified conclusion.** ● Include your own opinion together with your own reasoning. ● **Include evaluation.** Explain why you think one viewpoint is stronger than the other or why they are equally strong. ● Do not just repeat arguments you have already used without explaining how they apply to your reasoned opinion/conclusion.	*In conclusion, I would agree with the statement that the just war theory is the right religious response. I have sympathy with the views of pacifists, and ideally war should be avoided, but in the real world there are always countries that will bully other countries or try to take their land or resources, so war is sometimes necessary. It is better to have rules that limit the damage war can do, and the just war theory helps in that way.*

TIP

It is good practice to show that you know what the just war theory is before saying if it is a good response to whether it is right to fight in a war.

TIP

The conclusion does not always have to come down on one side of the argument or the other. In this example the student shows they understand the complexity of the moral issue of whether it is right to fight.

12 'Religion is the main cause of wars.'

Evaluate this statement. In your answer you:

- should give reasoned arguments in support of this statement
- should give reasoned arguments to support a different point of view
- should refer to religious arguments
- may refer to non-religious arguments
- should reach a justified conclusion.

[12 marks]
[+3 SPaG marks]

REASONED ARGUMENTS IN SUPPORT OF THE STATEMENT ● **Explain why some people would agree with the statement.** ● Develop your explanation with more detail and examples. ● Refer to religious teaching. Use a quote or paraphrase or refer to a religious authority. ● **Evaluate the arguments.** Is this a good argument or not? Explain why you think this.	
REASONED ARGUMENTS SUPPORTING A DIFFERENT VIEW ● **Explain why some people would support a different view.** ● Develop your explanation with more detail and examples. ● Refer to religious teaching. Use a quote or paraphrase or refer to a religious authority. ● **Evaluate the arguments.** Is this a good argument or not? Explain why you think this.	
CONCLUSION ● **Give a justified conclusion.** ● Include your own opinion together with your own reasoning. ● **Include evaluation.** Explain why you think one viewpoint is stronger than the other or why they are equally strong. ● Do not just repeat arguments you have already used without explaining how they apply to your reasoned opinion/conclusion.	

> TIP
> When evaluation questions ask whether something is the 'main' cause or 'best' response or whether a religious belief is the 'most important' belief, they are asking you to think about whether other causes/responses/beliefs are more significant or whether there can be many of equal merit.

13 'Religious people should be the main peacemakers in the world today.'

Evaluate this statement. In your answer you:

- should give reasoned arguments in support of this statement
- should give reasoned arguments to support a different point of view
- should refer to religious arguments
- may refer to non-religious arguments
- should reach a justified conclusion.

[12 marks]
[+3 SPaG marks]

Check your answers using the mark scheme on page 163–164. How did you do?
To feel more secure in the content you need to remember, re-read pages 116–123.
To remind yourself of what the examiner is looking for, go to pages 7–13.

9.1 Crime and punishment

Essential information:

☐ Crime and punishment are both governed by the law.

☐ Not all good actions are required by law and not all evil actions break the law.

What are crime and punishment?

- A **crime** is an offence that breaks the law set by the government. People who commit crimes face legal consequences.
- In the UK, people who commit crimes are arrested and questioned by police.
- They then appear before a court where a judge or jury determines their **punishment** (something done legally to somebody as a result of being found guilty of breaking the law).
- In the UK, the most serious crimes are punished with a life sentence in prison, while less serious ones might result in a shorter time in prison, community service or a fine. No legal punishment is allowed to deliberately cause harm to the offender.

Good and evil actions and intentions

Good actions and intentions	Evil actions and intentions
• Some people assume a good action is an action that does not break a law. However, there are many good actions that people perform which exist outside the law (such as giving to charity or helping people in need). • Actions encouraged by genuine religious faiths are usually considered to be good.	• Evil actions usually go against the law (such as murder and child abuse). However, there are some actions which are legal but might be considered evil by some people (such as adultery and abortion). • In the UK, the intentions of the criminal (the plan they have before they act) will often be taken into account when setting a punishment. A criminal who commits an evil action but has good intentions may receive a more lenient punishment. • Jews and Christians believe evil actions are wrong and offensive to God, regardless of the intentions behind the action. • Many Christians and Jews believe God created people to be good but humans have a tendency to use their free will to do evil things. • Teachings in the Bible (such as Matthew 5:27–28) warn against having any evil thoughts or intentions, as these will lead to evil actions.

> ❝You have heard that it was said, 'You shall not commit adultery.' But I tell you that anyone who looks at a woman lustfully has already committed adultery with her in his heart.❞
>
> *Matthew 5:27–28 [NIV]*

 A **Explain the difference** between evil actions and evil intentions.

 B 'Intentions are more important than actions.'

Write a developed argument to support **each** side of this statement. Elaborate your arguments with religious teaching.

TIP

When faced with a statement that you strongly agree or disagree with, you must also focus on an alternative opinion and explain why a person might hold it.

RECAP

Essential information:

- [ ] Religious believers think crime is hardly ever justified, no matter the reason.

- [ ] Some reasons why people commit crimes include **poverty** (being without money, food or other basic needs), **mental illness** (a medical condition that affects a person's emotions or moods), **addiction** (a physical or mental dependency on a substance or activity) and **greed** (a selfish desire for something).

Reasons why some people commit crimes

Reason	Development	Christian view	Jewish view
Poverty	There are millions of people in the UK who live in poverty and cannot always afford to buy food or other essentials. Some believe the only way out of this is to steal.	Stealing for any reason is wrong, but society should ensure that nobody has to steal because of poverty. Christians support action that helps those in poverty.	Jews have an obligation to help each other so nobody should face poverty. Committing crimes out of need is discouraged.
Upbringing	Some people grow up in a household where crime is a way of life. A troubled upbringing might also lead a person to turn to crime.	Parents should teach their children the right way to behave through their own words and actions.	Children should be brought up in the faith and its morality.
Mental illness	Some forms of mental illness may lead people into crime. E.g. anger management problems may lead to violence.	Treating the causes of the illness is the most loving and compassionate thing to do.	Jews are expected to care for the mentally ill and cater for their needs.
Addiction	Taking illegal drugs is a crime, even when the person is addicted. They may commit further crimes to be able to buy drugs. Legal drugs, e.g. alcohol, can also play a part in crimes such as violence, rape and drunk driving.	Christians are against taking illegal drugs and support rehabilitation. Most Christians believe alcohol is acceptable in moderation.	People should be helped to overcome their addiction. Drinking alcohol is allowed in Judaism but discouraged in excess.
Greed	Some people want personal possessions that they do not need and cannot afford. Their greed for them may lead them to steal.	The Ten Commandments forbid envy and it is envy that often causes greed. ❝ You shall not covet [...] anything that belongs to your neighbour. ❞ *Exodus 20:17* [NIV]	Greed is discouraged by the Ten Commandments.
Hate	Hate, the opposite of love, can lead to violence or aggression.	Jesus taught Christians to love everybody.	Hatred is against Jewish morality.
Opposition to an unjust law	Some people break laws they believe to be unjust in order to protest against them. These could be laws based on inequality or that deny basic human rights.	Some Christians may agree with this but only if no violence is involved and nobody is harmed.	Jews do not encourage this but if a law is against Jewish morality they may work to change it.

Even though some people believe they have a justified reason for committing crimes, everybody must obey the law. This helps society to live in peace without fear of danger. Christians believe God put the system of government in place to rule every citizen.

> ❝ Let everyone be subject to the governing authorities, for there is no authority except that which God has established. ❞ *Romans 13:1* [NIV]

Regardless of the reasons why crimes are committed, most crimes are selfish because they harm innocent people in order that the criminal can get what they want or need.

APPLY

 A   Explain **two** reasons why people commit crimes.

 B   'Addiction is the only good reason for committing crimes.'
Write down your own thoughts about this and **develop them by adding religious views**.

RECAP

Essential information:

☐ Many Christians and Jews condemn the crimes people commit but do not hate the people who commit them.

Attitudes to lawbreakers

Christian views	Jewish views
• Christians believe the law should be respected. • Offenders must be punished by the law according to the seriousness of the crime. • Offenders have basic rights and so should not be given a punishment that is inhumane or harmful. Through their punishment they should be helped to become a useful member of society so they do not re-offend. • The parable of the Sheep and the Goats makes it clear that helping prisoners is helping Jesus: 🎧 I was in prison and you came to visit me. 🎧 *Matthew 25:36 [NIV]* • Some Christians think the punishment should be as severe as the crime committed.	• The law of a country should be respected provided it does not contradict Torah law. • Lawbreakers should be given punishments as dictated by the law. • The punishment should reflect the severity of the crime in order to deter others. • However, punishments should also be merciful and not be unreasonably harsh. • Offenders should be helped so they do not re-offend. • Individuals should take responsibility for their own behaviour and if they do wrong, they should try to make amends for their crime. 🎧 the wickedness of the wicked shall be accounted to him alone 🎧 *Ezekiel 18:20 [Tenakh]*

Different types of crime – hate crime, theft and murder

- **Hate crimes** often involve violence and are usually targeted at a person because of their race, religion, sexuality, disability or gender. The murder of six million Jews in the Holocaust during the Second World War, along with members of other minority groups, is considered to be the worst hate crime the world has seen.
- **Theft** is less serious than some other crimes but it still results in a victim suffering loss.
- **Murder** is one of the worst crimes. Some murders involve the victim being put in great pain before they die. Some murders are classed as hate crimes.

Religious attitudes to different types of crime

- Hate crimes are widely condemned by both Christians and Jews. The teaching of 'love your neighbour' refers to showing compassion, care and respect for everybody. No crime shows this sort of love towards the victim.
- Christians and Jews believe murder is wrong because only God has the right and authority to take life. It also goes against the Ten Commandments.

🎧 You shall not murder. 🎧
Exodus 20:13 [NIV]

🎧 Do to others what you want them to do to you. 🎧
Matthew 7:12 (the Golden Rule) [NIV]

- Similarly, theft is not permitted in the Ten Commandments. Neither Christians nor Jews justify theft caused by the need to supply food for a family.

> **TIP**
> See page 129 for Christian and Jewish beliefs about poverty as a reason for crime.

APPLY

(A) **Explain** the similarities and differences between a hate crime and murder.

(B) Should religious believers hate the crime but not the criminal who has committed it? **Explain your opinion** and elaborate it with religious teachings.

> **TIP**
> When elaborating a developed idea with religious teachings, you should show how the teachings are relevant.

RECAP

Essential information:

☐ Three aims of punishment are retribution, deterrence and reformation.

TIP

To protect other people in the community is another aim of punishment that you can use if you wish.

Aims of punishment

Aim	Explanation	Christian views	Jewish views
Retribution – to get your own back	• Society, on behalf of the victim, is getting its own back on the offender. • Criminals should be made to suffer in proportion to how serious their crimes are. • For example, in the case of murder, the murderer should be killed as a punishment.	• Paul teaches, 'Do not be overcome by evil, but overcome evil with good' (Romans 21:21 [NIV]). • Many Christians focus on other aims of punishment, which they believe are less harmful and more positive. • Some Christians support the death penalty by quoting, 'life for life, eye for eye, tooth for tooth' (Exodus 21:23–24 [NIV]). But most think this means, for example, that murderers should be punished severely but not killed.	• Many Jews do not interpret the 'eye for eye' teaching literally. They reject the idea of retribution as it goes against Jewish teachings. ❝You shall not take vengeance or bear a grudge against your countrymen. Love your fellow as yourself: I am the LORD.❞ *Leviticus 19:18* [Tenakh]
Deterrence – to put people off committing crimes	• The idea of deterrence is to use punishment as an example and warning to others. • If the punishment is harsh, it may deter the offender from repeating the crime and others from copying it. • In some countries, punishments are carried out in public as a form of deterrence.	• Although most Christians agree with deterring people from committing crimes, they do not support punishments that cause physical or mental harm to the offender or infringe their rights. • They oppose public punishments because they think offenders should be treated with respect, despite what they have done.	• The belief that humans should be treated with respect, regardless of what they have done, discourages Jews from making examples of offenders in order to deter others. • Punishment as a deterrent is acceptable if it is necessary, but it should always be humane.
Reformation – to change someone's behaviour for the better	• Reformation aims to use punishment that helps offenders to give up crime and realise their behaviour is harmful. • This may involve counselling, community service and meeting the victims. • It is hoped offenders will change their attitude to become law-abiding citizens.	• Most Christians favour reformation over other aims of punishment. • It is positive rather than negative and works with individuals to improve their life chances. • It is not a replacement for punishment but should happen alongside punishment, even for the worst offenders.	• Most Christians favour reformation over other aims of punishment. • Punishment should be compassionate as an example of correct behaviour. • Punishment should help offenders to turn their lives around. • Reformation should not replace punishment.

APPLY

(A) **Explain** what each of the three aims of punishment are.

(B) **Write a detailed argument** to support your own opinion about whether offenders should be punished severely. Try to include some religious teaching.

TIP

The three aims of punishment may be useful to develop your ideas if writing about other aspects of punishment.

RECAP

Essential information:

☐ Suffering can be caused by natural events (such as illness or an earthquake) or by human behaviour (such as an assault or a car crash).

☐ Christians and Jews believe they must not ignore any suffering they have caused to others, and they should repair any damage they may have caused.

☐ Suffering is an unfortunate part of life that no one can avoid.

Religious attitudes to suffering

Christian beliefs	Jewish beliefs
• Whatever the cause, Christians believe they have a duty to help those who are suffering. • Paul, who suffered greatly at some points in his life, wrote: ❝We also glory in our sufferings, because we know that suffering produces perseverance; perseverance, character; and character, hope.❞ *Romans 5:3–4 [NIV]* • Christians try to follow the example of Jesus. He helped many whom he saw were suffering and told his followers to do the same.	• Jews believe they should try to help anyone who is suffering. • The Holocaust has caused Jews to question why such suffering can have happened to people chosen by God. • They accept that suffering is caused by human evil as a result of free will, not by God. • Suffering provides an opportunity for Jews to care for others.

Why does a loving God allow people to suffer?

• Theists believe it is wrong to blame God for the suffering that results from human actions.

• This is because God has given humans **free will** (the ability to make decisions for themselves), and has also given guidance about how to use that free will responsibly.

• The role of the law is to give more guidance about the best way to use free will, together with punishments for those who cause suffering by committing crimes.

Religious attitudes to causing suffering to others

Christian beliefs	Jewish beliefs
• Jesus taught that people should love and respect each other and not use violence in self-defence because it may increase suffering. • However, this does not always work and on occasions, maybe accidentally, Christians do cause others to suffer. • If and when this happens, Christians are taught to apologise and to try to repair the damage they have caused in order to restore relationships. For example, at Jesus' arrest, one disciple cut off the High Priest's servant's ear. Jesus rebuked the disciple and healed the servant. • So Christians can try to heal the wrong that has been done and the suffering that has been caused.	• Jews are opposed to causing people to suffer. • As no person is perfect, it is inevitable that at times they may cause others to suffer, possibly by accident or by having an unclear mind. • If a person causes another to suffer, they should try to repair the damage caused. ❝Do not do to others that which you would not want them to do to you.❞ *Rabbi Hillel*

APPLY

 A **Explain** carefully what Christians and Jews believe about free will and how it should be used.

B 'Using violence in self-defence only causes more suffering.'

Think carefully about this and **write a developed argument** to support your opinion about it.

9.6 The treatment of criminals – prison, corporal punishment and community service

Essential information:

☐ You need to know about three forms of punishment: **prison** (a secure building where offenders are kept for a period of time), **corporal punishment** (punishment of an offender by causing them pain, now illegal in the UK) and **community service** (punishing offenders by making them do unpaid work in the community).

☐ Christian and Jewish beliefs and attitudes to the treatment of criminals vary.

You might be asked to compare beliefs on corporal punishment between Christianity (the main religious tradition in Great Britain) and another religious tradition.

Forms of punishment for criminals

	Christian beliefs	Jewish beliefs
Prison • A punishment for serious crimes • The main punishment is a loss of liberty • Prisoners have no real choice about how to spend their time – everything is controlled for them • They are locked in cells, fed and allowed exercise and interaction with other prisoners at set times • They work in the prison for very little money or take part in training or education programmes	Many Christians believe that prisoners should be treated well when in prison. They are keen to help prisoners make their stay in prison useful by encouraging positive activity. They believe it is important that conditions within prisons are humane and civilised.	The Torah makes no mention of prisons but most Jews today agree with the use of prisons for those who commit serious crimes. Prisoners should be treated well and have the opportunity to reflect on their actions. Showing remorse and making positive resolutions for the future are important.
Corporal punishment • Punishes offenders by inflicting physical pain • Illegal in the UK and many other countries • Some Muslim countries such as Iran and Saudi Arabia use corporal punishment, such as caning for some offences and amputation of the hand for theft • Punishments often take place in public • Considered to be a breach of human rights	Most Christians do not support corporal punishment. It does not seek to reform an offender and it physically harms the person, so it is seen as a negative and harmful punishment.	The Torah and Talmud both allow corporal punishment but most Jews today do not agree with its use. Instead they emphasise the importance of positive discipline that does not cause harm but encourages the offender to reform their ways.
Community service • A punishment for minor offences • Allows offenders the chance to reform • Includes 'community payback' which involves doing supervised work in the community, such as cleaning graffiti off buildings • Can include treatment for addiction or medical conditions, counselling or educational opportunities • In some cases, and with the agreement of the victim, a meeting may be set up so the victim can give their side of the story and the offender can apologise for their actions	Christians agree with community service for offenders who are likely to benefit from it. It allows offenders to make up for what they have done wrong (reparation), deters them from committing offences in the future and reforms them by making them realise the consequences of their actions. No harm is done to the offender, which is a positive step.	Many Jews see community service as an opportunity for an offender to repair the damage they have caused. It can help offenders to reform and although it can involve hard work, it is not harmful.

A Explain **two** similar religious beliefs about corporal punishment.

B 'Criminals should not be treated well.'

What **religious arguments** would you include when evaluating this statement?

RECAP

Essential information:

☐ Christians and Jews believe that **forgiveness** (showing mercy and pardoning someone for what they have done wrong) is important for living a peaceful life.

☐ Christians and Jews do not think forgiveness is a replacement for punishment.

 You might be asked to compare beliefs on forgiveness between Christianity (the main religious tradition in Great Britain) and another religious tradition.

Christian attitudes to forgiveness

- Forgiveness is a key belief in Christianity, but many Christians also believe that forgiveness should not be a replacement for punishment. They believe the offender should be forgiven as far as possible, but should also be punished to ensure justice is done.
- When he was dying on the cross, Jesus forgave those who crucified him:

> ❝Father forgive them, for they do not know what they are doing.❞
>
> *Luke 23:34 [NIV]*

- God expects Christians to show forgiveness to others, no matter what they may have done. In turn, they believe that God will forgive them for any sinsthey may commit. This is emphasised in the Lord's Prayer:

> ❝Forgive us our sins as we forgive those who sin against us.❞
>
> *The Lord's Prayer*

- Jesus also told his followers that there is no upper limit to the amount of forgiveness they should show to someone.

> ❝'Lord, how many times shall I forgive my brother when he sins against me? Up to seven times?' Jesus answered, 'I tell you, not seven times, but seventy-seven times.'❞
>
> *Matthew 18:21–22 [NIV]*

Jewish attitudes to forgiveness

- Forgiveness is an important teaching in Judaism, but it is not expected to be an automatic response from the person who has been wronged.
- Instead, offenders should show remorse to their victims and sincerely ask for their forgiveness before they expect to be forgiven by their victim or by God.
- Showing forgiveness is a duty if an offender genuinely asks for it.
- The Ten Days of Repentance between Rosh Hashanah and Yom Kippur are a traditional time to ask for forgiveness in advance of God's forgiveness on Yom Kippur.
- Forgiveness is not a replacement for punishment.

> ❝Come, let us reach an understanding,
>
> —says the LORD.
>
> Be your sins like crimson,
> They can turn snow-white;
> Be they red as dyed wool,
> They become like fleece.❞
>
> *Isaiah 1:18 [Tenakh]*

TIP
Remember that forgiveness is a core belief in Christianity and Judaism, although many would argue that it is not a replacement for punishment. In the UK, a person convicted of murder will receive a lengthy prison sentence regardless of whether friends and family of the victim have forgiven them.
Part of repentance is accepting punishment as an opportunity to reform.

APPLY

(A) **Explain** how Christian beliefs about forgiveness are different from Jewish ones.

(B) 'Nobody should expect to be forgiven more than once.'

Write a logical chain of reasoning that agrees with this statement and another one that gives a different point of view.

TIP
Knowing and using an example of someone who has forgiven is a good way to develop your answer.

RECAP

Essential information:

☐ The **death penalty** (when a criminal is put to death for their crime) is illegal in the UK but still exists in some other countries.

☐ Many Christians and Jews oppose the death penalty.

You might be asked to compare beliefs on the death penalty between Christianity (the main religious tradition in Great Britain) and another religious tradition.

Arguments for and against the death penalty

The death penalty was abolished in the UK in 1969. It is illegal in most of Europe, but still exists in some states in the USA, in China and in some Middle Eastern countries, such as Saudi Arabia. Arguments for and against the death penalty include the following:

Viewpoint	Explanation
For	• The **principle of utility** states an action is right if it produces the maximum happiness for the greatest number of people affected by it. • If the use of the death penalty is proven to protect society – therefore creating happiness for a greater number of people – it can be justified.
	• It is **justified retribution** for people who commit the worst possible crimes.
	• It **protects society** by removing the worst criminals so they cannot cause harm again.
Against	• There is a chance of **killing an innocent person**. • E.g. three people executed in the UK in the 1950s have since been pardoned, because new evidence has cast serious doubt over their guilt.
	• There is **little evidence the death penalty is an effective deterrent**. • E.g. the UK murder rate is no higher than in countries that have the death penalty. • Often the threat of punishment does not enter into the murderer's thinking.
	• It is **not right to take another person's life**. This does not show forgiveness or compassion.
	• Society can still be protected by **imprisoning criminals** instead of executing them.

Religious attitudes to the death penalty

Most Christians and Jews do not support the death penalty, although some do. Their views may be based partly on the arguments given above, and partly on the religious teachings given below.

Christian views	Jewish views
• The **sanctity of life** is the idea that all life is holy as it is created by God, and only God can take it away. This teaching is used to oppose the death penalty. • Ezekiel 33:11 teaches that wrongdoers should be reformed (not executed). • Some Christians agree with the death penalty and use teachings from the Old Testament to support their views. ❝Whoever sheds human blood, by humans shall their blood be shed.❞ *Genesis 9:6 [NIV]*	• The Torah identifies 36 offences that should be punishable by death, but the Talmud lays down conditions that make it very difficult to pass the death sentence. • Israel abolished the death penalty in 1954 for everything except Nazi Holocaust offences and treason in war. • Many Jews refer to the sanctity of life to argue against the death penalty. • Some Jews believe retribution and deterrence are valid reasons for the death penalty. They may refer to passages in the Torah such as Genesis 9:6.

APPLY

(A) Give **two** religious teachings about the death penalty.

(B) **Write a paragraph to support the statement**, 'No religious believer should support the death penalty'. Include religious teachings.

9 Exam practice

Test the 1 mark question

1   Which **one** of the following punishments is illegal in the UK?

    A   Corporal punishment   B   Prison   C   Paying a fine   D   Community service   **[1 mark]**

2   Which **one** of the following reflects the principle of utility, which suggests an action is right if it promotes maximum…?

    A   Pain   B   Sadness   C   Happiness   D   Profit   **[1 mark]**

Test the 2 mark question

3   Give **two** aims of punishment.   **[2 marks]**

    1) _____

    2) _____

4   Give **two** different reasons why some people commit crimes.   **[2 marks]**

    1) _____

    2) _____

Test the 4 mark question

5   Explain **two** contrasting beliefs in contemporary British society about whether the death penalty should be restored in the UK.

In your answer you should refer to the main religious tradition of Great Britain and one or more other religious traditions.   **[4 marks]**

● **Explain one belief.**	Some Christians believe that the death penalty is correct because it follows the Old Testament teaching of 'eye for eye, tooth for tooth'.
● Develop your explanation with more detail/an example/ reference to a religious teaching or quotation.	'Eye for eye, tooth for tooth' means that an offender should receive back the same as he or she has done, so if he has murdered someone, he should be killed.
● **Explain a second belief.**	Many Jews do not support the death penalty as they believe only God has the right to take life, because he gave life in the first place.
● Develop your explanation with more detail/an example/ reference to a religious teaching or quotation.	The prophet Ezekiel said that it is not God's desire that the wicked should die, but instead they should turn away from their wickedness and be reformed.

6   Explain **two** contrasting beliefs about community service.

In your answer you must refer to one or more religious traditions.   **[4 marks]**

● **Explain one belief.**	
● Develop your explanation with more detail/an example/ reference to a religious teaching or quotation.	
● **Explain a second belief.**	
● Develop your explanation with more detail/an example/ reference to a religious teaching or quotation.	

9 Exam practice

7   Explain **two** similar religious beliefs that support retribution as an aim of punishment.
    In your answer you must refer to one or more religious traditions.   **[4 marks]**

Test the 5 mark question

8   Explain **two** religious beliefs about reformation as an aim of punishment.
    Refer to sacred writings or another source of religious belief and teaching in your answer.   **[5 marks]**

● **Explain one belief.**	*One Christian belief is that reformation is a preferable aim of punishment because it seeks to help offenders change their behaviour.*
● Develop your explanation with more detail/an example.	*This means they are less likely to commit any further offences, so they won't hurt anybody else or need to be punished again.*
● **Explain a second belief.**	*A second Christian belief is that reformation is a compassionate response towards wrongdoing.*
● Develop your explanation with more detail/an example.	*Christians believe that to show compassion for others is to follow the teachings of Jesus, who told his disciples to turn the other cheek.*
● Add a reference to sacred writings or another source of religious belief and teaching. If you prefer, you can add this reference to your first belief instead.	*The words of Paul in Romans support this idea: 'do not be overcome by evil, but overcome evil with good.'*

TIP
When using scripture, try to show the examiner that you understand its relevance to the question.

9   Explain **two** religious beliefs about forgiveness.
    Refer to sacred writings or another source of religious belief and teaching in your answer.   **[5 marks]**

● **Explain one belief.**	
● Develop your explanation with more detail/an example.	
● **Explain a second belief.**	
● Develop your explanation with more detail/an example.	
● Add a reference to sacred writings or another source of religious belief and teaching. If you prefer, you can add this reference to your first belief instead.	

10 Explain **two** religious beliefs about hate crimes.
    Refer to sacred writings or another source of religious belief and teaching in your answer.   **[5 marks]**

Test the 12 mark question

11 'It is right to forgive all offenders whoever they are and whatever they have done.'

Evaluate this statement. In your answer you:

- should give reasoned arguments in support of this statement
- should give reasoned arguments to support a different point of view
- should refer to religious arguments
- may refer to non-religious arguments
- should reach a justified conclusion.

[12 marks]

[+3 SPaG mark

REASONED ARGUMENTS IN SUPPORT OF THE STATEMENT • **Explain why some people would agree with the statement.** • Develop your explanation with more detail and examples. • Refer to religious teaching. Use a quote or paraphrase or refer to a religious authority. • **Evaluate the arguments.** Is this a good argument or not? Explain why you think this.	*Christians should always forgive anybody who wants to be forgiven. When the disciples asked Jesus how many times they should forgive, suggesting that seven was a fair number, Jesus told them it should be seventy-seven times. In other words, there should be no maximum. Jesus even asked God to forgive the people who crucified him because they didn't know what they were doing. So it should not matter how many times, who is asking to be forgiven or what they have done to be forgiven for.* *If someone is forgiven, there is a better chance that they will be reformed and try hard to make sure that whatever they have done is never repeated. This is what repentance is about and forgiveness and repentance are closely linked. No sin is unforgiveable and so people, especially religious people, should always forgive, especially as this does not mean that the sinner is not punished because they have been forgiven.*
REASONED ARGUMENTS SUPPORTING A DIFFERENT VIEW • **Explain why some people would support a different view.** • Develop your explanation with more detail and examples. • Refer to religious teaching. Use a quote or paraphrase or refer to a religious authority. • **Evaluate the arguments.** Is this a good argument or not? Explain why you think this.	*Some people who are victims of serious crimes find it very difficult to forgive. They cannot imagine how they can ever feel anything but hatred for someone who has wronged them so horribly. A victim of rape may find it hard to forgive their attacker and they are highly unlikely to ever forget it. Judaism teaches that people should show remorse and sincerely ask for forgiveness before they are forgiven by their victim or God. This suggests that offenders should not be forgiven if they are not sorry for what they did. Many Jews find it impossible to forgive the Nazis for the Holocaust and why should they be expected to?*
CONCLUSION • **Give a justified conclusion.** • Include your own opinion together with your own reasoning. • **Include evaluation.** Explain why you think one viewpoint is stronger than the other or why they are equally strong. • Do not just repeat arguments you have already used without explaining how they apply to your reasoned opinion/conclusion.	*In my opinion, forgiveness is an ideal that religions want people to work towards. I think if they become the victims themselves, they may change their mind. We are only human. Maybe Jews are right in insisting that offenders show remorse and ask for forgiveness before being forgiven. To me, this seems fair.*

TIP
The first paragraph not only shows good knowledge of the Bible's teaching on forgiveness but also makes its meaning clear. The next paragraph develops the argument by relating the teaching directly to the statement being evaluated.

TIP
In this case the student has used religious perspectives throughout the answer. It is important to use religious arguments in the answer to reach the higher levels, but you may also use non-religious arguments. For example, non-religious people might see no reason to forgive all offenders, because they would not be guided by religious teachings about forgiveness.

12 'The idea of the sanctity of life shows the death penalty is wrong.'

Evaluate this statement. In your answer you:

- should give reasoned arguments in support of this statement
- should give reasoned arguments to support a different point of view
- should refer to religious arguments
- may refer to non-religious arguments
- should reach a justified conclusion.

TIP
Don't forget that the focus of the statement is on the <u>sanctity of life</u> and the death penalty, not just whether the death penalty is wrong.

[12 marks]
[+3 SPaG marks]

REASONED ARGUMENTS IN SUPPORT OF THE STATEMENT ● **Explain why some people would agree with the statement.** ● Develop your explanation with more detail and examples. ● Refer to religious teaching. Use a quote or paraphrase or refer to a religious authority. ● **Evaluate the arguments.** Is this a good argument or not? Explain why you think this.	
REASONED ARGUMENTS SUPPORTING A DIFFERENT VIEW ● **Explain why some people would support a different view.** ● Develop your explanation with more detail and examples. ● Refer to religious teaching. Use a quote or paraphrase or refer to a religious authority. ● **Evaluate the arguments.** Is this a good argument or not? Explain why you think this.	
CONCLUSION ● **Give a justified conclusion.** ● Include your own opinion together with your own reasoning. ● **Include evaluation.** Explain why you think one viewpoint is stronger than the other or why they are equally strong. ● Do not just repeat arguments you have already used without explaining how they apply to your reasoned opinion/conclusion.	

13 'There is no good reason why anyone should commit a crime.'

Evaluate this statement. In your answer you:

- should give reasoned arguments in support of this statement
- should give reasoned arguments to support a different point of view
- should refer to religious arguments
- may refer to non-religious arguments
- should reach a justified conclusion.

TIP
Don't forget to include a logical chain of reasoning.

[12 marks]
[+3 SPaG marks]

Check your answers using the mark scheme on page 164–165. How did you do?
To feel more secure in the content you need to remember, re-read pages 128–135.
To remind yourself of what the examiner is looking for, go to pages 7–13.

10.1 Social justice and human rights

RECAP

Essential information:

☐ **Social justice** means ensuring that society treats people fairly whether they are poor or wealthy, and protects people's **human rights** – the basic rights and freedoms to which all humans should be entitled.

☐ All people have a **responsibility** (a duty of care) not to harm the rights of others.

Human rights and responsibilities

- In 1948, the United Nations adopted the **Universal Declaration of Human Rights** (UDHR).
- This sets out the rights to which every person should be entitled.
- The UK government is obliged to provide these rights to people living in the UK.

People can only have human rights if they acknowledge the responsibility to make sure these rights are available. This includes the responsibility to **respect other people's rights**, and the responsibility to **help create access to those rights**. For example:

- Humans have the right to freedom of speech, but the responsibility not to say something that causes offence.
- Children have the right to protection from cruelty, but the responsibility not to bully or harm each other.

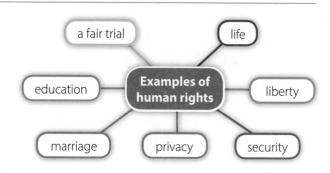

Examples of human rights: a fair trial, life, education, liberty, marriage, privacy, security

Social justice

Social justice is about trying to protect people's rights and opportunities so the least advantaged members of society are treated with the same justice and compassion as more advantaged people.

Christian views	Jewish views
• There are many teachings in the Bible about the importance of social justice and caring for others. • Jesus stressed the need to help others, for example in his teaching 'love your neighbour as yourself' (Mark 12:31 [NIV]), and in the parable of the Sheep and the Goats (Matthew 25:31–46).	• Following the teaching of 'love your fellow as yourself' (Leviticus 19:18 [Tenakh]), Jews believe it is important to work for the good of the community and to treat all people with fairness, honesty and kindness. ❝ let justice well up like water, Righteousness like an unfailing stream ❞ *Amos 5:24 [Tenakh]*

APPLY

(A) **Explain** how social justice may influence the way a religious person lives.

(B) 'Everybody's human rights should be protected.'

Write a detailed argument agreeing with this statement and a contrasting argument to support a different opinion.

TIP
If you are including scripture in your answer, don't worry if you can't remember the quote exactly. Summarise or paraphrase it instead.

10.2 Prejudice and discrimination

Essential information:

- [ ] Christians and Jews believe in **equality** – that humans are of equal value and status.

- [ ] **Prejudice** (holding biased opinions about an individual or group without knowing all the facts) and **discrimination** (the actions or behaviour that result from prejudice) go against Christian and Jewish teaching.

> **TIP**
> Remember: biased attitudes (thinking) = prejudice, biased actions and behaviour (doing) = discrimination.

Equality

- Christians and Jews both believe that being created in God's image makes people very special and precious.
- Whatever their status, religion or gender, they are equally valuable and can have the same relationship with God.
- People should only be judged on how well they live their lives in obedience to God, not on wealth or status.

> **"** There is neither Jew nor Gentile [non-Jew], neither slave nor free, nor is there male or female for you are all one in Christ Jesus. **"**
>
> *Galatians 3:28 [NIV]*

- Jesus was repeating the Jewish teaching 'love your fellow as yourself' (Leviticus 19:18 [Tenakh]) when he taught people to treat everyone as having equal value, saying, 'love your neighbour as yourself' (Mark 12:31 [NIV]).

Christian and Jewish views on prejudice based on sexuality

- Christianity and Judaism have traditionally taught that heterosexual relationships (between a man and a woman) are what God intended, following the example and teaching in Genesis about Adam and Eve.
- Homosexual relationships (between man and man, and woman and woman) are more controversial.

Christian views	Jewish views
• Some Christians think homosexual relationships are sinful as they go against teachings in the Bible and cannot lead to procreation. • Others think homosexual relationships are morally acceptable, and it is not loving to condemn people for their sexual orientation.	• Orthodox Judaism teaches that homosexual relationships are wrong, following teachings in the Torah such as Leviticus 18:22, but that all people should be treated with respect. • Some Liberal and Reform Jews accept homosexual relationships.

- Those who think homosexual relationships are acceptable focus more on the love between a couple, rather than on the sexual act, which is of lower importance.
- As of 2018, same-sex marriage is legal in the UK (except for Northern Ireland). It is illegal for a homosexual couple to marry in Israel, but their marriage is recognised if the wedding takes place in another country where it is legal.

> **TIP**
> For more religious beliefs about human sexuality go to page 80.

 (A) **Explain** the difference between prejudice and discrimination.

(B) **Write a developed argument** for agreeing that all people are born equal and another argument that expresses a different opinion.

> **TIP**
> In a question such as this, there is no need for you to express your opinion.

RECAP

Essential information:

☐ Christians and Jews generally believe people should have **freedom of religion** (the right to believe or practise whatever religion one chooses) and **freedom of religious expression** (the right to worship, preach or practise one's faith in whatever way one chooses).

You might be asked to compare beliefs on freedom of religious expression between Christianity (the main religious tradition in Great Britain) and another religious tradition.

Religious freedom

- Christianity is currently the main religious tradition in Great Britain.
- The government protects the freedom of religious expression, which gives all individuals the right to follow whichever faith they choose or none.
- Laws forbid the persecution of members of any faith.
- Any person can encourage anybody else to follow their faith, provided they do not preach hatred and intolerance.
- These freedoms are protected in the Universal Declaration of Human Rights.

> ❝Everyone has the right to freedom of thought, conscience and religion; this right includes freedom to change his religion and belief, and freedom [...] to manifest his religion or belief in teaching, practice, worship and observance. ❞
> *Universal Declaration of Human Rights*

- In some parts of the world governments do not allow their citizens such freedoms.
- In Britain there are some people who discriminate against members of particular religious traditions.
- Those found guilty of such behaviour in Britain can be punished by a court.
- Conflict based on politics and a divide between Protestants and Catholics in Northern Ireland during the second half of the twentieth century has largely been ended.

Religious teachings on freedom of religion

Christian beliefs	Jewish beliefs
• Christian teaching encourages tolerance and harmony. • Different Christian denominations fighting each other or other religions are not following Paul's words in the New Testament: ❝If it is possible, as far as it depends on you, live at peace with everyone. ❞ *Romans 12:18* [NIV] ❝Watch out for those who cause divisions and put obstacles in your way that are contrary to the teaching you have learned. Keep away from them. ❞ *Romans 16:17* [NIV]	• Judaism is not a missionary religion and does not set out to convert others to the faith. • Nearly all Jews are born into the faith, but it is possible to become a Jew if the person is sincere in their choice. • Jews in the UK have the freedom to follow their faith in whatever way their tradition dictates. • Some Jews face anti-Semitism (prejudice against the Jewish faith). ❝Or, if you are loath to serve the LORD, choose this day which ones you are going to serve – the gods that your forefathers served beyond the Euphrates, or those of the Amorites in whose land you are settled; but I and my household will serve the LORD. ❞ *Joshua 24:15* [Tenakh]

In Britain, some Christians and Jews are involved in interfaith organisations. They promote constructive dialogue that highlights what faiths have in common to develop harmony rather than division.

APPLY

 A **Explain** the attitudes to freedom of religion from the main religious tradition of Great Britain and one or more other religious traditions.

 B **Explain, with reference to religion**, whether you think people should be free to follow any religion they choose without any interference from anybody else.

RECAP

Essential information:

- [ ] Christians and Jews oppose racial prejudice and other forms of discrimination.

- [ ] **Positive discrimination** (treating people more favourably because they have been discriminated against in the past) can help to ensure equality of opportunity.

Racism

- **Racism** means showing prejudice against someone because of their ethnic group or nationality.
- In Britain, racism was made illegal in the 1976 Race Relations Act.

Christian beliefs	Jewish beliefs
• Christians oppose racism. It denies equality of opportunity to people purely because of where they come from or the colour of their skin. **"** There is neither Jew nor Gentile, neither slave nor free, nor is there male and female for you are one in Christ Jesus. **"** *Galatians 3:28* [NIV] • At the time Paul wrote these words, this was a revolutionary way of thinking. The fact that discrimination is still a problem in some parts of the world shows that Paul's vision is still not completely accepted. • In the twentieth century, races were kept apart with black people being discriminated against in countries such as South Africa and the USA. • The actions of Christians such as Archbishop Desmond Tutu (South Africa) and Dr Martin Luther King Junior (USA), with the help of others, persuaded their respective governments that racist policies were unfair and needed to be changed.	• Judaism teaches that all people should be treated fairly and with respect, because everybody is made in the image of God. **"** You shall not wrong a stranger or oppress him, for you were strangers in the land of Egypt. **"** *Exodus 22:20* [Tenakh] • Jewish beliefs have been shaped by the persecution aimed at them throughout history. • During the Holocaust in the Second World War, Jews were wrongly identified by the Nazis as an inferior race. Discrimination against them started with laws preventing Jews from working in many jobs, developed into the destruction of businesses and synagogues, and culminated in the murder of around six million Jews in concentration camps.

Positive discrimination

The use of positive discrimination can help groups that have previously been discriminated against to gain equal access to opportunities.

- For example, people with physical disabilities sometimes experience discrimination and often do not have equal access to physical spaces. Many people support the use of positive discrimination in such circumstances, e.g. giving wheelchair users front-row positions at a football ground so they can see the match.
- Some political parties in Britain may use positive discrimination to give more women the chance to be elected to Parliament, because there have always been many more male MPs than female ones.

APPLY

A **Explain** why religious believers disagree with racial prejudice.

B 'All discrimination is wrong.'

Write a chain of reasoning in support of this statement and another one for a different point of view. Give your opinion with a reason, then develop and elaborate it with some religious teaching.

> **TIP**
> You might find a statement such as this is difficult to argue against. In this instance, positive discrimination could help you to come up with such an argument.

RECAP

Essential information:

☐ Both Christians and Jews believe that women and men have equal status in the eyes of God. They are of equal value and will be held equally accountable for their actions.

☐ The roles of women within religions vary as attitudes have changed through the years.

TIP

Being equal does not mean everybody is the same.

Christian views on the status and roles of women in religion

- At the time of the early Christians (first century CE), attitudes to women were very different from today. Paul wrote:

> "Women should remain silent in the churches. They are not allowed to speak […] for it is disgraceful for a woman to speak in the church."
>
> 1 Corinthians 14:34–35 [NIV]

- He also wrote that just as Christ is the head of man, so a man is head of a woman.
- Many Christians believe that Paul's writings are a reflection of the times he lived in, and should not be strictly followed today.
- However, the Catholic and Orthodox Churches still do not allow women to be priests. They argue that men and women are equal but have different roles.
- Other Christian denominations are happy to ordain women, arguing that the Church should adapt to reflect the importance of equality in today's society. In 1993 women were allowed to become priests in the Church of England and in 2014 Rev Libby Lane became the first female bishop.

You might be asked to compare beliefs on the status of women in religion between Christianity (the main religious tradition in Great Britain) and another religious tradition.

Jewish views on the status and roles of women in religion

- Judaism teaches that women and men have equal value and status as both were made in the image of God.
- However, women and men traditionally have different roles. For men this involves providing for the family; for women it involves looking after the home and family, ensuring the dietary laws are kept, and bringing up children in the faith.

Orthodox Judaism	Reform and Liberal Judaism
• Orthodox Jews are more traditional in their interpretation of the role of women. Bringing up children in the Jewish faith is highly valued. • Men and women sit separately in the synagogue and the rabbi must be male. • The attendance of women at worship is voluntary, whereas for men it is a duty.	• Reform and Liberal Jews have less defined roles for men and women. Many share the duties in the home and both may have paid jobs. • In Reform and Liberal synagogues, men and women sit together and women can take important roles in worship, including becoming a rabbi. • Coming of age ceremonies are celebrated for girls as well as for boys.

APPLY

(A) Explain **two** religious beliefs about the status and roles of women in religion.

(B) 'It is unfair to treat people differently due to their gender or sexuality.'

Give reasoned arguments to support this statement. Include religious teaching in your answer.

TIP

For more about religious views on sexuality and gender equality, go to pages 80 and 87.

RECAP

Essential information:

☐ Christians and Jews believe that wealth is a gift from God and should be used responsibly.

You might be asked to compare beliefs on the uses of wealth between Christianity (the main religious tradition in Great Britain) and another religious tradition.

Christian principles

- The Bible teaches that wealth is a blessing from God (1 Chronicles 29:12).
- The Bible also teaches that wealth is associated with dangers like greed and selfishness.

> ❝For the love of money is a root of all sorts of evil.❞
> *1 Timothy 6:10* [NIV]

TIP
If you use this quote in your exam, you must include the words 'For the love of' at the beginning, otherwise you change its meaning.

- Jesus did not teach that it is wrong to be wealthy, but said that focusing on wealth brings the danger of ignoring God and neglecting the spiritual life.

> ❝You cannot serve both God and money.❞
> *Matthew 6:24* [NIV]

Jewish principles

- Wealth is a blessing from God and a reward for following his commands.

> ❝Remember that it is the LORD your God who gives you the power to get wealth❞
> *Deuteronomy 8:18* [Tenakh]

- Jews are taught to focus on God and fulfilling religious duties, not on acquiring wealth.
- In the Torah, King Solomon does not show greed when offered a choice of any gift by God. Jews aim to follow his example.

> ❝And I also grant you what you did not ask for – both riches and glory all your life❞
> *1 Kings 3:13* [Tenakh]

- Some Jews follow the teaching about paying tithes in Deuteronomy 14:22 by paying ten per cent of their income to charity.
- Jews believe that working honestly is the right way to earn money and laziness is not encouraged.

What is the responsible use of wealth?

Christian views	Jewish views
• While everyone needs money to live, Christians believe that those with excess money should give it to the Church for its upkeep and mission, including providing for the poor. • The parable of the Rich Man and Lazarus ends with the rich man in hell for not sharing his wealth with the poor beggar (Luke 16:19–31). • The parable of the Sheep and the Goats states that those who help the poor are rewarded with a place in heaven.	• Wealth should be shared with others in need; it is important not to be selfish. • Many homes have a pushke – a collecting box used to save money for charity. • Using money to show kindness is called tzedakah. This is a religious duty that helps to promote justice. • The best way of giving is when neither the giver nor the recipient knows the other's identity.

TIP
You do not have to believe any teachings you use. If they are relevant and help you to develop your answer, you should use them.

APPLY

A Explain **two** religious teachings about wealth.

B 'Giving to charity should be compulsory.'

Write a developed argument in support of the statement.

RECAP

Essential information:

☐ **Exploitation** is the misuse of power or money to get other people to do things for little or unfair reward.

☐ The poor are exploited worldwide in various ways, including by being paid unfairly, being charged excessive interest on loans, and being involved in people-trafficking.

Fair pay

- An important way to stop exploitation of the poor is to make sure they receive **fair pay** for the work they do.
- In the UK, the National Minimum Wage sets the lowest amount an employer can pay a worker per hour.
- In many developing countries, large companies pay their workers very low wages in order to increase their profits.
- For example, in West Bengal in India, hundreds of thousands of people work on tea plantations for around £1 per day, which is about half of what they are legally entitled to.

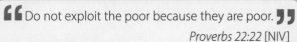

Religious responses

- Most Christians support fair pay for everyone as this contributes to an equal and just society.

> ❝ Do not exploit the poor because they are poor. ❞
>
> *Proverbs 22:22* [NIV]

- Teachings in the Torah mean that Jewish businesses consider it a duty to pay fair wages to their employees, in full and on time. Any exploitation should be avoided.

Excessive interest on loans

- Poor people sometimes have little choice but to borrow money from loan companies that charge very high rates of interest (**excessive interest on loans**).
- If they cannot repay the loans fast enough, the huge interest rates mean they can quickly end up in debt, as they end up owing much more than the amount they borrowed.

Religious responses

- The Christian Church opposes charging excessive interest on loans. This stems in part from Old Testament teachings such as Psalm 15:5.
- Judaism prohibits charging any interest on loans because it believes it is not fair to vulnerable people who need to borrow money. (However, this does not apply to businesses or banks.)

People-trafficking

- **People-trafficking** is the illegal movement of people, typically for the purposes of forced labour or commercial sexual exploitation.
- People who are desperate for a better way of life may pay smugglers to get them into a more prosperous country.
- Once in the new country, they have few rights and may be forced by the smugglers to work in poor conditions for little pay.
- Some are kidnapped and forced to work against their will.

Religious responses

- For Christians and Jews, people-trafficking goes against the sanctity of life. This teaches that every person has value and should be respected.
- People-trafficking also goes against the teaching to 'love your neighbour as yourself', which is important to both Christians and Jews.

APPLY

A Explain **two** ways in which poor people might be exploited.

B 'Developed countries requiring cheap goods are to blame for exploitation.'

Write two chains of reasoning, one supporting the statement and one supporting a different opinion. For each, give an opinion with a reason, develop it and elaborate it with religious teaching.

TIP
When including religious teaching try to make it relevant and include your thoughts about it.

RECAP

Essential information:

☐ Christians and Jews have a religious duty to help the poor.

☐ They also encourage those in need to use their own talents and abilities to help themselves out of poverty, where this is possible.

Giving aid

There are two main types of help that can be given to the poor – short-term (emergency) aid and long-term aid.

- **Short-term aid** is help given to communities in a time of disaster or crisis.
- For example, after an earthquake or outbreak of conflict, organisations such as **Christian Aid** and **World Jewish Relief** will mobilise their workers, many of whom are volunteers, to provide emergency supplies such as food, water, blankets, basic shelter and medical supplies.
- Giving money directly to homeless people on the streets is another type of short-term aid.
- Short-term aid is important for immediate survival but does not tackle the underlying causes of poverty.
- **Long-term aid** is help given to communities over a longer period of time, which has a more lasting effect.
- Examples include providing education to help people find better-paid work, or providing farmers with tools to improve their efficiency.
- Although it may take time to have an effect, long-term aid helps people to become more self-reliant and helps to solve the root causes of poverty.

Christian and Jewish responses

Christians and Jews believe they have been given a responsibility by God to look after the world and the poor (stewardship). Teachings such as 'love your neighbour as yourself' also encourage Christians and Jews to help those in poverty. Ways they might do this include:

Buying Fairtrade products. These are made by workers who are paid fairly and work in good conditions.	Supporting or volunteering for soup kitchens, food banks, and charities that help those in poverty.	Supporting campaigns that promote greater equality and a just society, such as the Living Wage campaign.

Responsibilities of those living in poverty

- Christianity and Judaism teach that everybody has talents and abilities to help themselves out of poverty if they have the opportunity to do so. Providing such opportunities is an important part of helping people to provide for themselves.
- Proverbs 6:6–11 warns that laziness leads to hunger and poverty. Both Christians and Jews encourage the poor to help themselves by working, but realise there are some who are unable to do so, for example due to a lack of qualifications, a disability, or having to care full-time for young children.
- Christians and Jews are keen to help the poor to develop their skills and education so they can better support themselves. While they believe it is important to show generosity and compassion to those in poverty, they recognise that helping the poor to provide for themselves is also essential.

APPLY

A Explain **two** ways in which long-term aid helps people to provide for themselves.

B 'Religious believers don't do enough to help the poor.'

Write one paragraph supporting this view and another which expresses a different point of view.

10 Exam practice

Test the 1 mark question

1 Which **one** of the following best describes prejudice?

A Doing something to someone which is unfair B Misusing power to get people to do things

C Unfairly judging someone before knowing the facts D Using violent action to harm someone **[1 mark]**

2 Which **one** of the following is **not** an action which goes against human rights?

A People-trafficking B Promoting tolerance C Racial prejudice D Exploiting the poor **[1 mark]**

Test the 2 mark question

3 Give **two** ways in which the poor are exploited. **[2 marks]**

1) _____

2) _____

4 Give **two** ways in which a religious person should use their wealth. **[2 marks]**

1) _____

2) _____

Test the 4 mark question

5 Explain **two** contrasting beliefs in contemporary British society about what role women should be allowed in worship.

In your answer you should refer to the main religious tradition of Great Britain and one or more other religious traditions. **[4 marks]**

● **Explain one belief.**	*The main religious tradition of Great Britain is Christianity and many denominations believe that women should have the right to take a full and active role in leading worship.*
● Develop your explanation with more detail/an example/reference to a religious teaching or quotation.	*For example, Libby Lane became an Anglican bishop, and in the United Reformed and Methodist denominations, women are also allowed to be preachers and ministers.*
● **Explain a second belief.**	*In contrast in Orthodox Judaism, although men and women are seen as equals they are believed to have been given different roles by God.*
● Develop your explanation with more detail/an example/reference to a religious teaching or quotation.	*Orthodox Judaism only allows men to become rabbis. For men prayer in the synagogue is a duty, but for women it is voluntary.*

TIP
This is a good start to the answer. It immediately identifies Christianity as the main religious tradition of Great Britain.

6 Explain **two** contrasting religious beliefs about prejudice based on sexuality.

In your answer you must refer to one or more religious traditions. **[4 marks]**

● **Explain one belief.**	
● Develop your explanation with more detail/an example/reference to a religious teaching or quotation.	
● **Explain a second belief.**	
● Develop your explanation with more detail/an example/reference to a religious teaching or quotation.	

TIP
Do not confuse prejudice based on sexuality with gender prejudice.

7 Explain **two** similar religious beliefs about the importance of human rights.

In your answer you must refer to one or more religious traditions. **[4 marks]**

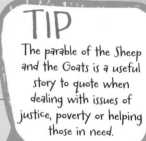

Test the 5 mark question

8   Explain **two** religious beliefs about social justice.

Refer to sacred writings or another source of religious belief and teaching in your answer.   **[5 marks]**

● **Explain one belief.**	Jews believe social justice is important because people should be treated as equals.
● Develop your explanation with more detail/an example.	In promoting equality, Jews challenge what is unjust and show kindness and honesty, aiming to never exploit others in their business dealings.
● **Explain a second belief.**	Christians believe that working to promote social justice brings them closer to God.
● Develop your explanation with more detail/an example.	So, many Christians have campaigned to improve human rights, for example Martin Luther King Jr, who led a peaceful movement to achieve social justice for black people who were discriminated against in America.
● Add a reference to sacred writings or another source of religious belief and teaching. If you prefer, you can add this reference to your first belief instead.	The parable of the Sheep and the Goats supports this Christian belief: 'Take your inheritance, the kingdom prepared for you since the salvation of the world. For I was hungry and you gave me something to drink, I was a stranger and you invited me in...' (Matthew 25:34–36)

> **TIP**
> The parable of the Sheep and the Goats is a useful story to quote when dealing with issues of justice, poverty or helping those in need.

9   Explain **two** religious beliefs about the duty to tackle poverty.

Refer to sacred writings or another source of religious belief and teaching in your answer.   **[5 marks]**

● **Explain one belief.**	
● Develop your explanation with more detail/an example.	
● **Explain a second belief.**	
● Develop your explanation with more detail/an example.	
● Add a reference to sacred writings or another source of religious belief and teaching. If you prefer, you can add this reference to your first belief instead.	

10   Explain **two** religious beliefs about the dangers of wealth.

Refer to sacred writings or another source of religious belief and teaching in your answer.   **[5 marks]**

Test the 12 mark question

11 'All religious believers should give to charities that help the poor.'

Evaluate this statement. In your answer you:

- should give reasoned arguments in support of this statement
- should give reasoned arguments to support a different point of view
- should refer to religious arguments
- may refer to non-religious arguments
- should reach a justified conclusion.

[12 marks]

[+3 SPaG mark

REASONED ARGUMENTS IN SUPPORT OF THE STATEMENT ● **Explain why some people would agree with the statement.** ● Develop your explanation with more detail and examples. ● Refer to religious teaching. Use a quote or paraphrase or refer to a religious authority. ● **Evaluate the arguments.** Is this a good argument or not? Explain why you think this.	*If all religious believers gave to charities it would go a long way to ending a lot of poverty in the world. So many people are suffering because they do not have enough money to buy food, clothes and provide a home for themselves. While a lot of food is thrown away in rich countries other people struggle to have one meal a day. Thousands have to survive on less than £1 a day. So if all religious believers were generous in their giving it would make life a lot more bearable for the poor. Some people are poor because of natural disasters or are refugees from war. They need emergency aid and religious believers should respond and it should be their duty to give to charities that are helping.*
REASONED ARGUMENTS SUPPORTING A DIFFERENT VIEW ● **Explain why some people would support a different view.** ● Develop your explanation with more detail and examples. ● Refer to religious teaching. Use a quote or paraphrase or refer to a religious authority. ● **Evaluate the arguments.** Is this a good argument or not? Explain why you think this.	*However, some religious believers are poor themselves, so will not be able to afford to help others. They are struggling to survive and have no extra money to give to charity. So you can't expect those religious believers to starve in order to give to the poor. Some may prefer to do work to help the charities like distributing and collecting envelopes for Christian Aid. Not all religious believers have to give money; they can help in other ways.*
CONCLUSION ● **Give a justified conclusion.** ● Include your own opinion together with your own reasoning. ● **Include evaluation.** Explain why you think one viewpoint is stronger than the other or why they are equally strong. ● Do not just repeat arguments you have already used without explaining how they apply to your reasoned opinion/conclusion.	*It is true that charities do a lot of good in helping those who are poor. However, it is unfair just to expect religious believers to donate money to the charities. Everyone should try and help if they can whether they are religious or not. Not all religious believers are able to donate money but they can pray or give their time to help charities.*

TIP

A key word in the statement is 'all'. It hints that some religious believers might <u>not</u> have a duty to give to charities. The student explains that not all believers can afford to help as some are poor themselves. The question doesn't mention money, it just says 'give to charities', so the student has rightly explained other ways people could help, for example by helping raise money for the charity.

TIP

This answer refers to the actions of religious believers but this is not backed up with religious teachings. As a result, it would be unlikely to be awarded the highest level.

12 'Discrimination is always wrong.'

Evaluate this statement. In your answer you:

- should give reasoned arguments in support of this statement
- should give reasoned arguments to support a different point of view
- should refer to religious arguments
- may refer to non-religious arguments
- should reach a justified conclusion.

[12 marks]
[+3 SPaG marks]

REASONED ARGUMENTS IN SUPPORT OF THE STATEMENT ● **Explain why some people would agree with the statement.** ● Develop your explanation with more detail and examples. ● Refer to religious teaching. Use a quote or paraphrase or refer to a religious authority. ● **Evaluate the arguments.** Is this a good argument or not? Explain why you think this.	
REASONED ARGUMENTS SUPPORTING A DIFFERENT VIEW ● **Explain why some people would support a different view.** ● Develop your explanation with more detail and examples. ● Refer to religious teaching. Use a quote or paraphrase or refer to a religious authority. ● **Evaluate the arguments.** Is this a good argument or not? Explain why you think this.	
CONCLUSION ● **Give a justified conclusion.** ● Include your own opinion together with your own reasoning. ● **Include evaluation.** Explain why you think one viewpoint is stronger than the other or why they are equally strong. ● Do not just repeat arguments you have already used without explaining how they apply to your reasoned opinion/conclusion.	

TIP
Don't forget that your spelling, punctuation and grammar are assessed in 12 mark questions.

13 'Everybody should have the freedom to follow whichever religion they wish to.'

Evaluate this statement. In your answer you:

- should give reasoned arguments in support of this statement
- should give reasoned arguments to support a different point of view
- should refer to religious arguments
- may refer to non-religious arguments
- should reach a justified conclusion.

[12 marks]
[+3 SPaG marks]

Check your answers using the mark scheme on page 165. How did you do?

To feel more secure in the content you need to remember, re-read pages 140–147.

To remind yourself of what the examiner is looking for, go to pages 7–13.

Apply answers

1 Christianity: Beliefs and teachings

Please note that these are suggested answers to the Apply questions, designed to give you guidance, rather than being definitive answers.

Where questions have been taken from AQA specimen papers, these suggested answers have neither been provided nor approved by AQA, nor do they constitute the only possible solutions.

1.1 **A** 'We believe in one God' (the Nicene Creed)/ first of the Ten Commandments. **B** *You might include:* Christians are inspired to follow the teaching of the Bible/ believe they have a relationship with God/ communicate with God through prayer/ find comfort in God in challenging times/ pray and worship/ try to follow Jesus' example.

1.2 **A** Creating humans/ caring for humans/ sending his son, Jesus, to live among humans/requiring justice. **B** Suffering was brought into God's perfect world by Adam and Eve's disobedience/ the result of human free will/ a test of faith/ without suffering people can't show positive human qualities such as compassion/ by overcoming suffering humans learn to be strong and appreciative of good in the world. *Remember to develop each point with more detail.*

1.3 **A** 1: These persons are God the Father, the Son (Jesus) and the Holy Spirit/ these three persons are named in the Apostles Creed and the Nicene Creed. 2: God the Father is the creator of all life/ acts as a good father towards humankind, who are his children/ is omnipotent, omnibenevolent, omniscient and omnipresent. **B** *Arguments for:* 1, 2, 4, 6, 7. *Arguments against*: 3, 5, 8. *In your justified conclusion you should weigh up both sides of the argument and then say which side you personally find more convincing and why.*

1.4 **A** They value every human being as created by God/ they believe people should look after the natural world. **B** *You might conclude that this is a strong argument because it is true that Christians believe in God's omnipotence and the truth of the Bible. But you might think it is a weak argument because theories of evolution and the Big Bang are widely accepted by many Christians despite not being 'proved'. It doesn't matter whether you think the argument is weak or strong, the important thing is to carefully explain why you think it is weak or strong.*

1.5 **A** Jesus was God in human form/ 'The Word became flesh and made his dwelling among us' (John 1:14 [NIV])/ Jesus was born of a virgin, Mary. **B** *E.g. 'The belief that Jesus was conceived by the Holy Spirit is given in Matthew's Gospel which says, 'His mother Mary was pledged to be married to Joseph, but before they came together, she was found to be pregnant by the Holy Spirit.'*

1.6 **A** 1: Jesus' death restored the relationship between people and God. 2: God understands human suffering because Jesus, who is God, experienced it. **B** When Jesus died he took the sins of everyone on himself (the atonement)/ if Jesus had not died he would not have risen from the dead. *The answer could be improved by developing reasons why the crucifixion is an important belief rather than merely describing what took place.*

1.7 **A** The women were told by angels that Jesus had risen/ Jesus appeared to the disciples. **B** Paul wrote, 'And if Christ has not been raised, our preaching is useless and so is your faith' (1 Corinthians 15:14 [NIV])/ 'He rose again according to the scriptures' (the Nicene Creed)/ the resurrection shows the power of good over evil and life over death/ Christians will be resurrected if they accept Jesus/ 'I look for the resurrection of the dead and the life of the world to come' (the Nicene Creed).

1.8 **A** Gives hope of life after death with Jesus/ inspires Christians to live in the way God wants. **B** *In your paragraph you should weigh up both sides of the argument and then say which side you personally find more convincing and why.*

1.9 **A** Christians believe that when they die God will judge them on their behaviour and actions during their lifetime/ as well as their faith in Jesus/ God will judge people based on how they serve others unselfishly. *Refer to the parable of the Sheep and the Goats to support your points.* **B** *You might include*: the promise of heaven inspires people to be kind to others/ people want to be with Jesus when they die so they follow his teachings/ on the other hand, no one can be sure there is an afterlife so it is not a good way to get people to behave/ an atheist would question how a loving God could punish people forever in hell. *In your justified conclusion you should weigh up both sides of the argument and then say which side you personally find more convincing.*

1.10 **A** A loving God would not condemn people to hell/ God is forgiving so would offer everyone a second chance to repent. **B** *Arguments in support might include*: the promise of heaven would encourage good behaviour/ the threat of hell would prevent bad behaviour/ belief in heaven takes away the fear of death/ gives hope that people will experience eternal happiness even if their life on earth has been hard. *Other views might include*: atheists don't believe in heaven or hell but still have moral principles/ most people do not consider belief in the afterlife when deciding how to behave/ morality is formed in childhood by parental teaching/ if heaven and hell were made up to encourage good behaviour, it hasn't worked.

1.11 **A** Salvation by grace of God freely given through faith in Jesus/ 'For it is by grace you have been saved' (Ephesians 2:8 [NIV])/ Salvation by doing good works/ 'In the same way, faith by itself, if it is not accompanied by action, is dead' (James 2:17 [NIV]). **B** *In deciding whether you find this argument convincing, try to think of what others might say against it.*

1.12 **A** Jesus' death made up for the original sin of Adam and Eve/ Jesus' resurrection was proof that his sacrifice was accepted by God. **B** *There is no 'right' order, but suggested arguments in support*: 4, 5, 2, 8. *Arguments against*: 1, 6, 7, 3. *Missing from this evaluation is any reference to specific Christian teaching, for example a reference to sacred writing. A justified conclusion is also needed.*

2 Christianity: Practices

Please note that these are suggested answers to the Apply questions, designed to give you guidance, rather than being definitive answers.

Where questions have been taken from AQA specimen papers, these suggested answers have neither been provided nor approved by AQA, nor do they constitute the only possible solutions.

2.1 **A** Private prayer/ singing hymns of praise in church. **B** *Arguments in support might include*: a set ritual is familiar to people/ provides a powerful emotional bond/ liturgical worship may be more formal, so more dramatic/ give a powerful sense of tradition. *Arguments in support of other views might include*: spontaneous worship is more powerful as it comes from the heart/ charismatic worship involves speaking in tongues so is a powerful emotional experience/ the silence of a Quaker service may be more powerful than one that uses words and hymns/ it depends on an individual Christian's point of view whether one type of service is more powerful than another.

2.2 **A** It is the prayer Jesus taught his disciples/ it is a model of good prayer as it combines praise to God with asking for one's needs. **B** *You might include an example*: a Christian may wish to pray for something personal using their own words, such as the strength to overcome an illness. *Or add a religious teaching*: Jesus said to pray in your room with the door closed so that God who sees in secret will reward you (Matthew 6:6).

2.3 **A** 1: Believers' baptism: full immersion in a pool/ person is old enough to make a mature decision about their faith. 2: Infant baptism: blessed water is poured over the baby's head/ parents and godparents make promises of faith on behalf of the child. **B** *Arguments in support might include*: at baptism the parents promise to bring up the child as a Christian so they would be lying/ it is hypocritical/ the symbolic actions have no meaning for them. *Arguments against might include*: they may not be religious themselves but that doesn't mean they should not give their child a chance to be a member of the Church/ the child receives grace at baptism regardless of their parents' future actions/ the child is cleansed from sin.

2.4 **A** 1: Christians receive God's grace/ by joining in the sacrifice of Jesus/ their faith is strengthened/ they become closer to God. 2: Communion brings the community of believers together in unity by sharing the bread and wine/ this provides support and encouragement for those going through a difficult time/ encourages church members to love others in practical ways. **B** *In your paragraph you should weigh up both sides of the argument and then say which side you personally find more convincing and why.*

2.5 **A** 1: An Orthodox Holy Communion is mainly held behind the iconostasis/ the priest distributes the consecrated bread and wine on a spoon. 2: Holy Communion in the United Reformed Church has an 'open table' so anyone can receive communion/ bread is broken and passed around the congregation/ wine is distributed in small cups. **B** *Arguments for the statement might include*: the ministry of the Word is very important because it focuses on the life and teaching of Jesus/ reminds people of sacred writing in the Old Testament/ provides spiritual education for the congregation through the sermon given by the priest/ allows the community to pray for themselves and others. *Arguments against might include*: Holy Communion services should focus on the consecration and sharing of bread and wine because that is the most important part of the service/ people receive the body and blood of Jesus/ recall Jesus' death and resurrection which saved them from sin.

2.6 **A** 1: Lourdes: pilgrims go there to seek healing, both spiritual and physical/ to help the sick bathe in the waters/ to strengthen their faith/ to take part in services with people speaking many different languages from many countries/ it is a busy place with crowds of people, unlike Iona which is quieter and more remote. 2: Iona: pilgrims wish to spend time in quiet prayer, reading the Bible or meditating/ to enjoy the natural beauty of the place so they feel closer to God who created nature/ to worship with others who are like-minded/ some prefer to feel God's presence in silence and solitude rather than in a busy place like Lourdes. **B** On a pilgrimage there are many opportunities for prayer and meditation/ for reading the scriptures/ for reflecting on one's life/ whereas on a holiday people usually spend time enjoying themselves and reading novels rather than scriptures, etc. *A Christian teaching that supports pilgrimage might include*: Jesus withdrew to a lonely place when he wanted to pray/ Bernadette was told by Mary in a vision to build a church in Lourdes and pray for sinners, so Christians are following their traditional teaching by going there.

2.7 **A** By attending services which emphasise Jesus is risen/ by celebrating with family and friends/ giving Easter eggs to children to symbolise new life. **B** *Arguments for might include*: Christmas is very commercialised/ many people think about food, presents and seeing their relatives, not about Jesus/ not many people go to church on Christmas/ some think that in multicultural Britain, celebrating Christmas as a religious festival might offend others. *Arguments against might include*: Christmas is still a religious holiday in Britain/ the royal family go to church on Christmas Day and many Christians attend Midnight Mass/ carol services are held to prepare for the coming of Jesus into the world/ schools have nativity plays about Jesus' birth and often collect presents to give to children who are less fortunate.

2.8 **A** 1: The community of Christians/ holy people of God/ Body of Christ. 2: A building in which Christians worship. **B** The Church is the Body of Christ and as such has a duty to help the needy/ Christians are taught to love their neighbour/ the parable of the Sheep and the Goats/ the parable of the Good Samaritan.

2.9 **A** Patrol streets in urban areas to support vulnerable people/ challenge gang and knife crime/ listen to people's problems/ help young people who have had too much to drink and may end up in trouble/ try to stop anti-social behaviour/ in this way they show love of neighbour/ 'Faith by itself, if it is not accompanied by action, is dead' (James 2:17 [NIV]). **B** *Two religious arguments might include*: Jesus taught that Christians should help others by showing agape love towards them/ this means being unselfish, caring and putting others' needs before your own, including praying for your neighbours' needs/ Jesus taught Christians should give practical help to others in the parable of the Sheep and the Goats/ he said to feed the hungry, clothe the naked, etc. *Non-religious arguments against the statement might include*: praying is pointless/ not a practical action/ no one will know if prayer works to help them/ Christians should not have to be street pastors or social workers/ it is the police and social services' responsibility, not the Church's responsibility.

2.10 A By telling non-believers that Jesus Christ, the Son of God, came into the world as its saviour/ by spreading the Christian faith through evangelism. **B** *Arguments for:* 1, 3, 5. *Arguments against:* 2, 4, 6. *You should weigh up both sides of the argument and then say which side you personally find more convincing.*

2.11 A Through organisations that promote evangelism, such as Christ for all Nations/ through personal witness and example. **B** *You should weigh up the argument and suggest how it could be improved – e.g. by referring to the Great Commission (which suggests all Christians have a duty to spread the gospel), or by considering arguments for the statement.*

2.12 A 1: The Church works on a personal level to try to restore relationships between individuals/ between conflicting groups in the community. 2: The Church has sponsored different organisations that work for reconciliation/ e.g. the Irish Churches Peace Project. **B** Jesus taught, 'Love the Lord your God with all your heart and with all your soul and with all your mind. This is the great and first commandment.' (Matthew 22: 37–38 [NIV])/ therefore reconciliation to God is most important/ reconciliation to one's neighbour is second: 'Love your neighbour as yourself' (Matthew 22:39 [NIV]).

2.13 A Smuggling Bibles into the USSR to give comfort to persecuted Christians/ sending money to projects that support persecuted Christians. **B** *A religious argument might include:* it is possible for a Christian to be happy even in times of persecution because they believe they are sharing in the sufferings of Jesus/ their courage can inspire others to become Christians/ persecution strengthens their faith. *A non-religious argument might include:* no one can be happy while being persecuted/ they may be angry at the injustice of their treatment and turn to violence or stop believing in God.

2.14 A 1: Emergency relief includes food, shelter and water to people suffering from a natural disaster or sudden war/ parables such as the Rich Man and Lazarus and the Good Samaritan encourage Christians to help the needy. 2: Long-term aid may include education or new farming equipment that helps to make people independent of aid/ 'If anyone has material possessions and sees a brother or sister in need but has no pity on them, how can the love of God be in that person?' (1 John 3:17 [NIV]). **B** *Arguments for the statement might include:* religious charities can respond quickly to emergencies but it is not their role to provide long-term aid/ the countries themselves should be helping their own people/ long-term aid might make people dependent on religious charities. *Arguments against might include:* religious charities should provide long-term aid because people are still in need/ it will give independence eventually/ it is better to teach people how to make a living for themselves than merely to feed them for a short period of time/ the parable of the Sheep and the Goats teaches that God will judge people on whether they have helped their fellow humans because helping them is helping Jesus Christ.

3 Judaism: beliefs and teachings

3.1 A 'Hear, O Israel! The Lord is our God, the Lord alone. You shall love the Lord your God with all your heart and with all your soul and with all your might.' For Jews, this passage confirms the belief there is only one God/ a single, whole, indivisible being/ who they should show complete loyalty, love and dedication towards. **B** *Arguments could include:* The belief in God as One also means that God is a single, indivisible being (not three Persons, as in Christianity)/ that God is the source of all Jewish morality, beliefs and values/ that everything in the universe has been created and is sustained by God/ that God is always present in people's lives/ that everything Jews see and experience is a meeting with God.

3.2 A A more literal interpretation is that the events in Genesis actually happened about 6000 years ago/ i.e. God took six days to create the universe and everything in it/ a more liberal interpretation is that God is the creator of everything/ but the universe is much older and life has evolved over many years. **B** *Your answer should explain whether you think the statement is true or not, giving the reasons why. You should refer to specific knowledge of Judaism, and consider arguments for and against the statement. Arguments in support of the statement might include:* Jews believe that evil exists because God gave people free will/ if free will didn't exist, there would be no evil/ so Jews would not be able to do bad things that displease God/ so they would have a better relationship with God. *Arguments in support of other views might include:* if free will didn't exist, Jews would not be able to actively choose to do good/ actively choose God/ but choosing God is clearly important to God, otherwise he would not have created free will/ so without this choice, any relationship with God would be meaningless.

3.3 A On the journey through the wilderness to Canaan, e.g. when the Jews were led by a pillar of fire or a cloud/ in the Temple in Jerusalem, e.g. when Isaiah saw God 'seated on a high and lofty throne' (Isaiah 6:1 [Tenakh]). **B** *Arguments for the statement could include:* Jews believe God has given them many laws to follow (the mitzvot) and will judge them for how well they follow these laws/ this has a great impact on their lives today as they are expected to follow these laws in their daily lives/ particularly if they are Orthodox Jews/ the laws cover the worship of God but also other areas such as the types of food they can eat/ and how they should treat other people/ so affect almost every aspect of their lives. *Arguments in support of other views could include:* if God is the creator of the universe then he must also be omnipotent, omniscient and omnipresent/ which gives him the power to know if Jews are following his laws and to judge them accordingly/ which gives Jews motivation to follow his laws, so impacting on their lives today/ Jews celebrate God's role as the creator every week during Shabbat/ understanding God as the creator of free will and evil helps Jews to know why his laws are important in the first place/ knowing that God is the creator of everything means he is the only God that should be worshipped/ which is a fundamental belief in Judaism, and impacts upon how Jews worship and relate to God in their daily lives.

3.4 A Some Jews believe they will be judged by God as soon as they die (Ecclesiastes 12:7)/ others believe God will judge everyone on the Day of Judgement (Daniel 12:2).

B *You might finish the first paragraph as follows:* it matters if there are different beliefs about life after death within a religion because then believers don't know how to live their lives in a way that would guarantee them a good afterlife. For example, if there are different ideas about how to gain entry to heaven then believers might get confused or doubt which teachings are best to follow. In addition, if there is no clear idea about what heaven is like (as in Judaism), this could discourage believers from trying their hardest to please God to end up in heaven when they die. *You might finish the second paragraph as follows:* it doesn't matter if there are different beliefs about life after death within a religion because it is more important to focus on the present. For example, Jews are not too concerned with the afterlife because they think it is more important to focus on living in a way that pleases God, whereas focusing on the afterlife might mean believers don't make the most of their lives. And if it is impossible to know what happens in the afterlife, then there is not too much point in worrying about it – living in a way that pleases God should lead to the best afterlife possible, whatever it is.

3.5 A Reform Jews believe there will be a future Messianic age, but this will be achieved by everyone working together, rather than as the result of leadership from the Messiah/ whereas Orthodox Jews believe there is a descendent of King David in every generation who has the potential to become the Messiah, who will lead the Jews during the Messianic age. **B** *Arguments for the statement could include:* the idea of a Messianic age is not relevant because there are too many problems in the world today/ they could not be solved by the leadership of one person/ there are always wars somewhere in the world, so a time of perfect peace and harmony is impossible/ it is impractical to think that all Jews could be gathered back to the land of Israel/ the rebuilding of the Temple in Jerusalem would create conflict, not a peaceful age/ a leader from the Jews or any religious leader would not have sufficient authority in an increasingly atheist and materialistic world. *Arguments against the statement could include:* the idea of a Messianic age is relevant because it encourages Orthodox Jews to work towards being worthy of redemption/ encourages Reform Jews to work together to create world peace/ this is particularly important at a time when there is much division and conflict in the world/ the hope for a Messianic age provides comfort for Jews facing persecution and hardship/ it is important for all people to have an ideal to work towards/ all humanity and religious groups agree that there should be lasting justice and peace.

3.6 A 'I give all the land that you see to you and your offspring forever' (Genesis 13:15 [Tenakh]). **B** *Arguments could include:* Abraham tried to convince people in Ur to worship God rather than idols/ he travelled from Haran to Canaan after God told him to continue his journey/ he agreed to the covenant with God/ which required him to 'walk in [God's] ways and be blameless' (Genesis 17:1 [Tenakh]), i.e. to show dedication and obedience to God/ he accepted this by being circumcised himself and circumcising all the males in his household.

3.7 A *You could include any two of:* I am the Lord your God/ you shall have no other Gods besides Me/ you shall not make for yourself a sculptured image, or any likeness/ you shall not swear falsely by the name of the Lord your God/ remember the Sabbath day and keep it holy/ honour your father and your mother/ you shall not murder/ you shall not commit adultery/ you shall not steal/ you shall not bear false witness against your neighbour/ you shall not covet *(Simplified versions of these commandments would also be accepted).* **B** *In the paragraph arguing for the statement, points could include:* the covenant at Sinai requires Jews to follow God's laws/ including the Ten Commandments and all of the mitzvot/ which not only affect the worship of God but other areas of a Jew's life, such as what they eat/ while this means that in return, God will protect them and be their God/ some people might question whether it is possible or fair to ask Jews to obey all of the 613 mitzvot in the Torah. *In the paragraph arguing against the statement, points could include:* the covenant at Sinai means the Jews are God's chosen people/ that God will protect them from harm and be their God/ this is worth having to obey all of God's laws/ because God sustains the world/ brings Jews protection/meaning/happiness/the hope of an afterlife in heaven.

3.8 A A belief in healing the world motivates Jews to help achieve social justice/ volunteer for a charity such as World Jewish Relief/ help protect the environment/ obey the mitzvot/ try to become closer to God. **B** *Arguments could include:* justice requires treating the poor and vulnerable fairly/ which means showing them kindness/ healing the world involves taking actions to help God's work in sustaining the world/ for many Jews it means helping to make the world a better and more just place/ e.g. by volunteering for a charity that helps those living in poverty/ which contributes to social justice and shows kindness to others/ therefore creating justice and healing the world both reinforce each other/ and rely on showing kindness to others.

3.9 A Breaking Shabbat law by doing work that is not normally allowed during Shabbat/ e.g. rescuing a child from the sea/ putting out a fire/ driving a sick person to hospital/ performing a life-saving operation. **B** *In the paragraph arguing for the statement, points could include:* Jews believe in the sanctity of life/ which means life is sacred and holy because it has been created by God/ so only God has the right to take it away/ if God chooses to take away a person's life, he must have a reason for this/ God is omniscient/omnipotent/benevolent so knows what is best for a person and shouldn't be challenged/ belief in God should mean accepting all of his decisions for a person, including when to end their life. *In the paragraph arguing against the statement, points could include:* sometimes it is difficult to know what God's plan for a person is/ and whether trying to save a patient is interfering with his plan or not/ e.g. some Jews think the duty to preserve life means a patient should be kept alive at all costs/ whereas others think a patient's death shouldn't be prolonged if they are in great pain/ pikuach nefesh emphasises how valuable human life is/ so Jews should try to save lives because this may be part of God's plan/ as this is the most loving thing to do.

3.10 A Genesis 3 teaches that free will exists/ God has given humans free will/ which is shown in the fact that Adam and Eve are able to use their free will to disobey God and eat from the forbidden tree/ Genesis 3 also teaches that using free will to go against God has serious consequences/ which is shown in the fact that God banished Adam and Eve from the Garden of Eden as a result of their disobedience. **B** *A good* answer would include an explanation of your opinion on the statement, which refers to specific knowledge of Judaism. If you agree with the statement, points might include: it is very important for Jews to show love to their neighbour/ 'Love your fellow as yourself' (Leviticus 19:18 [Tenakh])/ and to show kindness to others/ obeying the mitzvot between man and man makes other people happier as well/ and strengthens the Jewish community/ by showing love towards others, Jews are also showing love for God/ so obeying these mitzvot has two benefits: improving relationships with other people and pleasing God. If you disagree with the statement, points might include: a Jew's relationship with God is more important than their relationship with other people/ so they should focus on the mitzvot that are concerned with how to worship God/ this will help to ensure that God judges them favourably/ worshipping God correctly should be the most important thing in Judaism, as God is the most important thing to Jews. Your answer should also explain why someone else might agree with the statement when you have disagreed with it, or vice versa, by referring to some of the points made above.

4 Judaism: practices

4.1 **A** By the use of Jewish symbols such as a menorah (many-branched candlestick)/ Star of David (six-pointed star that represents King David). **B** Your answer should explain whether you think the statement is true or not, giving the reasons why. You should refer to specific knowledge of Judaism, and consider arguments for and against the statement. Arguments in support of the statement might include: the synagogue is sometimes called the 'house of prayer'/ Jews believe it is best to pray in a group/ certain prayers can only be said in the presence of a minyan (a group of at least 10 adults)/ so having a space for communal prayer is very important/ prayer brings Jews closer to God than any other activity in the synagogue. Arguments in support of other views might include: the synagogue is also called the 'house of study' or 'school'/ it is possible for Jews to pray at home/ an equally important role is to strengthen the Jewish community/ e.g. through social activities/ another important role is to help educate Jews in their faith/ e.g. by providing classes in Hebrew for young Jews/ e.g. by giving Jews access to books and scriptures they might not be able to find elsewhere.

4.2 **A** The Ark (Aron Hakodesh) is the cabinet where the Torah scrolls are kept, and the holiest place in the synagogue/ the ner tamid (ever-burning light) is a light that sits above the Ark, which is kept on at all times to symbolise God's presence/ the bimah (reading platform) is the raised platform from where the Torah is read. **B** Arguments could include: the holiest place in the synagogue is the Ark, which represents the first Ark that held the Ten Commandments in the Temple/ when Jews face the Ark in the synagogue, they face Jerusalem (where the Temple was built)/ the ner tamid is a reminder of the menorah that was lit every night in the Temple/ the bimah is a reminder that the altar was the central feature of the courtyard in the Temple/ all of these features in the prayer hall are reminders of the Temple, which shows how important it is to Jews.

4.3 **A** Orthodox Jews believe the Torah was given directly to Moses by God/ so the laws in the Torah should be strictly followed, including laws about how to worship/ men and women should have different roles in worship/ Reform Jews believe the Torah was inspired by God but written by humans/ so it can be adapted for modern times/ this means there is more individual choice/freedom in how to worship/ and men and women are able to take on the same roles in worship. **B** Points might include: Reform services are in Hebrew and the country's own language, which makes them easier to understand for Jews who are not fluent in Hebrew/ however, Orthodox services in Hebrew are inclusive and accessible to all Orthodox Jews, whatever their language/ the person leading the service in Reform Judaism faces the congregation most of the time, which may help people to understand what is happening than if the person has their back to the congregation (as in Orthodox Judaism)/ Reform services are more structured, which may help people to understand what each part of the service means.

4.4 **A** Your answer might include two of the following: the opening prayers might consist of a series of prayers and psalms that praise and give thanks to God/ after this the Shema is recited and accompanied by blessings/ the Amidah (standing prayer) is prayed in silence while standing and facing Jerusalem; it consists of a series of blessings/ the Amidah is sometimes followed by a reading from the Torah/ the final prayers include the closing Aleinu prayer, which gives praise and thanks to God. **B** Arguments in support of the statement might include: prayer is vital for communicating with God/ and reminds Jews what their faith is all about/ this helps them to become closer to God/ it strengthens their relationship with God/ and with the rest of the Jewish community/ without prayer Jews would not be able to have a personal relationship with God. Arguments in support of other views might include: healing the world is also very important to Jews/ it also brings Jews closer to God, just through actions rather than prayer/ it is a practical way to help God sustain the world he created/ Jews should not just have faith in God, they should also live in a way that pleases God, which involves helping others/ Jews are only able to focus on prayer if they live in a safe environment.

4.5 **A** Your answer could include two of the following actions (with explanations of their significance): the congregation stands when the Ark is opened to reveal the Torah scrolls/ as a reminder of how the Jews stood at the bottom of Mount Sinai when Moses returned with the Ten Commandments/ the Torah is dressed with a cover and various ornaments/ as a reminder of the vestments worn by priests in early Judaism/ the Torah is paraded round the synagogue/ to represent the march through the wilderness, when the original Ark was carried from Mount Sinai to Jerusalem/ many Jews touch the Torah with their prayer book or prayer shawl, then touch their lips/ recalling that God's words should be on their lips and sweet like honey (Ezekiel 3:3). **B** Points could include: Jews believe Shabbat is a time to celebrate that God has kept his promises in the covenant between God and the Jews/ and to celebrate God's creation/ as it recalls the Genesis creation story, when God created everything in six days and rested on the seventh day/ God commanded the Jews to celebrate Shabbat in the fourth commandment (Exodus 20:8)/ the fact that no work is done on Shabbat gives Jews time to focus on God and all he has

given them/ including their families, as Shabbat is a time when Jews should enjoy eating together and spending time with the rest of the family.

4.6 **A** Your answer could include two of the following preparations (with explanations of their significance): the house is cleaned/ made neat and presentable/ Jews change into smart clothes/ to welcome in Shabbat, which is seen as being like welcoming a special bride or queen into the home/ the food and house are prepared before Shabbat begins/ as most types of work are not allowed during Shabbat/ at least two candles are placed on the table/ to represent the two commandments to remember and observe Shabbat/ two loaves of challah bread are placed on the table/ to represent the food that God provided for the Jews when they were wandering in the wilderness/ wine is placed on the table/ to symbolise joy and celebration. **B** Arguments for the statement could include: most types of work are not allowed during Shabbat, as stated in the fourth commandment/ 'you shall not do any work' (Exodus 20:10 [Tenakh])/ so Jews are expected to relax and enjoy the day/ the Friday evening meal is an important part of Shabbat celebrations/ which gives families time to enjoy eating a meal together/ and telling religious stories or singing songs/ families also spend time together on the Saturday, e.g. by sharing another special meal. Arguments against the statement could include: Shabbat is most important as a time to remember and worship God/ and give thanks for God's creation/ as Shabbat recalls the Genesis creation story, when God created everything in six days and rested on the seventh day/ the emphasis on worshipping God is why Jews attend the synagogue on Friday evening and Saturday morning/ why parents may study the Torah on Saturday afternoon/ why blessings/ prayers/religious stories are a part of the Friday meal/ why Jews are reminded of God through the food they eat during Shabbat/ e.g. the challah bread reminds Jews of the food that God provided for them in the wilderness.

4.7 **A** Your answer could include two of the following: by praying in the home/ through Shabbat celebrations (e.g. the Friday evening meal/the Havdalah ceremony)/ by touching the mezuzah/ by following the Jewish dietary laws when cooking. **B** Your answer should explain whether you think the statement is true or not, giving the reasons why. You should refer to specific knowledge of Judaism, and consider arguments for and against the statement. Arguments in support of the statement might include: the Talmud explains how to interpret the Torah and apply its laws to everyday life/ e.g. it gives advice on how to follow the dietary laws or the laws of Shabbat/ so Jews should study it carefully to get a more complete understanding of the Torah/ be able to follow the laws in the Torah correctly/ Orthodox Jews believe studying the Talmud is important/ the authority of the early rabbis means their beliefs and thoughts should be respected/considered. Arguments in support of other views might include: the Torah is more important/ as it forms the basis of Jewish law/ the discussions and debates in the Talmud might just confuse interpretation of the Torah/ some Reform Jews do not believe the Talmud needs to be carefully studied/ as they do not believe the laws in the Torah have to be followed as closely as possible in order to please God/ Jews can learn how to please God in other ways/ e.g. from their parents/ from attending classes or services in the synagogue.

4.8 **A** Your answer might include two of the following: the Orthodox naming ceremony usually happens on the first Shabbat after the baby's birth, whereas the Reform ceremony may be held at another time/ both parents take part in a Reform naming ceremony, whereas the father recites the Torah blessing and asks God for the good health of his wife and baby in an Orthodox ceremony/ some Orthodox Jews give a small amount of money 31 days after the birth of their firstborn son, but this is not a usual Reform practice. **B** Arguments might include: Brit Milah recalls the covenant God made with Abraham/ as circumcision 'would be a sign of the covenant between Me and you' (Genesis 17:11 [Tenakh])/ it reminds Jews they are God's chosen people/ but to be God's chosen people, they are expected to follow his laws/ during the redemption of the firstborn son, prayers are said asking that the child may 'enter into Torah, into marriage, and into good deeds'/ this reminds Jews of the importance of following the laws in the Torah.

4.9 **A** Your answer might include two of the following: a Jew might read from the Torah/ lead part of the service/ say prayers/ make a short speech. **B** You might finish the first paragraph as follows: I agree with this statement because the Bar or Bat Mitzvah ceremony marks the point when a Jewish person has to take full responsibility for following Jewish law/ This may have a significant impact on their life, as they may have to start following new laws/ or think more carefully about the laws their parents are already helping them to follow./ It is also when a Jewish person is seen to become an adult,/ and when they are allowed to become part of the minyan./ Jews may view it as a significant moment as it helps to bring them closer to God. You might finish the second paragraph as follows: I disagree with this statement because there are other moments in a Jewish person's life that some might think are equally significant. For example, the Brit Milah ceremony is when a male Jew is circumcised as a reminder that they are one of God's chosen people./ This reminder stays with them for their whole life./ Some Jews might think their marriage is equally or more significant, because it is when they get to marry the person they love and this brings holiness into their everyday lives.

4.10 **A** In Judaism, 'betrothal' is a period of engagement/ which typically lasts for the year before a wedding/ which can only be broken by death or divorce/ when the couple do not live together, but prepare for their future lives together. **B** Arguments for the statement might include: both the bride and groom may fast before the wedding to cleanse themselves of sin/ the bride and groom both recite two blessings over wine/ In Reform weddings, the bride and groom exchange rings/ a Reform marriage contract usually describes mutual hopes for the marriage, which are the same for the bride and groom/ the rabbi blesses both the bride and groom. Arguments against the statement might include: in Orthodox weddings, the groom gives the bride a ring but the bride doesn't give the groom a ring/ an Orthodox marriage contract may suggest unequal expectations or treatment/ e.g. it may cover the husband's duties to his wife, but not the wife's duties to her husband/ the groom breaks a glass under his heel to show regret for the destruction of the Temple in Jerusalem, but the bride doesn't do this.

4.11 **A** They make a small tear in their clothes/ to follow the example of Jacob, who 'rent his clothes, put sackcloth on his loins, and observed mourning for his son many days' (Genesis 37:34 [Tenakh])/ they say a blessing that refers to God as the true judge/ which shows they accept God's decision to take the person's life. **B** *A good answer would include an explanation of your opinion on the statement, which refers to specific knowledge of Judaism. If you agree with the statement, points might include:* in Judaism there are set periods of mourning that decrease in intensity over the period of a year/ these help to give structure to a person's mourning/ and give them enough time to grieve fully but also help them to get back to normal life/ during the first period of mourning, Jews do not have to worry about following certain Jewish laws/ during shiva (the second period of mourning), mourners stay at home to pray together and support each other/ mirrors are covered so they can't focus on their appearance, helping them to focus instead on coming to terms with a person's death. *If you disagree with the statement, points might include:* mourning/grieving is very personal and some people might find the structure or rigidity of Jewish mourning customs unhelpful/ e.g. they might need longer than 24 hours to mentally prepare themselves for the funeral/ they might need more than a week before returning to work/ they might want to mourn alone during shiva/ they might find that listening to music brings them solace, but are unable to do so during the third period of mourning/ they might find that going to parties helps to distract them after a person's death, but are unable to do so for the first year of mourning.

4.12 **A** *Your answer might explain one of the following passages from the Torah:* 'But make sure that you do not partake of the blood; for the blood is the life, and you must not consume the life with the flesh' (Deuteronomy 12:23 [Tenakh])/ this means Jews should not eat food containing blood/ so they should only eat kosher meat (where the blood has been drained from it)/ 'You shall not boil a kid in its mother's milk' (Exodus 23:19 [Tenakh])/ this means Jews should not eat meat and dairy products at the same time/ and several hours must pass between eating meat and anything containing milk/ which means Jews have to be very careful about preparing food. **B** *Your answer should explain whether you think the statement is true or not, giving the reasons why. You should refer to specific knowledge of Judaism, and consider arguments for and against the statement. Arguments in support of the statement might include:* the dietary laws mean Jews can only eat certain kosher foods/ and have to keep dairy products and meat separate/ which ideally means having a kitchen with two sets of utensils and crockery, two sinks and two food preparation areas/ some Jews may not be able to afford to have a special kitchen like this/ the dietary laws also make it hard to eat out at restaurants/ and to buy food in supermarkets/ Jews with busy lifestyles, allergies or those who live in non-Jewish communities may find it particularly hard/ the laws are outdated in modern society/ the original reasons for the laws may no longer apply/ there are more meaningful ways to show obedience to God/ some Reform Jews don't follow the dietary laws but still follow God. *Arguments in support of other views might include:* if Orthodox Jews manage to follow the laws then they can't be too difficult to follow/ Jews can buy meat from kosher butchers or foods with kosher labels on them, so they know they are buying the right food/ the laws test a person's self-control and obedience to God/ – if the laws were relaxed then that would defeat the point of them/ the laws remind Jews daily of their faith/ – if they were relaxed they would lose these reminders/ the laws mark Jewish people out as different from others and should be kept for this reason.

4.13 **A** *Your answer might include two of the following differences:* during Rosh Hashanah, Jews will try to take actions to improve their relationships with others – e.g. by making up for any harm they have caused other people – whereas Jews will spend much of Yom Kippur in the synagogue in order to improve their relationship with God/ Jews celebrate Rosh Hashanah with a festive meal, but fast during Yom Kippur/ Jews wear white during Yom Kippur, but wear any smart clothes for Rosh Hashanah.
B *Points could include:* some Jews believe it is important to show kindness during Rosh Hashanah in particular because this may influence God's judgement/ and affect their fortunes for the coming year/ Rosh Hashanah is a particularly good time to mend or improve relationships with other people/ which involves showing them kindness/ but some Jews may argue it is important to show kindness all year round/ as instructed in Leviticus ('love your fellow as yourself')/ and suggesting this is more important during Rosh Hashanah suggests it is less important at other times, which is not true.

4.14 **A** To prepare for Pesach, Jews remove leaven from their homes/ this recalls how the Jews did not have time to let their bread rise when they escaped from Egypt/ some firstborn sons fast before Pesach starts/ in thanksgiving for the firstborns' escape from death in Egypt/ recalling the story of the final plague, which killed the firstborn children of the Egyptians but not the Jews/ during the Passover Seder, the story of the escape from Egypt is told from a book called the Haggadah/ the different foods symbolise different aspects of the Jews' escape from Egypt/ e.g. the green vegetable symbolises new life in the Promised Land. **B** *The following points could be included in the paragraph supporting the statement:* it is important for religious believers to understand the history of their faith/ knowing about the escape from slavery in Egypt might help Jewish children to appreciate God more/ feel more willing to obey God's laws, as they know what God has done for them/ passing on the history of a religion to the next generation is important for its continuity/ Pesach rituals do this in a fun way, e.g. by finding bread crumbs to burn. *The following points could be included in the paragraph supporting a different point of view:* Pesach rituals are important to older Jews as well/ help Jews to celebrate and give thanks to God/ are more than just an opportunity to teach Jewish history/ help Jews to feel empathy with those who are oppressed.

5 Relationships and families

Please note that these are suggested answers to the Apply questions, designed to give you guidance, rather than being definitive answers.

5.1 **A** 1: Some Christians believe it is the quality of the relationship between the two people, not their gender that is important/ homosexual relationships should show Christian qualities of love, commitment, faithfulness, etc. 2: Heterosexual relationships

are part of God's plan for humanity/ the Torah teaches that homosexual relationships are wrong (Leviticus 18:22). **B** *Examples of religious arguments:* Christians believe sex expresses a deep, lifelong union and casual sex does not represent this/ Jews believe the only place for a sexual relationship is within marriage, which is a blessing from God. *Examples of non-religious arguments:* the acceptance of contraception and legal abortion has made casual sex more common/ sex has not been devalued in British society except by those who use it irresponsibly.

5.2 **A** 1: The wedding vows include the promise to forsake all others and be faithful to each other as long as you both shall live. 2: 'You shall not commit adultery [...] You shall not covet your neighbour's wife' (Exodus 20:14, 17 [NIV]). **B** *In support:* it can be a valid expression of love for each other/ the couple may intend to marry but just can't afford it at the time. *Against:* 'your bodies are temples of the Holy Spirit' (1 Corinthians 6:19 [NIV])/ Orthodox Judaism teaches that sex is a gift from God which should always be reserved for marriage. *A development may be:* The Torah warns against promiscuity and sexual conduct that harms others/ Orthodox Jews follow guidance in the Talmud which forbids pre-marital sex.

5.3 **A** Catholics believe the use of artificial contraception within marriage goes against the natural law/ Jews accept the use of contraception within marriage to help with family planning, but not to avoid having children altogether. **B** *Arguments for might include:* the decision of whether or when to have children is up to the couple/ no one else knows their particular circumstances/ it is wrong to bring a baby into deprivation/ contraception prevents unwanted pregnancies and the spread of sexually transmitted infections. *Arguments against might include:* religious authorities have a duty to guide their followers to carry out God's will/ it is a Catholic and Jewish belief that God intended married couples to have a family/ children are a blessing from God/ so guidance about the proper use of contraception is needed to help people make correct choices.

5.4 **A** Marriage is God's gift to humans at creation/ a lifelong union blessed by God/ a covenant before God/ the proper place to enjoy a sexual relationship/ to raise children. **B** Marriage is a legal contract/ society is more stable if the rights of all people are protected/ cohabitation does not protect the children or remaining parent if one partner decides to leave the relationship/ 'The Church sees marriage between a man and a woman, as central to the stability and health of human society' (House of Bishops of the General Synod of the Church of England)/ many Jews believe that a sexual relationship should only take place within marriage, so cohabitation is not considered ideal/ could undermine having a family, through which the Jewish faith is passed down.

5.5 **A** The Catholic Church teaches that marriage is permanent/ a sacrament/ cannot be dissolved by civil divorce/ vows made before God must be kept/ therefore oppose remarriage while a partner is still alive/ other Christians believe that sometimes divorce is the lesser of two evils/ the Church should reflect God's forgiveness/ people should have a second chance for happiness/ approve of remarriage as long as the couple take the vows seriously/ divorce is allowed in Judaism if both partners agree/ Jews are encouraged to remarry after a divorce. **B** *For:* children are badly affected by divorce and parents have a duty to their children/ marriage is a sacrament and reflects the love Christ has for his Church/ Jesus taught that anyone who divorced and remarried was committing adultery (Mark 10:11–12)/ 'whenever anyone divorces his first wife even the altar [God] in the Temple sheds tears' (Babylonian Talmud, Sanhedrin 22a). *Against:* continual arguments or abuse can damage children more than divorce/ atheists and humanists do not believe vows are made before God/ some Christians think the Church should reflect God's forgiveness and allow couples a second chance for happiness/ Christianity and Judaism allow divorce.

5.6 **A** Members of a Christian family should 'love one another', as it is in the family that a child learns to love/ a nuclear family allows Christians to follow God's plan for humanity/ a Christian family is where a child learns faith in God and Jesus/ Jews believe the family shapes the faith, moral values and character of their children. **B** *For:* many non-religious people and some Christians agree the gender of the parents makes no difference to a child's upbringing/ a same-sex couple that gives love and security to their children will make just as good parents as heterosexual ones/ it is the quality of their parenting that matters. *Against:* all religions agree children should grow up in a loving, secure family, but not all would agree the gender of the parents makes no difference/ some people think children should have male and female role models as they grow up/ Christians and Jews who oppose homosexual relationships would disagree with same-sex parents because of their homosexuality, they might argue that homosexual parents would not provide a good example for their children.

5.7 **A** 1: E.g. children are taught to 'love your neighbour as yourself' (Mark 12:31 [NIV])/ to follow commandments such as 'Honour your father and your mother' (Exodus 20:12 [NIV]). 2: Jewish parents, particularly mothers, teach their children how to pray/ welcome Shabbat/ follow the mitzvot/ celebrate festivals/ the Torah instructs parents to teach God's law to their children/ 'Take to heart these instructions [...] Impress them upon your children' (Deuteronomy 6:6-7 [Tenakh]). **B** *For the statement:* children should do more for their parents when they get older, as their parents cared for them when they were younger/ many elderly relatives today live alone and need the extra support/ Christians and Jews are taught to respect their elderly parents/ 'Listen to your father, who gave you life, and do not despise your mother when she is old' (Proverbs 23:22 [NIV])/ 'Honour your father and your mother' (Exodus 20:12 [NIV]). *Against the statement:* families in the UK are already doing a lot for their elderly relatives/ e.g. even if they live far away, children might contribute to their care or contact them regularly/ Christians and Jews already support their elderly relatives because of teachings such as, 'Honour your father and mother' (Exodus 20:12 [NIV]). *You should weigh up both sides of the argument and then say which side you personally find more convincing.*

5.8 **A** Prejudice is unfairly judging someone before the facts are known/ holding biased opinions about people based on their gender or race etc./ discrimination is acting on the prejudice/ doing something which treats someone unfairly, e.g.

not giving a job to a woman who has children. **B** Despite the Sex Discrimination Act making gender discrimination illegal, women still get paid less than men for similar jobs/ there are still more men than women in senior positions/ some areas of employment are considered inappropriate for women or men/ Paul taught that this was wrong when he said, 'There is neither… male nor female, for you are all one in Christ Jesus' (Galatians 3:28 [NIV])/ Judaism also teaches that men and women are equal as they are both created in the image of God/ 'And God created man in His image, in the image of God He created him; male and female He created them' (Genesis 1:27 [Tenakh]).

6 Religion and life

Please note that these are suggested answers to the Apply questions, designed to give you guidance, rather than being definitive answers.

6.1 **A** Literally; creation happened just as the Genesis story records/ symbolically; the main message of the story is that God created the universe and humans were created to look after the earth/ the 'days' are longer periods of time/ the story is a myth that should not be taken as truth. **B** *Agree*: God has the power to do anything so creation through the Big Bang is possible/ if religious creation stories are not read literally then it is possible for the Big Bang to be the method through which God created the universe. *Disagree*: religious creation stories must be literally true, so it is not possible to believe the Big Bang theory/ the Big Bang was triggered by random chance, not God.

6.2 **A** Looking after something on behalf of somebody else, e.g. looking after the earth for God. **B** This must be true because God would or could not create anything that is not wonderful and valuable/ the earth inspires awe and wonder/ provides everything needed to live/ people learn about God through creation, so it must be wonderful and valuable to achieve this learning/ the earth must be valuable if God has made humans stewards of it.

6.3 **A** Pollution causes harm to living things including humans/ is not good stewardship and therefore against God's wishes (Genesis 1:28)/ may lead to God's fair judgement being harsh (the parable of the Talents). **B** E.g. *'I agree because many are still using vehicles that cause a lot of pollution and they don't always dispose of their waste in a way that does not harm the earth. It is important for religious believers to do as much as they can to help the environment, not only to protect it for future generations, but also because the teachings of their religion require it (such as the teaching of stewardship) and because it shows respect for God's creation. So they should try to do things like recycle more and use their cars less.'*

6.4 **A** It is cruel because it harms animals/ it is unnecessary because scientists can use other methods to test products/ experimenting on animals is not good stewardship/ most Christians and Jews believe it should only be used for essential human needs/ some Christians believe humans have dominion over animals, so can use them for their own needs. **B** All killing of living beings is cruel/ animals bred for experimentation have no freedom in their lives/ experimenting on animals is not good stewardship/ there are alternatives that are not harmful to animals/ Christians and Jews believe that cruelty to animals does not respect or value living creatures which God has made.

6.5 **A** The origins of human life are exactly as recorded in scripture/ evolution is a biological principle and not opposed to Christianity or Judaism/ God created original life which has evolved naturally as science teaches/ evolution is correct for all creatures except humans/ God continues to preside over evolution/ evolution is false because God made humans as descendants of Adam and Eve. **B** *E.g. for the statement: 'The story of Adam and Eve is more important than evolution because it teaches religious believers valuable lessons. For example, that humans are equally created in God's image, that heterosexual relationships are part of God's plan, and that misusing God's free will has serious consequences. In order to follow God it is more important to understand these lessons than to know how life began.' E.g. against the statement: 'The belief that life evolved on earth is more important than the story of Adam and Eve because this story cannot be proved. It is likely the story was made up to help people believe in God, as it seems difficult to believe human life simply started with a man and woman created by God. It is more important to understand how life really developed than to know about a story that is probably not true.'*

6.6 **A** Abortion is taking away life given by God (Psalm 139:13)/ the sanctity of life means life should be valued and respected/ Jews have a duty to save and preserve life wherever possible (pikuach nefesh). **B** *For*: being brought up with a poor quality of life is not loving/ cruel/ possibly not the child's preferred option had they been able to choose/ abortion removes the possibility of a life of suffering. *Against*: preventing life is never the best option/ the sanctity of life/ 'You shall not murder' (Exodus 20:13 [NIV])/ the family should be supported to improve the child's quality of life/ better a poor quality of life than no life.

6.7 **A** *An argument in favour*: drugs used to end life are God-given/ people should have the choice to end their own life/ most loving and compassionate thing to do/ may allow a painless death. *How religious beliefs disagree*: against the sanctity of life/ murder/ suffering may be for a purpose/ against predestination/ not a right reason for killing/ a sin against God. **B** It is murder/ sinful/ interferes with God's plan/ open to abuse/ disrespects the sanctity of life/ only God should take life/ may be against the will of the person suffering/ suffering can bring a person closer to God/ *see 6.7 A for other reasons.*

6.8 **A** God judges a person's behaviour, including their faith in following Jesus/ God's judgement results in the person spending eternity in heaven with God or in hell without God. **B** *E.g. 'I agree with this statement. Some people believe that human life is valuable but are more concerned about their own destiny than other people. They want to go to heaven rather than hell because they believe that eternity with God is the best option. Because the Bible says that God made life in his image, they feel that valuing human life by helping the poor will be rewarded with a better life after death. The sacrifice they make by helping others is worth it.Others recognise that God made all humans in his image and so see it as their duty to God to value life. This means that if they do all they can to help others maintain and improve their valuable life, they are serving God. This is their main motivation rather than doing what they think God wants in order to get into heaven. However, being granted a place in heaven isn't just about helping others. God knows people's thoughts and reasoning and his decision is final.'*

7 The existence of God and revelation

Please note that these are suggested answers to the Apply questions, designed to give you guidance, rather than being definitive answers.

7.1 **A** *Christian/Jewish Design argument*: the world is beautiful and made up of complex, independent parts/ it must have been designed and only God is powerful enough to do this. *William Paley*: the intricacy and complexity of earth shows it cannot have appeared by chance. *Isaac Newton*: the thumb is evidence of design because it allows precise delicate movement. *Thomas Aquinas*: only an intelligent being could keep everything in the universe in a regular order. *F.R. Tennant*: everything in the universe is perfect to sustain life. **B** *See the answers to 7.1 A for arguments to agree with the statement. Arguments against could include*: natural selection happens by chance/ species are developed by evolution, not a designer/ suffering proves there is no designer God/ order and structure in nature is imposed by humans, not God.

7.2 **A** If everything has a cause, what caused God?/ the universe could be eternal/ the universe may not need a cause/ the Big Bang was random chance/ religious creation stories are myths and not actually true. **B** *For the statement*: everything (including the universe) has a cause to explain its existence/ to cause everything to exist there must be something existing that is eternal and without a cause/ this can only be God, so God must exist/ this means God caused everything to exist, possibly by causing the Big Bang. *Against the statement: see the answers to 7.2 A.*

7.3 **A** E.g. God provided fire to light Elijah's sacrifice, defeating the priests of Ba'al (I Kings 18:38–39)/ the incarnation of Jesus: an angel appeared to Mary and Joseph telling them that they would have a child/ Mary became pregnant by virgin conception and gave birth to Jesus. **B** *E.g. 'There is never enough evidence to prove that miracles are the work of God, instead of having a (perhaps unknown) scientific explanation. People who claim to have witnessed miracles are making them up or mistaken about what they have experienced. On the other hand, anyone who has witnessed a miracle is unlikely to remember it wrongly and there are 69 recorded miracles at Lourdes alone. They cannot all have been remembered wrongly. If Jesus had not performed miracles, they wouldn't have been written down in the Bible, and people who were there at the time would have spoken out if they thought the miracles were made up.'*

7.4 **A** If God was loving, he would not allow suffering/ evil exists because God does not/ an all-knowing and all-powerful God would know about suffering and do something to prevent it/ God would not have created an earth that causes suffering through natural disasters. **B** *E.g. 'Science is correct to challenge the existence of God because it can provide explanations for things that used to be explained with God, which means God is no longer needed as the explanation for these things. For example, some people would say the Big Bang theory removes the need to believe that God created the universe. Science also challenges the accuracy of religious creation stories. However, others believe science can help to explain God's creation. For example, the Big Bang theory explains how God created the universe, and the theory of evolution explains how God brought life to earth and developed it to what it is like now. Science does not have to challenge religious creation stories if these are not interpreted literally.'*

7.5 **A** A specific experience of God such as a dream, vision, prophecy or miracle. *Any example from scripture, tradition, history or the present day can be given, for example God appearing to Moses and communicating with him through the burning bush.* **B** *E.g. 'I disagree with this statement because visions can have a profound effect on people's lives, which would be unlikely to happen if they were not real. For example, Saul converted to Christianity after he saw a blinding light and heard Jesus' voice. The way he changed his life as a result of this vision means it probably did happen. Also, he certainly did not expect to experience God in this way because he was very opposed to Christianity.'*

7.6 **A** God's presence in nature/ reason, conscience or morality/ worship/ reading scriptures/ the lives of religious leaders. *Include examples.* **B** *E.g. 'Over the centuries, what was originally written is unlikely to have been changed, because believers were not prepared to change what they thought was the word of God. Even though the world has changed over time, people believe that scripture is still relevant nowadays because God's words are timeless, and can still help people to believe in God.'*

7.7 **A** Omniscient: all-knowing, aware of everything that has happened/ omnipotent: all-powerful, capable of doing anything/ transcendent: beyond and outside life on earth, etc. **B** *E.g. 'I agree it is not possible to properly express God's nature in words because God's nature is outside the comprehension of any other being, because nobody but God is all-powerful, all-knowing or eternal. Humans are subject to limits, God is not. God is infinite, humans are finite. Because language is finite, there are no words to fully express God. However, some people might argue it is possible to express God's nature in words because the Bible and the Tenakh do a good job of telling Christians and Jews what God is like . Words such as 'omnipotent', 'immanent' and 'transcendent' can also teach us something about the nature of God, even if they cannot describe him fully.*

7.8 **A** Drugs or alcohol can make a person lose touch with reality/ wishful thinking means people can persuade themselves that something has happened purely because they want it to/ hallucinations can be symptoms of some illnesses/ some people might lie to become famous or rich, as it is hard to disprove their lies/ some may genuinely believe they have had a revelation but there may be a perfectly normal explanation that they do not know about. **B** *E.g. 'There is no way to prove that a revelation means God does exist. There are perfectly normal explanations for what people say are revelations, so they cannot be considered as evidence for God. For example, they might just be hallucinations caused by illness, or made up by someone to get attention. There is no way to know if a person's 'revelation' is genuine or not, so it cannot act as proof that God exists.'*

8 Religion, peace and conflict

Please note that these are suggested answers to the Apply questions, designed to give you guidance, rather than being definitive answers.

8.1 **A** Christians believe God sent Jesus to save people from sin, so Jesus' sacrifice on the cross gives hope to Christians that their sins will be forgiven if they sincerely repent/ Christians should forgive others as Jesus forgave his enemies on the cross/ Jews believe that at Yom Kippur they must atone for any harm they have done/ express sorrow for sin/ seek God's forgiveness/ both Christians and Jews believe God offers forgiveness to all who ask in faith. **B** *Arguments for*: the Christian Church teaches that killing is wrong/ Jesus' teaching does not support war/ Jesus told people to love their enemies/ Jewish scriptures give laws and guidance to promote peace/ the prophet Isaiah looks forward to a time when God will bring peace (Isaiah 2:4). *Arguments against*: Christians believe in the just war theory/ it is sometimes necessary to take part in war for self-defence/ Jews believe fighting in self-defence or in defence of the faith can be justified/ it is a Jewish duty to fight when attacked.

8.2 **A** There is an injustice/ they believe in loving their neighbours/ defending the faith if it is attacked. **B** *You might wish to use recent terrorist attacks as examples/* 'You shall not murder' (Exodus 20:13 [Tenakh])/ 'love your neighbour as yourself' (Mark 12:31 [NIV]).

8.3 **A** d) Forgiveness. **B** *Agree*: if attacked, a country has the right to retaliate/ the enemy started the conflict so they should expect a response/ the Bible teaches, 'An eye for an eye, a tooth for a tooth'/ justice must prevail. *Disagree*: retaliation is wrong because it is just getting back at someone, which is likely to prolong rather than resolve the conflict/ Jesus taught retaliation was wrong when he told people to 'turn the other cheek'/ Jesus taught forgiveness and reconciliation were needed to bring about peace/ the Torah says 'Do not take vengeance or bear a grudge against your countrymen. Love your fellow as yourself' (Leviticus 19:18 [Tenakh]).

8.4 **A** *Beliefs must be contrasting*. All religions are against the use of weapons of mass destruction/ Christians believe life is sacred (sanctity of life)/ only God has the right to end life/ God created the earth and it should not be destroyed with WMD/ nothing can justify the use of WMDs which target innocent people/ some Christians and Jews agree with the possession of nuclear weapons as a deterrent/ to maintain peace and prevent attack/ some people think the use of nuclear weapons in war can be justified/ e.g. they ended the Second World War. **B** 'You shall not murder' (Exodus 20:13 [NIV])/ only God has the right to end life (sanctity of life)/ 'violence begets violence [...] nuclear proliferation benefits no one' (Rabbi David Saperstein).

8.5 **A** If the cause of the war is just/ if the war is fought in self-defence/ if the faith is under attack. **B** Quakers believe war is never justified/ Jesus taught that even the anger that leads to violence is wrong (Matthew 5: 21–22)/ Jesus did not try to resist arrest and told Peter to put his sword away/ Judaism teaches that war should be a last resort/ 'When you approach a town to attack it, you shall offer it terms of peace' (Deuteronomy 20:10 [Tenakh]).

8.6 **A** Fighting for God or a religious cause/ authorised by a high religious authority. **B** *The argument is very brief. It could be supported by points such as*: in a democracy people are entitled to freedom of speech/ there is no need to turn to violence to defend religion/ religious freedoms are guaranteed by Human Rights legislation/ God does not want people to fight each other/ Jesus taught people to 'turn the other cheek'. *A different point of view might be*: if a particular religious group is constantly attacked, they may feel justified in using violent means to respond/ although this is not what is really meant by 'holy war'.

8.7 **A** *Beliefs must be contrasting*. Many Christians are not pacifists because they believe war can be justified under certain circumstances/ as explained by the just war theory/ the Quakers strongly support pacifism/ believe that conflict should always be settled through peaceful means/ many Jews believe fighting in self-defence is a duty of the faith. **B** Conflict is often caused by injustice/ if people feel their rights are being denied they may wish to take violent action to achieve equality of opportunity/ e.g. racist laws in some countries have provoked violent clashes with the authorities/ it is better to make sure people are treated with equal dignity and respect so that conflict is avoided/ Christians and Jews believe all human beings are created by God so should be treated fairly/ Christian charities like Christian Aid and Caritas campaign to establish human rights in the hope that wars will not be necessary to bring about justice.

8.8 **A** By raising money to help refugees through organisations such as Caritas and Magen David Adom UK/ by going to war-torn areas to deliver emergency supplies to victims. **B** *Agree*: if a country has taken the serious decision to go to war, it should try to defeat the enemy as quickly as possible to prevent more loss of innocent life/ it is sometimes not practical to take the enemy prisoner to help them survive. *Disagree*: according to the conditions of a just war, only appropriate force should be used, so if the enemy tries to surrender they should not be killed/ Jewish rules for a just war state that innocent civilians on the enemy side must be protected and helped to survive/ St Paul teaches, 'Do not repay anyone evil for evil [...] If it is possible [...] live at peace with everyone' (Romans 12:17–18 [NIV]).

9 Religion, crime and punishment

Please note that these are suggested answers to the Apply questions, designed to give you guidance, rather than being definitive answers.

9.1 **A** Evil actions are wicked things some people do which usually cause serious harm to other living creatures/ evil intentions are what the offenders hope to achieve by behaving in a wicked or destructive way. **B** *For the statement*: intentions are the reasons for actions/ loving and compassionate intentions usually bring about good actions/ 'But I tell you that anyone who looks at a woman lustfully has already committed adultery with her in his heart' (Matthew 5:28 [NIV]). *Against the statement*: nobody is helped or harmed by intentions but they may be by actions / 'faith by itself, if it is not accompanied by action, is dead' (James 2:17 [NIV]).

9.2 **A** Poverty can lead people to steal food/ a person's upbringing may lead them to view crime as acceptable/ people may break a law in order to protest against it/ greed may prompt someone to steal something they want, etc. **B** *Arguments for the statement could include*: addiction takes away choice/ a person may need to commit crimes to fund their addiction/ addiction may cause illegal actions because the offender doesn't realise what they are doing. *Arguments against the statement could include*: addicts should be helped to defeat their addiction so they do not commit crimes/ Christianity and Judaism discourage the consumption of addictive drugs/ there is no good reason for committing crimes/ poverty and mental illness are also understandable reasons for committing crimes.

9.3 **A** Hate crimes usually involve violence and possibly killing/ murder is unlawful killing/ hate crimes result from prejudice, murder can have other reasons/ murder is generally considered to be worse/ some murders are classed as hate crimes. **B** *For*: hatred of a criminal is not constructive/ reasons why the criminal committed the crime should be considered/ love and compassion are religious teachings that should extend even to criminals. *Against*: criminal actions can cause great harm and upset/ some victims never fully recover from a criminal action/ 'let everyone be subject to the governing authorities, for there is no authority except that which God established' (Romans 13:1 [NIV])/ crimes break Christian and Jewish teachings and morality.

9.4 **A** *Retribution*: getting your own back/ the offender should receive the same (not greater) injuries and harm that their actions caused. *Deterrence*: putting people off from committing crimes/ the punishment should be severe enough to prevent repetition of the offence. *Reformation*: changing someone's behaviour for the better/ offenders are helped to change so they do not reoffend. **B** *For*: severe punishment can help prevent future crimes/ the criminal deserves severe punishment for what they have done/ 'eye for an eye' means punishment should equal harm caused, so more serious crimes deserve severe punishment. *Against*: less severe punishment may lead more easily to repentance and change/ positive methods (e.g. reformation) are more likely to have a lasting effect/ 'Do not take revenge, my dear friends' (Romans 12:19 [NIV])/ 'it is not My desire that the wicked shall die, but that the wicked turn from his [evil] ways and live' (Ezekiel 33:11).

9.5 **A** Free will is given by God to allow humans to make their own choices and decisions/ it does not mean humans can choose to do whatever they want; there are good or bad consequences to every action/ temptation makes free will harder to use properly/ religious beliefs and teachings encourage the responsible use of free will, as does the law and human conscience. **B** *For*: all violence causes suffering/ violence is not loving and doesn't show respect, even in self-defence/ better to try to repair damage that has been done rather than responding with further violence/ Jesus gave an example during his arrest when he healed the High Priest's servant/ there is a duty in Christianity and Judaism to help relieve suffering, not cause and increase it. *Against*: using violence in self-defence may cause less harm than allowing an attack to continue/ e.g. the use of atom bombs helped to end the Second World War.

9.6 **A** *Beliefs must be similar*. Christians oppose all punishment that causes harm to offenders/ corporal punishment has no element of reform/ although the Torah and Talmud allow corporal punishment, most Jews today do not agree with its use/ positive discipline that encourages reformation is preferred. **B** *Against*: Christians and Jews believe in compassion and 'love your neighbour' so criminals should be treated well/ all humans are deserving of respect as they are created by God. *For*: 'eye for an eye' suggests to Christians that offenders who commit serious crimes should receive severe punishment/ Christians and Jews see God as a fair and just judge.

9.7 **A** Christians should forgive a person no matter what they have done/ Jesus said there is no limit to the number of times a person should forgive/ Jews do not believe forgiveness should be automatic/ instead offenders must show remorse and ask for forgiveness before God will forgive. **B** *E.g. 'I agree that nobody should expect to be forgiven more than once because they should have learned from their original mistake. If they were punished on the first occasion they should have used the chance to repent and promised not to offend again. Christians who deliberately reoffend break promises to God. On the other hand, Christians are taught they should forgive again. When asked how many times they should forgive, Jesus said, 'not seven times, but seventy-seven times.' Because of this Christians should forgive as many times as necessary, even if the offender does not expect it. They should also try to help the offender not to commit offences in future.'*

9.8 **A** Some Bible passages agree with retribution (e.g. Genesis 9:6)/ others with reform (e.g. Ezekiel 33:11)/ 'You shall not murder' (Exodus 20:13 [NIV])/ death penalty does not reform the offender, which Christians and Jews believe is an important aim/ does not respect the sanctity of life/ the Torah identifies 36 offences that should be punishable by death, but the Talmud lays down conditions that make it very difficult to pass the death sentence. **B** The death penalty is not loving or compassionate/ may kill an innocent person by mistake/ life is sacred and only God has the right to take it/ evidence suggests that it does not deter/ a dead offender cannot be reformed/ the victim's family may not want it to happen.

10 Religion, human rights and social justice

Please note that these are suggested answers to the Apply questions, designed to give you guidance, rather than being definitive answers.

10.1 **A** They might treat others fairly/ make sure people's human rights are protected/ encourage people to act with respect and compassion/ work to create a more equal society. **B** *For*: everyone is entitled to have rights/ they allow the more disadvantaged to be treated with justice and compassion, which are both teachings of Christianity and Judaism/ supported by the parable of the Sheep and the Goats/ 'Let justice well up like a river, Righteousness like an unfailing stream' (Amos 5:24 [Tenakh])/ allow people freedom to live their lives as they wish/ not protecting human rights goes against responsibilities to others and God. *Against*: some people (e.g. murderers) do not deserve rights/ rights should be earned/ those who do not respect the rights of others should have no rights themselves.

10.2 A Prejudice is an attitude that some people are superior to others because of their gender, race, sexuality, etc./ discrimination is acting on prejudiced opinions. **B** *For*: religious creation stories say all people are born equal/ everyone is born in the same way, without possessions and completely dependent/ all have equal value as humans/ all have the same access to God/ 'you are all one in Christ Jesus' (Galatians 3:28 [NIV]). *Against*: some are born into wealthy countries or families and some into poor ones, so life opportunities are unequal/ historically certain groups have been seen as dominant, giving better opportunities (e.g. men and women are not always treated equally).

10.3 A In Great Britain, nobody is forced to be a Christian/ other faiths are welcomed in Christian countries/ everybody has the right to choose a faith (or none)/ the persecution of members of any faith and preaching religious hatred or intolerance are against mainstream Christian teaching/ Jews believe religious freedom is part of God's design and agree with Christian attitudes/ Judaism does not attempt to convert people to be Jews and it is difficult to become a Jew unless born into the faith. **B** *Use of any answers to 10.3 A that are relevant to support an opinion*/ it is a basic human right to be allowed to follow a faith/ following any faith can only be helpful to a person and society as a whole/ some sects and interpretations of major faiths may be harmful and so should be avoided.

10.4 A It is unjust/ 'You shall not wrong a stranger or oppress him, for you were strangers in the land of Egypt' (Exodus 22:20 [Tenakh])/ the Holocaust was mainly caused by racial prejudice and resulted in 6 million Jews being murdered/ it denies belief in equality/ 'there is neither Jew nor Gentile, neither slave nor free, nor is there male and female for you are one in Christ Jesus' (Galatians 3:28 [NIV])/ it is harmful/ illegal/ not loving or compassionate/ against the will of God. **B** *E.g. 'I believe all discrimination is wrong because it can cause great harm to people. It is also completely unjust because Christians and Jews believe all humans are created by God, in his image, and with equal rights. Behaving in any other way shows no love and respect to others and makes them feel that they are in some way inferior and wrong through no fault of their own. However, positive discrimination is an exception because it is not harmful. This means to treat people of some minority groups better than others, for example by giving disabled people special areas of seating in sports stadiums and theatres. This allows them equal opportunity to see sports or arts performances because it removes problems with access. Some Christians and Jews see this as fulfilling the prophecy of Amos: 'Let justice roll on like a river and righteousness like a never-failing stream' (Amos 5:24 [NIV]).'*

10.5 A Men and women have equal status in the eyes of God/ despite this, Catholic and Orthodox Christianity and Orthodox Judaism believe men and women should have different roles in religion, so they do not allow women to be priests/rabbis/ women have the responsibility to teach their children the basics of Judaism, including customs and practices/ Reform and Liberal Jews have less defined roles for men and women, and allow women to become rabbis. **B** It is not treating people equally/ it goes against Christian and Jewish teachings/ Galatians 3:28/ gender or sexuality is not a choice/ it is based on prejudice, which is a negative attitude/ it goes against justice, love and compassion, which are central values to all faiths.

10.6 A Wealth is a blessing from God/ 'Remember that it is the LORD your God who gives you the power to get wealth' (Deuteronomy 8:18 [Tenakh])/ excess wealth should be shared with those who have less/ wealth can be dangerous/ can cause greed and selfishness/ wealth can cause neglect of the spiritual life/ it is not possible to serve both God and money/ 'For the love of money is the root of all sorts of evil' (1 Timothy 6:10 [NIV]). **B** *E.g. 'Charities are desperate for money so they can carry out their work. They rely on people's generosity to give them money. If giving to charity was compulsory, it is likely they would receive more than they do at present, so could help more people in need throughout the world. Some Christians and Jews follow instructions in the Bible and Torah to give tithes to the poor (10 per cent of their earnings), so the idea of compulsory giving is not unknown.'*

10.7 A By not being paid fairly for the work they do/ by being forced to work in poor conditions/ by being charged excessive interest on loans/ by being exploited by people-traffickers. **B** *E.g. 'Developed countries that prefer to buy cheap goods do cause exploitation. In order to have cheap goods, the cost of making them has to be reduced to a minimum. This means exploiting workers by paying them next to nothing. If people in developed countries were prepared to pay a little more, the workers could be paid more. Exploitation goes against religious ideas of justice, compassion and love, and shows that Amos' vision that justice should flow like a river and righteousness like a stream has not yet been reached. However, another opinion is that it is the multinational companies that make the goods, and the shops that sell the goods, who are to blame. Designer goods are often made in poor countries by people who are exploited, yet they are expensive to buy because the producers and shops are keen to make ever bigger profits because they are so greedy. Christianity and Judaism warn against greed and hoarding money, and in 1 Timothy it says, 'the love of money is the root of all evil'. So exploitation of poor countries is caused by the greed of rich people, not poor people who want to buy decent things at prices they can afford.'*

10.8 A Long-term aid educates people in skills such as literacy, numeracy and basic training to allow them to access work/ teaches them agricultural methods to grow their own crops/ provides assistance for setting up a small business to earn enough to provide for their needs. **B** *Arguments in support*: The fact that so many people are still poor shows that much more still needs to be done/ some religions do not set a good example to believers because they invest a lot of wealth in places of worship rather than giving it to the poor/ 'The one who is unwilling to work shall not eat' (2 Thessalonians 3:10 [NIV]). *Arguments for a different point of view*: religions have a history of giving to charity/ have set up charities that work with the poor at home and abroad/ many religious believers do all they can to help the poor/ they may be poor themselves so they don't have the money to spare.

Exam practice answers

1 Christianity: Beliefs and teachings

Test the 1 mark question

1. B) Incarnation
2. C) Benevolent

Test the 2 mark question

Suggested answers, other relevant answers would be credited. 1 mark for each correct point.

3. Through good works/ through the grace of God/ through faith/ through Jesus' death/ through obeying the Ten Commandments/ through loving one's neighbour/ through prayer/ through worship/ through the Holy Spirit.

4. Christians believe everyone will be raised from the dead (resurrection)/ face judgement of God/ immediately or at the end of time/ Judgement Day/ Second Coming of Christ/ Jesus rose from the dead/ people will be judged on how they lived their lives/ sent to heaven, hell or purgatory/ resurrection of the body/ restoration to glorified bodies.

Test the 4 mark question

Suggested answers, other relevant answers would be credited. 1 mark for each simple contrasting or similar point, another mark for developing each point, so a maximum of 4 marks for two developed points.

6. Christians may show respect towards all of God's creation/ actively work for conservation/ show stewardship/ take practical steps like recycling/ be energy efficient.

Christians may treat others with respect/ all are created 'in imago dei' (in God's image)/ work for peace between people/ support charities that help people in need/ reflect God in all they do.

Christians may take care of themselves (both body and soul)/ adopt healthy lifestyles/ develop spiritual practices/ prayer/ worship/ meditation.

7. Christians believe that because God is loving, God wants the best for them/ they accept God's will as being for their benefit, even if it does not appear to be so/ they love others because God loves them.

God's greatest act of love was sending his Son Jesus/ to save people from sin/ to gain eternal life/ so they are grateful to God/ express their thanks through worship or praise.

God is love/ qualities of love described in Paul's letter to the Corinthians/ patient/ kind/ not easily angered/ Christians try to live according to these descriptions of love.

Test the 5 mark question

Suggested answers, other relevant answers would be credited. 1 mark for each simple contrasting or similar belief, another mark for developing each belief, so 4 marks for two developed beliefs, 1 extra mark for a correct reference to a source of religious belief or teaching.

9. Christians believe God is omnipotent (all-powerful)/ has supreme authority/ can do all things/ 'Nothing is impossible with God' (Luke 1:37 [NIV])/ is loving (benevolent)/ wants good for God's creation/ wants people to love God freely in return/ 'God so loved the world that he gave his one and only Son, that whoever believes in him shall not perish but have eternal life' (John 3:16 [NIV])/ is just (fair/righteous)/ wants people to choose good over evil/ punishes wrongdoing/ is the perfect judge of human character.

Christians believe there is only one God/ 'The Lord is our God, the Lord alone' (Deuteronomy 6:4 [NIV])/ but within God there is a Trinity of persons/ Father, Son (Jesus), Holy Spirit/ 'Our Father in heaven' (Lord's Prayer)/ the Spirit's presence at Jesus' baptism.

God is the creator of all that is/ 'In the beginning, God created the heavens and the earth' (Genesis 1:1 [NIV])/ the Spirit was present at creation/ the Word of God (the Son) was involved in creation too.

10. Christians believe Jesus restored the relationship between God and humanity/ Jesus atoned for the sins of humankind/ God accepted his death as atonement for sin by raising Jesus from the dead/ 'Jesus Christ […] is the atoning sacrifice for our sins, and not only for ours but also for the sins of the whole world' (1 John 2: 1–2 [NIV]).

Through the atonement of Jesus, humans can receive forgiveness for sin/ be able to get close to God/ gain eternal life/ sin has been defeated/ 'For the wages of sin is death, but the gift of God is eternal life in Christ Jesus our Lord' (Romans 6:23 [NIV]).

Jesus' death atoned for the original sin of Adam and Eve/ Adam chose to disobey God, but Jesus chose to offer his life as a sacrifice/ 'For since death came through a man, the resurrection of the dead also comes through a man. For as in Adam all die, so in Christ all will be made alive' (1 Corinthians 15:21 [NIV]).

Test the 12 mark question

Suggested answers shown here, but see page 11 for guidance on levels of response.

1 Arguments in support

- Hell is not a place/ exploration of the earth and space have not discovered a place where spirits are punished forever/ although hell is shown in paintings as a place of fire and torture ruled by Satan (the devil) somewhere beneath the earth, no such place exists.

- The idea of hell is inconsistent with a benevolent God/ Christians believe God is loving/ a loving God would never send anyone to eternal damnation in hell/ like a loving Father, God will give people another chance if they repent.

- The idea of hell is just a way of comforting those who want to see justice/ some people get away with many bad things and seem not to receive punishment in this life/ the idea of hell ensures the idea of justice being done, but it does not really exist.

Arguments in support of other views

- Today hell is more often thought to be an eternal state of mind being cut off from the possibility of God/ the state of being without God, rather than a place/ a person who did not acknowledge God or follow his teachings would necessarily end up without God in the afterlife.

- Christians believe God is just/ it is only fair that someone who has gone against God's laws should be punished eventually/ it is a just punishment for an immoral life.

- Jesus spoke about hell as a possible consequence for sinners/ 'But I tell you that anyone who is angry with a brother or sister will be subject to judgment […] And anyone who says, 'You fool!' will be in danger of the fire of hell.' (Matthew 5:22 [NIV])/ 'If your right eye causes you to stumble, gouge it out and throw it away. It is better for you to lose one part of your body than for your whole body to be thrown into hell.' (Matthew 5:29 [NIV])/ 'For if God did not spare angels when they sinned, but sent them to hell, putting them in chains of darkness to be held for judgment' (2 Peter 2:4 [NIV]).

2   Arguments in support

- Salvation means deliverance from sin and admission to heaven brought about by Jesus/ saving one's soul/ sin separates people from God who is holy/ the original sin of Adam and Eve brought suffering and death to humankind/so God gave the law so that people would know how to stay close to him/ Jesus' teaching takes the law even further.

- One way of gaining salvation is through good works/ by having faith in God and obeying God's laws/ obeying the Ten Commandments (Exodus 20:1–19) is the best way of being saved because by doing so the Christian is avoiding sin/ following other Christian teachings such as the Beatitudes (Matthew 5:1–12) helps gain salvation through good works/ being merciful/ a peacemaker.

- Christians believe God gave people free will to make moral choices/ following God's law shows the person is willing to use their free will wisely.

Arguments in support of other views

- The best way of gaining salvation is through grace/ grace is a free gift of God's love and support/ it is not earned by following laws/ faith in Jesus is all a person needs to be saved/ 'For it is by grace you have been saved, through faith – and this is not from yourselves, it is the gift of God – not by works, so that no one can boast.' (Ephesians 2:8–9 [NIV]).

- Merely following the law is a legalistic approach/ it can hide sinfulness inside a person/ Jesus criticised the Pharisees for following the law but having evil hearts/ Jesus said, 'The teachers of the law and the Pharisees sit in Moses' seat. So you must be careful to do everything they tell you. But do not do what they do, for they do not practice what they preach.' (Matthew 23:2–3 [NIV]).

- Most Christians believe both good works and grace (through faith in Jesus) are needed to be saved/ you can't prove you have faith unless you show it in your outward behaviour/ a danger in believing in salvation through grace alone is that people can feel specially chosen so look down on others/ not feel they have to obey God's law as they are already 'saved'.

2 Christianity: Practices

Test the 1 mark question

1.   D) Liturgical worship

2.   C) Christmas

Test the 2 mark question

Suggested answers, other relevant answers would be credited. 1 mark for each correct point.

3.   By setting up charities/ Christian Aid/ CAFOD/ Tearfund/ by raising or donating money/ by working overseas in poor countries/ by praying for justice for the poor/ by campaigning for the poor.

4.   Prayer helps Christians communicate with God/ develop and sustain their relationship with God/ thank God for blessings/ praise God/ ask God for help for oneself or others/ find courage to accept God's will in difficult times.

Test the 4 mark question

Suggested answers, other relevant answers would be credited. 1 mark for each simple contrasting or similar point, another mark for developing each point, so a maximum of 4 marks for two developed points.

6.   *Ways must be contrasting*:

Infant baptism: Catholic, Orthodox, Anglican, Methodist and United Reformed Churches baptise babies/ 'I baptise you in the name of the Father, and of the Son, and of the Holy Spirit'/ blessed water poured over the baby's head/ sign of cross on baby's forehead/ anointing with oil/ white garment/ candle/ godparents' and parents' promises.

Believers' baptism: others such as Baptist and Pentecostal Christians baptise those who are old enough to make their own decision about baptism/ baptise people who have made a commitment to faith in Jesus/ full immersion in pool/ minister talks about meaning of baptism/ candidates are asked if they are willing to change their lives/

Bible passage/ brief testimony from candidate/ baptised 'in the name of the Father, and of the Son, and of the Holy Spirit'.

7.   *Interpretations must be contrasting*:

Catholic, Orthodox and some Anglican Christians believe the bread and wine become the body and blood of Christ/ Jesus is fully present in the bread and wine/ a divine mystery/ those receiving become present in a mystical way at the death and resurrection of Christ/ receive God's grace/ Holy Communion is a sacrament.

Protestant Christians see Holy Communion as a reminder of Jesus' words and actions at the Last Supper/ bread and wine are symbols of Jesus' sacrifice/ they help them reflect on the meaning of Jesus' death and resurrection for their lives today/ it is an act of fellowship.

Test the 5 mark question

Suggested answers, other relevant answers would be credited. 1 mark for each simple contrasting or similar belief, another mark for developing each belief, so 4 marks for two developed beliefs, 1 extra mark for a correct reference to a source of religious belief or teaching.

9.   Spreading the Christian gospel/ by public preaching/ by personal witness.

Evangelism is considered a duty of Christians because of the Great Commission/ 'Therefore go and make disciples of all nations, baptising them in the name of the Father and of the Son and of the Holy Spirit, and teaching them to obey everything I have commanded you' (Matthew 28:19–20 [NIV])/people have a desire to share the good news with others because they have experienced it themselves.

Christians believe they are called to do more than just know Jesus in their own lives/ they are called to spread the good news to non-believers that Jesus is the Saviour of the world.

When the early disciples received the Spirit at Pentecost they were given the gifts necessary to carry out the Great Commission/ the Spirit gives some people wisdom/ knowledge/ faith/ gifts of healing/ miraculous powers/ prophecy/ the ability to speak in tongues and understand the message of those who speak in tongues.

10.   Christians may work for reconciliation in their own lives by forgiving their enemies/ making up with people they have offended/ going to the sacrament of Reconciliation to be reconciled with God/ 'But I tell you, love your enemies and pray for those who persecute you' (Matthew 5:44 [NIV]).

Christians may work for reconciliation between political or religious groups through organisations/ e.g. through the Irish Churches Peace Project/ the Corrymeela Community/ which sought to bring Catholic and Protestant communities together in Northern Ireland/ through discussion and working on their differences together.

Christians could work for more global reconciliation through an organisation such as the Community of the Cross of Nails at Coventry Cathedral/ which works with partners in many countries/ to bring about peace and harmony in areas where conflict and violence are present.

Christians do this work because of Jesus' teaching and example/ as Paul says, 'For if, while we were God's enemies, we were reconciled to him through the death of his Son, how much more, having been reconciled, shall we be saved through his life!' (Romans 5:10 [NIV]).

Test the 12 mark question

Suggested answers shown here, but see page 11 for guidance on levels of response.

12.   **Arguments in support**

- Going to a place where Jesus or saints lived and died can inspire people/ it can teach people more about their religion's history/ can strengthen faith as it increases knowledge about holy people/ Christians make pilgrimages to the Holy Land as it is where Jesus lived, preached, died and resurrected from the dead/ Christians can experience for themselves what it was like to live there/ they follow in the footsteps of Jesus/ meet others who share their faith/ the effort and discipline needed strengthens their faith.

- Some Christians go on pilgrimage to places where miracles are said to have occurred/ e.g. Lourdes in France/ they pray to be healed from sin/ mental or physical illness/ to thank God for a special blessing/ to help others who are disabled or ill, putting into practice love of neighbour.

- Some Christians go on pilgrimage to a remote place/ e.g. Iona in Scotland/ they go to have quiet time to pray/ read scriptures/ connect with God through nature/ reflect on their lives/ particularly if facing a big decision/ refresh their spiritual lives in today's busy world.

Arguments in support of other views

- Pilgrimage does not always bring people closer to God/ some places are very commercialised/ it can disappoint people who had a certain mental image of a place to see that it is touristy/ it can be very crowded so not a place for reflection/ some people on the pilgrimage may just see it as a holiday, making it hard to concentrate on God.

- Pilgrimage can be expensive/ not everyone can afford going abroad/ not everyone has time to make a pilgrimage, e.g. getting time off work/ family commitments.

- Other ways of becoming closer to God are better than pilgrimage/ daily prayer in one's own home can bring the peace of mind and heart the person needs/ receiving Holy Communion brings people closer to God than any journey/ going to the sacrament of Reconciliation can be done locally.

13. **Arguments in support**

• The Church (meaning all Christians) has a mission to spread the good news/ that Jesus Christ is the Son of God/ came into the world to be its saviour/ the Great Commission/ 'Therefore go and make disciples of all nations, baptising them in the name of the Father and of the Son and of the Holy Spirit, and teaching them to obey everything I have commanded you' (Matthew 28:19–20 [NIV]).

• Christians believe they are called to do more than just know Jesus in their own lives/ they are called to spread the good news to non-believers that Jesus is the Saviour of the world.

• When the early disciples received the Spirit at Pentecost they were given the gifts necessary to carry out the Great Commission/ the Spirit gives some people wisdom/ knowledge/ faith/ gifts of healing/ miraculous powers/ prophecy/ the ability to speak in tongues and understand the message of those who speak in tongues/ Christians today receive the Holy Spirit at their Confirmation/ they are called to be disciples of Jesus, like the first disciples/ so they must spread the faith fearlessly as the disciples did.

Arguments in support of other views

• The main job of a Christian is to believe in Jesus/ follow the commandments/ worship God/ love one's neighbour as oneself/ live a good life in the hope of eternal life in heaven.

• Many Christians do not have the personality to preach to others about their faith/ do not have the time if working/ have family responsibilities/ are not public speakers/ do not want to antagonise people who are unsympathetic non-believers/ cannot go abroad to work as missionaries.

• There are other ways of showing one's faith to others without actually 'telling them'/ being a good neighbour/ helping those in need/ working with charities/ worshipping God/ showing integrity/ having high moral principles that make non-believers notice that faith makes a difference to the Christian believer.

3 Judaism: beliefs and teachings

Test the 1 mark question

1. A) Do not cause harm to anyone

2. A) Abraham

Test the 2 mark question

Suggested answers, other relevant answers would be credited. 1 mark for each correct point:

3. God created the universe and everything in it/ in six days/ about 6000 years ago/ God took four days to make the universe fit to support life/ and two days to create all living creatures/ God created the universe but it developed/evolved over a much longer period of time.

4. During Rosh Hashanah/ during Yom Kippur/ on the Day of Atonement/ as soon as they die/ on the Day of Judgement.

Test the 4 mark question

Suggested answers, other relevant answers would be credited. 1 mark for each simple contrasting or similar point, another mark for developing each point, so a maximum of 4 marks for two developed points:

6. The covenant at Sinai means Jews today have to obey God's laws/ including the Ten Commandments and the mitzvot in the Torah/ this influences how they worship God/ how they celebrate Shabbat and Jewish festivals/ the food they eat/ the covenant at Sinai also means Jews are considered to be the chosen people of God/ that God is the God of the Jews/ which inspires Jews to centre their lives around God/ e.g. by showing dedication and commitment to God in the way they live and worship.

7. Many Jews believe they will go to heaven/paradise/Gan Eden when they die/ if they follow their faith correctly/ heaven is where people are with God/ some Jews believe people who do not go to heaven go to Sheol/ a place of waiting where souls are cleansed/ some Jews believe they will be judged by God as soon as they die/ supported by Ecclesiastes 12:7/ others believe God will judge everyone on the Day of Judgement/ supported by Daniel 12:2/ some Jews believe in physical or spiritual resurrection/ but many do not.

Test the 5 mark question

Suggested answers, other relevant answers would be credited. 1 mark for each simple contrasting or similar point, another mark for developing each point, so 4 marks for two developed points, 1 extra mark for a correct reference to a source of Jewish belief or teaching:

9. Justice means bringing about what is right and fair, according to the law, or making up for a wrong that has been committed/ pursuing justice is a sacred duty for Jews/ 'to do justice and love goodness' (Micah 6:8 [Tenakh])/ the laws in the Torah give guidance to Jews on how to treat the poor and vulnerable, to help achieve justice/ healing the world means taking actions to help God's work in sustaining the world/ it may involve contributing to social justice or helping to protect the environment/ e.g. volunteering for a charity such as World Jewish Relief/ some Jews believe it also involves obeying the mitzvot and trying to become closer to God/ showing kindness to others means showing positive, caring actions towards all living things/ the Torah teaches that Jews should love others as they love themselves/ 'love your fellow as yourself' (Leviticus 19:18 [Tenakh]).

10. God is a single, whole, indivisible being/ not three Persons, as in Christianity/ God is the only being who should be praised and worshipped/ everything in the universe has been created and is sustained by God/ 'when God began to create the heaven and earth' (Genesis 1:1 [Tenakh])/ God is the source of all Jewish morality, beliefs and values/ including all of the laws Jews should follow (the mitzvot)/ Jews should show total loyalty, love and dedication towards God/ 'You shall love the Lord your God with all your heart and with all your soul and with all your might' (Deuteronomy 6:5 [Tenakh]).

Test the 12 mark question

Suggested answers shown here, but see page 11 for guidance on levels of response.

12. **Arguments in support:**

• Orthodox Jews believe there will be a future leader of the Jews (called the Messiah)/ who will bring about world peace and unite humanity together/ by ruling over humanity with kindness and justice/ and upholding and teaching the law in the Torah.

• The Messiah will bring about the Messianic age/ when war will end and people will live in peace and harmony/ 'Nation shall not take up sword against nation; They shall never again know war' (Micah 4:3 [Tenakh]).

• Global peace will not be achieved until the Messiah comes/ Jews will not be able to achieve this on their own/ so there is little point in trying to create world peace before then.

Arguments in support of other views:

• Reform Jews believe everyone should work together to achieve world peace/ and this will bring about the Messianic age/ rather than the leadership of one person.

• Orthodox Jews believe the Messiah will come if God deems the Jews to be worthy of redemption/ but perhaps Jews will only be worthy of redemption if they first try to make the world a better place.

• The moral principles of pursuing justice/ healing the world/ showing kindness to others all require Jews to help create a more peaceful, just society.

13. **Arguments in support:**

• Jews believe that God will judge them for how well they follow his laws/ both once a year during Rosh Hashanah, to determine their fortunes for the coming year/ and after they die, to determine how they spend their afterlife.

• This encourages and motivates Jews to obey God's laws/ including the 613 mitzvot in the Torah/ which has a large influence on how they live their lives/ e.g. what food they eat, how they worship God, how they celebrate Shabbat, how they treat others.

• Focusing on God's role as judge emphasises the importance of living in a good way and following God's laws/ which might be helpful for Jews who struggle to follow all of the laws, or do not see the importance of following all of the laws.

• It may also help Jews who feel wronged/ because they know God's judgement will be fair.

Arguments in support of other views:

• It is hard to understand God as the judge without also understanding God as the lawgiver/ as Jews need to know what they are being judged on.

• It is equally/more important to understand God as the creator/ who created everything in the universe, including human life/ as this influences belief in the sanctity of life/ the obligation to save a life (pikuach nefesh)/ means that everything Jews see and experience is a meeting with God.

• Understanding God as the creator of free will helps Jews to understand the need for God's laws/ because the laws help Jews to use their free will correctly/ without this knowledge Jews might question the necessity of the laws.

• Understanding God as the creator and sustainer encourages Jews to help improve society and protect the world/ to fulfil God's plan for the world he created/ helps to explain the importance of healing the world.

4 Judaism: practices

Test the 1 mark question

1. C) Ner tamid

2. B) Amidah

Test the 2 mark question

Suggested answers, other relevant answers would be credited. 1 mark for each correct point:

3. By holding a Bar Mitzvah ceremony/ the boy reads from the Torah at a service in the synagogue/ wears a tallit for the first time/ may lead part of the service/ makes a short speech/ his father gives a speech thanking God/ there is a meal or party/ the boy receives gifts.

4. Orthodox synagogues usually hold daily services; Reform ones often don't/ Orthodox services are in Hebrew; Reform ones are in Hebrew and the country's own language/ in Orthodox services the leader has their back to the congregation; in Reform services they mostly face the congregation/ in Orthodox services men and women sit separately; in Reform ones they sit together/ Reform services tend to be shorter than Orthodox ones/ but more rigidly structured/ Orthodox men and married women always cover their heads, Reform men and women might not/ the singing is unaccompanied in Orthodox services but may be accompanied in Reform ones.

Test the 4 mark question

Suggested answers, other relevant answers would be credited. 1 mark for each simple contrasting or similar point, another mark for developing each point, so a maximum of 4 marks for two developed points:

6. To learn more about the history of Judaism/ e.g. the Tenakh contains accounts about the early history of the Jews, such as the escape from Egypt/ to learn more about God's laws/ as obeying these correctly is an important part of the Jewish faith (particularly for Orthodox Jews)/ to learn how to apply God's laws to everyday life/ the Talmud helps Jews to interpret the Torah and apply it to their lives today.

7. By doing good actions such as charity work/ as Jews believe this will improve God's judgement/ by sharing a special meal with their families/ this includes symbolic foods, e.g. apples dipped in honey to symbolise hope for a sweet new year/ by attending services in the synagogue/ where prayers are said asking God to continue to be the king of the world for the coming year.

Test the 5 mark question

Suggested answers, other relevant answers would be credited. 1 mark for each simple contrasting or similar point, another mark for developing each point, so 4 marks for two developed points, 1 extra mark for a correct reference to a source of Jewish belief or teaching:

9. In the naming ceremony the baby is formally introduced to the community and God/ Orthodox babies are blessed in the synagogue on the first Shabbat after their birth/ the father recites the Torah blessing and asks God for the good health of his wife and baby/ a baby girl's name is announced/ both Reform parents take part in the ceremony/ in the Brit Milah ceremony a baby boy is circumcised/ when he is eight days old/ placed on a chair that symbolises the presence of the prophet Elijah/ placed on the knee of the companion of the child/ blessed by his father/ formally named/ there is a festive meal/ recalls the covenant God made with Abraham/ circumcision 'would be a sign of the covenant between Me and you' (Genesis 17:11 [Tenakh])/ in the redemption of the firstborn son, some Orthodox Jews give money to redeem their firstborn son from Temple service/ five silver coins are given to a kohen/ prayers are said asking for the child to 'enter into Torah, into marriage, and into good deeds'/ 'but you shall have the first-born of man redeemed [...] Take as their redemption price [...] the money equivalent of five shekels' (Numbers 18:15–16 [Tenakh]).

10. Kosher food is acceptable to eat, trefah food is not/ it is not acceptable to eat food containing blood/ 'But make sure that you do not partake of the blood; for the blood is the life, and you must not consume the life with the flesh' (Deuteronomy 12:23 [Tenakh])/ dairy products and meat cannot be eaten together/ several hours must pass between eating meat and anything containing milk/ 'You shall not boil a kid in its mother's milk' (Exodus 23:19 [Tenakh])/ for this reason many Orthodox homes have kitchens with two sinks and two food preparation areas.

Test the 12 mark question

Suggested answers shown here, but see page 11 for guidance on levels of response.

12. Arguments in support:
• In Reform Judaism women and men can take on the same roles in worship/ e.g. both can become rabbis or be part of the minyan.
• Reform Jewish men and women can choose whether or not to wear a tallit and tefillin for prayer.
• Jewish men and women can attend the same services in the synagogue, or choose to pray at home.
• Both boys and girls may celebrate their coming of age in Reform Judaism.
• At Reform weddings, the marriage contract usually focuses on mutual hopes for the marriage that are the same for the husband and wife.
• In Orthodox Judaism both men and women follow the dietary laws.

Arguments in support of other views:
• In Orthodox Judaism women are not allowed to be rabbis.
• Orthodox Jewish men wear a tallit and tefillin for prayers but women do not.
• Orthodox boys celebrate their coming of age with a Bar Mitzvah ceremony but girls do not celebrate with a Bat Mitzvah ceremony/ in Reform Judaism, boys celebrate their coming of age at 13 and girls at 12.
• At Orthodox weddings, the marriage contract may detail aspects such as the husband's duties to his wife, and how he will provide for his wife if they get divorced, but not vice versa.
• During the third period of mourning after a death, male mourners say the kaddish daily in the synagogue but women do not.

13. Arguments in support:
• The set periods of time help to give structure to a person's mourning/ give them enough time to grieve fully but also help them to get back to normal life.
• When they first hear of the death Jews say a blessing that refers to God as the true judge/ this helps them to accept God's decision to take the person's life.
• During the first period of mourning, Jews do not have to worry about following certain Jewish laws
• During shiva (the second period of mourning), mourners stay at home to pray together and support each other/ mirrors are covered so mourners cannot focus on their appearance, helping them to focus instead on coming to terms with a person's death.

Arguments in support of other views:
• Mourning/grieving is very personal and some people might find the structure or rigidity of Jewish mourning customs unhelpful.
• Most Jews are buried as soon after death as possible/ but mourners might need longer than 24 hours to mentally prepare themselves for the funeral.
• The second period of mourning lasts for seven days/ when Jews stay at home and mourn together/ do not work/ but they might need more than a week before returning to work/ might want to mourn alone.

• During the third period of mourning Jews are not allowed to listen to music/ but they might find that listening to music brings them solace.
• During the first year after a person's death Jews are not allowed to go to parties/ but they might find that going to parties helps to distract them after a person's death.

5 Relationships and families
Test the 1 mark question
1. D) Stability
2. B) A couple and their children

Test the 2 mark question
Suggested answers, other relevant answers would be credited. 1 mark for each correct point.

3. Christians believe all people are created equal by God/ 'love your neighbour' applies to everyone/ Christians follow Jesus' example in treating women with equal value/ 'There is neither Jew nor Gentile, neither slave nor free, nor is there male and female, for you are all one in Christ Jesus' (Galatians 3:28 [NIV])/ men and women can have different roles in the family but this does not mean they are not equal in God's sight.

Jews believe God created all people equal/ in the image of God (Genesis 1:27)/ in Orthodox Judaism, roles are 'separate but equal': men support the family and women care for the children and home/ in Reform and Liberal Judaism, women can become rabbis/ sit with men in the synagogue/ handle the Torah scrolls/ have equality of opportunity in all other areas of life/ sharing duties within religion and the home.

4. Christians who oppose sex before marriage think cohabitation is wrong/ Catholic and Orthodox Churches believe a sexual relationship should only take place within marriage/ many Anglican and Protestant Christians accept that although marriage is best, people may live together in a faithful, loving, committed way without being married.

Traditionally, Jews consider sex before marriage as wrong and irresponsible/ it undermines the importance of creating a family through which Jewish religion and culture is passed down/ the Torah warns against promiscuity and sexual conduct that harms others/ Orthodox Jews, following laws in Leviticus and guidance in the Talmud, believe that pre-marital sex is forbidden, therefore cohabitation is wrong/ Reform and Liberal Jews may agree that although marriage is best, people may live together in a loving, committed way without being married.

Test the 4 mark question
Suggested answers, other relevant answers would be credited. 1 mark for each simple contrasting or similar point, another mark for developing each point, so a maximum of 4 marks for two developed points.

6. *Beliefs must be contrasting:*
Christians believe marriage is for life/ vows made in the presence of God should not be broken/ Jesus taught that anyone who divorced and remarried was committing adultery (Mark 10:11–12)/ except in the case of adultery (Matthew 5:32)/ for Catholics marriage is a sacrament that is permanent/ cannot be dissolved by civil divorce/ Catholics can separate but cannot marry someone else while their partner is still alive/ for some Christians divorce is the lesser of two evils/ Protestant Churches accept civil divorce and allow remarriage in church.

Jews accept divorce as a last resort/ marriage is a voluntary contract so a divorce ('get') is allowed if both people agree/ The Torah says a man can divorce his wife for shameful conduct (Deuteronomy 24:1), but today any reasons can apply/ couples should try reconciliation first but can divorce if they no longer love each other as 'one flesh'/ Jews are encouraged to remarry after divorce.

7. *Beliefs must be contrasting:*
Many Christians believe heterosexual relationships are part of God's plan for humans/ God created male and female/ told them to 'be fruitful and increase in number' (Genesis 1:28 [NIV])/ sex expresses a deep, life-long union best expressed in marriage/ some Christians oppose homosexual relationships because they go against God's plan/ the Catholic Church teaches that homosexual sex is a sinful activity/ some Christians think loving, faithful homosexual relationships are just as holy as heterosexual ones.

Judaism teaches that heterosexual relationships are the normal pattern of behaviour/ Jews are expected to marry and have a family/ the sexual relationship between husband and wife is a blessing from God/ for expressing love and companionship as well as for having children/ God created Eve as a companion for Adam (Genesis 2:18)/ Jewish law recognises the rights of both women and men to sexual fulfilment in marriage/ The Torah is clear that sex between men is forbidden (Leviticus 18:22)/ Orthodox Judaism considers homosexual relationships to be wrong/ Reform and Liberal Judaism think that loving, committed homosexual relationships are as valid as heterosexual ones.

Test the 5 mark question
Suggested answers, other relevant answers would be credited. 1 mark for each simple contrasting or similar belief, another mark for developing each belief, so 4 marks for two developed beliefs, 1 extra mark for a correct reference to a source of religious belief or teaching.

9. For Christians, procreation is an important purpose/ procreation is part of God's plan for humanity/ God created man and woman, blessed them and said, 'Be fruitful and increase in number; fill the earth and subdue it' (Genesis 1:28 [NIV])/ protection of children is an important purpose/ educating children about Christian values

is an important purpose/ 'Children thrive, grow and develop within the love and safeguarding of the family' (The Church of England website).

For Jews, procreation is an important purpose/ it is through the family that Jewish faith and culture is preserved/ bringing up their children in their faith is a duty placed on them by God/ the Shema instructs parents to teach children God's laws (Deuteronomy 6:6–7)/ children learn how to be a Jew from family life/ e.g. through stories of Jewish scripture and traditions/ through observing the Sabbath, festivals and dietary laws.

10. The Christian Church teaches that both parents and children have responsibilities in a family/ the commandment to 'Honour one's father and mother' (Exodus 20:12 [NIV]) applies to children of all ages/ it includes the respect and care given to the elderly members of the family/ children should obey their parents/ 'Children, obey your parents in everything, for this pleases the Lord' (Colossians 3:20 [NIV]).

Jews have a duty to respect and care for their parents as they get older/ 'Honour your father and your mother' (Exodus 20:12 [Tenakh])/ the Talmud explains this involves giving them food, drink, clothes and shoes/ elderly parents should be helped to go out and get home safely.

Test the 12 mark question

Suggested answers shown here, but see page 11 for guidance on levels of response.

12. Arguments in support

• Most Christians and Jews think marriage is the proper place to enjoy a sexual relationship/ sex expresses a deep, loving, lifelong union that first requires the commitment of marriage/ it is one of God's gifts at creation/ 'That is why a man leaves his father and mother and is united to his wife, and they become one flesh' (Genesis 2:24 [NIV]).

• Christians believe that sex is part of the trust between partners in marriage/ sex should not be a casual, temporary pleasure/ 'The sexual act must take place exclusively within marriage. Outside of marriage it always constitutes a grave sin.' (Catechism 2390).

• Paul urged sexual restraint: 'Flee from sexual immorality. All other sins a person commits are outside the body, but whoever sins sexually, sins against their own body. Do you not know that your bodies are temples of the Holy Spirit, who is in you, whom you have received from God? You are not your own.' (1 Corinthians 6:18–19 [NIV]).

• Marriage brings security/ protects each partner's rights/ the rights of children/ provides a stable environment in which to raise a family.

• For Jews, marriage is the foundation of family life/ the only place for a sexual relationship/ a faithful, lifelong partnership where both people take full responsibility for their children/ the best way to have a stable and secure sexual relationship/ the spiritual binding together of soulmates/ part of God's plan at creation.

Arguments in support of other views

• Society has changed/ many people do not see sex as requiring the commitment of marriage/ contraception has reduced the risk of pregnancy before marriage/ many people engage in casual sexual relationships.

• The cost of marriage prevents some people from marrying immediately/ some couples want to see if the relationship is going to work before marrying/ some people do not think a marriage certificate makes any difference to their relationship.

• Some Christians and Jews accept that for some people sex before marriage is a valid expression of their love for each other/ some Christians and Jews may accept cohabitation, particularly if the couple is committed to each other/ more liberal Christians and Jews may accept that people may live together in a faithful, loving and committed way without being married.

13. Arguments in support

• The Orthodox and Catholic Churches teach that using artificial contraception within marriage is wrong/ against natural law/ against the purpose of marriage to have children/ having children is God's greatest gift to a married couple/ 'Every sexual act should have the possibility of creating new life' (*Humanae Vitae*, 1968).

• God will not send more children than a couple can care for/ if Catholic couples wish to plan their families they should use a natural method, such as the rhythm method.

• Some Orthodox Jews think that using artificial contraception is wrong, as the size of a family is God's decision.

Arguments in support of other views

• Other Christians and Jews accept the use of artificial contraception provided it is not used to prevent having children altogether/ by mutual consent of the couple.

• Its use may allow a couple to develop their relationship before having children/ prevent sexually transmitted infections/ help reduce the population explosion.

• The Church of England approved the use of artificial contraception at the Lambeth Conference in 1930/ 'The Conference agrees that other methods may be used, provided that this is done in the light of Christian principles.'

• Orthodox Jews accept artificial methods if the wife's health is at risk/ to avoid serious financial difficulties/ to delay or space pregnancies/ but sterilisation is forbidden as it damages the body which God created.

6 Religion and life

Test the 1 mark question

1. C) A good or gentle death

2. B) Life is sacred

Test the 2 mark question

Suggested answers, other relevant answers would be credited. 1 mark for each correct point.

3. Christians believe the world is on loan to humans, who have been given the responsibility by God to look after it (Genesis 1:28)/ the parable of the Talents (Matthew 25:14–30) warns that God will be the final judge about how responsible humans have been in looking after the earth/ pollution is not loving towards others; Jesus teaches Christians to 'love your neighbour' (Luke 10:27 [NIV]).

Jews believe they are accountable to God for how they look after the earth/ the Torah instructs Jews to rest the land every seven years to help protect it and allow it to regain its fertility (Leviticus 25:4–5)/ Jews are instructed not to destroy trees in Deuteronomy 20:19.

4. A wonderful place where God resides/ paradise/ beautiful garden of physical and spiritual pleasures/ eternal/ opposite from hell/ no suffering (Revelation 4:2–6)/ for all who live a good life and obey the teachings of sacred writings/ a place after death for the faithful/ Gan Eden/ a temporary soul-cleansing process takes place before entry to heaven.

Test the 4 mark question

Suggested answers, other relevant answers would be credited. 1 mark for each simple contrasting or similar point, another mark for developing each point, so a maximum of 4 marks for two developed points.

6. *Beliefs must be similar:*

Animal experimentation makes sure products such as medicines and food are safe to use/ most Christians believe it is good stewardship of the earth's resources to use animals in this way/ some Christians believe humans are more important than animals as they have dominion over them/ so animal experimentation is acceptable if it saves human lives/ as long as the animals are treated as kindly as possible.

Most Jews believe animal experimentation should be allowed for essential human needs/ but not for cosmetic products/ the animals should not be made to suffer unnecessarily as this goes against stewardship and other Jewish principles.

7. *Beliefs must be contrasting:*

A minority of Christians believe that as God put people in charge of the world they can use the resources as they wish/ God gave humans dominion and created the natural resources so that they may be used/ 'Rule over the fish in the sea and the birds in the sky and over every living creature that moves on the ground.' (Genesis 1:28 [NIV])/ this has led in some cases to the overuse and abuse of natural resources.

Most Christians and Jews believe God has given them the role of stewards, so natural resources should be used responsibly/ damaging the earth goes against God's wishes/ on the Day of Judgement, humans will be judged by God for how well they have looked after the earth/ 'See to it that you do not spoil and destroy My world; for if you do, there will be no one else to repair it' (Ecclesiastes Rabbah 7:13).

Test the 5 mark question

Suggested answers, other relevant answers would be credited. 1 mark for each simple contrasting or similar belief, another mark for developing each belief, so 4 marks for two developed beliefs, 1 extra mark for a correct reference to a source of religious belief or teaching.

9. Christians and Jews believe God created the earth for humans to use and look after/ stewardship means humans have a responsibility to look after the earth on behalf of God/ God put Adam into the Garden of Eden 'to work it and take care of it' (Genesis 2:15 [NIV])/ 'See to it that you do not spoil and destroy My world; for if you do, there will be no one else to repair it' (Ecclesiastes Rabbah 7:13)/ it is an act of love to protect the earth for future generations.

10. Christians and Jews believe the universe was designed and made by God out of nothing/ the Bible and the Torah say that God made the universe and all life in it in six days/ 'In the beginning God created the heavens and the earth' (Genesis 1:1 [NIV])/ many believe God designed and used the Big Bang to create the universe/ the creation stories are symbolic and 'six days' refers to six longer periods of time.

Test the 12 mark question

Suggested answers shown here, but see page 11 for guidance on levels of response.

12. Arguments in support

• It would either make abortion easier (supporting pro-choice) or harder (supporting pro-life).

• Making abortion easier gives more rights to the mother/ the mother has to carry the baby, give birth to it and bring it up, so she should have the right to choose whether to continue with the pregnancy/ life does not begin until birth (or halfway down the birth canal), so abortion is not a form of killing.

• Making abortion stricter gives more rights to the unborn child/ respects the sanctity of life/ makes it harder to take away life given by God/ makes it harder to interfere with God's plan for people (Jeremiah 1:5).

• Some Christians and Jews would remove the law altogether to make abortion illegal.

Arguments in support of other views

• The current law is the best compromise between sides that support abortion and those that don't/ there is a reasonable balance between the rights of the mother and the unborn child/ the law respects the quality of life of both the mother and child.

• Making abortion illegal could endanger the life of the mother and the unborn child/ might prompt women to carry out unsafe abortions by themselves.

- For those who believe life starts at conception, making abortion easier would result in more killing of human life.

13. Arguments in support

- A minority of Christians believe humans were given dominion over the earth so can do what they want with it/ 'Rule over the fish in the sea and the birds in the sky and over every living creature that moves on the ground' (Genesis 1:28 [NIV]).

- If resources are destroyed or used up, scientists will develop alternatives.

- Humans need natural resources to sustain their way of life.

Arguments in support of other views

- Most Christians and Jews believe humans were put on the earth as stewards to look after it on behalf of God for future generations/ God put Adam into the Garden of Eden 'to work it and take care of it' (Genesis 2:15 [NIV])/ it is wrong to destroy something that belongs to someone else (i.e. God).

- Many of the earth's natural resources are non-renewable so there is only a limited supply of them/ using them up too quickly will probably make life much harder for future generations/ this shows a lack of love and respect for others.

7 The existence of God and revelation

Test the 1 mark question

1. C) Theist
2. B) Mortal

Test the 2 mark question

Suggested answers, other relevant answers would be credited. 1 mark for each correct point.

3. The argument contradicts itself/ it says everything has a cause, but what caused God to exist?/ if God is eternal, why can't the universe be eternal?/ the Big Bang was a random event, not caused/ just because events on earth have causes does not necessarily mean the universe itself has a cause.

4. Misuse of free will (e.g. war)/ natural causes (e.g. earthquakes, floods)/ disobedience of Adam and Eve.

Test the 4 mark question

Suggested answers, other relevant answers would be credited. 1 mark for each simple contrasting or similar point, another mark for developing each point, so a maximum of 4 marks for two developed points.

6. *Beliefs must be contrasting*:

An event performed by God which appears to break the laws of nature/ *an example of such an event*/ they confirm God's existence and power/ show God is at work in the world/ are answers to prayer.

They are not real/ they are lucky coincidences that have nothing to do with God/ may be made up for fame or money/ healing miracles may be mind over matter or misdiagnosis/ can be explained scientifically in a way we don't yet know.

7. *Beliefs must be similar*:

Comes through ordinary human experiences/ seeing God's creative work and presence in nature/ through reason or conscience/ through worship or scripture/ sacred writings help to reveal what God is like and how he wants people to live/ the power of the words in sacred writings are so strong that people can come to believe in God through reading or hearing them/ some who take sacred writings literally believe they are the actual word of God.

People are mistaken in interpreting normal events as general revelation/ nature is special but has nothing to do with revelation/ scriptures are opinions of their writers and not inspired by God/ scripture can be wrongly interpreted.

Test the 5 mark question

Suggested answers, other relevant answers would be credited. 1 mark for each simple contrasting or similar belief, another mark for developing each belief, so 4 marks for two developed beliefs, 1 extra mark for a correct reference to a source of religious belief or teaching.

9. For Christians, a way of God revealing something about himself/ direct experience of God in an event, such as a vision or prophecy/ e.g. Moses receiving the Ten Commandments, Mary finding out she is pregnant from the angel Gabriel, Saul's vision/ can have a great influence on people's lives.

God's special revelation to the Jews comes through the law, prophets and the covenant/ there are many stories in the Tenakh of prophets hearing the call of God and giving his message to others/ e.g. God's special revelation to Moses through the burning bush (Exodus 3:1–17).

10. Omnipotent/ omniscient/ benevolent/ immanent/ transcendent/ personal/ impersonal/ creator/ *any ideas in scripture related to creation, possibility of relationship with God through prayer, incarnation of Jesus, work of the Holy Spirit.*

Test the 12 mark question

Suggested answers shown here, but see page 11 for guidance on levels of response.

12. Arguments in support

- Miracles are events with no natural or scientific explanation that only God could perform/ only God is all-powerful and transcendent, so able to perform miracles.

- If they occur as a response to prayer, they are a response to asking God for something/ prove that God is listening and responding to prayers.

- They are usually good and God is the source of all that is good.

- The fact that some people convert to Christianity after experiencing a miracle is proof of God's existence.

- Miracles are recorded in sacred writings so they must be important.

- 69 healing miracles have officially been recognised as taking place at Lourdes.

- Miracles exist and are caused by God, therefore God exists.

Arguments in support of other views

- Miracles are lucky coincidences and nothing to do with God.

- Whether something counts as a miracle is a matter of interpretation.

- They may have scientific explanations we haven't yet discovered.

- Healings could be mind over matter or misdiagnosis.

- Some miracles are made up for fame or money.

- If God is involved in miracles, this means he is selective and unfair (as only a few people experience them)/ but God cannot be selective and unfair/ therefore he cannot be involved in miracles.

- If miracles don't exist or have other explanations, they are nothing to do with God, so do not prove he exists.

13. Arguments in support

- A loving God would not allow people to suffer.

- God should be aware of evil and suffering because he is omniscient/ if so, he should use his powers to prevent it because he is omnipotent/ because God does not do this, he cannot exist.

- If God made all of creation to be perfect then there would not be earthquakes, droughts, etc./ suffering caused by the natural world is an example of poor design, which no God would be responsible for.

Arguments in support of other views

- It is unfair to blame God for suffering because he doesn't cause it.

- Suffering is a result of the disobedience of Adam and Eve/ the result of humans misusing their free will.

- If there was no evil, no one would be able to actively choose good over bad/ learn from their mistakes/ show compassion and kindness towards others who are suffering.

- Humans are in charge of looking after the earth and God chooses not to interfere.

- The existence of evil doesn't necessarily prove God does not exist, but could suggest he is not all-loving or all-powerful.

8 Religion, peace and conflict

Test the 1 mark question

1. C) Justice
2. D) Conventional weapons

Test the 2 mark question

Suggested answers, other relevant answers would be credited. 1 mark for each correct point.

3. Just cause/ correct authority/ good intention/ last resort/ reasonable chance of success/ proportional methods used.

4. For Christians violent protest goes against Jesus' teachings not to use violence/ goes against the commandment 'You shall not murder' (Exodus 20:13 [NIV])/ does not show 'love of neighbour'/ goes against the sanctity of life/ goes against 'So in everything, do to others what you would have them do to you, for this sums up the Law and the Prophets' (Matthew 7:12 [NIV]).

For Jews, violence is only allowed in self-defence/ but protest is important to bring about change, as long as it is peaceful/ not protesting against injustice is almost agreeing with the injustice.

Test the 4 mark question

Suggested answers, other relevant answers would be credited. 1 mark for each simple contrasting or similar point, another mark for developing each point, so a maximum of 4 marks for two developed points.

6. *Beliefs must be contrasting*:

Christians who support pacifism (e.g. The Religious Society of Friends/Quakers) believe that war can never be justified/ all killing is wrong/ it breaks the commandment 'You shall not murder' (Exodus 20:13 [NIV])/ Jesus taught 'Blessed are the peacemakers, for they shall be called children of God' (Matthew 5:9 [NIV])/ conflicts should be settled peacefully.

Christians who do not support pacifism believe that war is sometimes necessary as a last resort/ they would fight in a 'just war'/ to stop genocide taking place/ to defend one's country or way of life/ to help a weaker country defend itself from attack.

Most Jews believe in peace but are not pacifists/ accept fighting in self-defence/ to defend their faith and family from attack/ the Tenakh advises people to 'Shun evil and do good, seek peace and pursue it' (Psalm 34:15 [Tenakh])/ the prophet Micah said that when God's kingdom of justice was established, war would not be necessary to settle disputes (Micah 4:3).

7. *Beliefs must be similar:*

Forgiveness is showing grace and mercy/ pardoning someone for what they have done wrong/ Christians believe forgiveness is important as in the Lord's Prayer it says 'Forgive us our sins as we forgive those who sin against us'/ this means God will not forgive if Christians do not forgive others/ Christians believe God sets the example by offering forgiveness to all who ask for it in faith/ some Christians believe repentance is needed for forgiveness/ forgiveness does not mean accepting wrongdoing.

Jews believe forgiveness should not be automatic/ offenders should show remorse and ask for forgiveness/ forgiveness is a duty if the offender asks genuinely/ Yom Kippur offers an opportunity to express sorrow for sin and seek God's forgiveness.

Test the 5 mark question

Suggested answers, other relevant answers would be credited. 1 mark for each simple contrasting or similar belief, another mark for developing each belief, so 4 marks for two developed beliefs, 1 extra mark for a correct reference to a source of religious belief or teaching.

9. Some Christians believe in the just war theory/ it is right to fight in a war if the cause is just/ war can be the lesser of two evils/ it can be justified if its purpose is to stop atrocities/ people have a right to self-defence/ 'If there is a serious injury, you are to take life for life, eye for eye, tooth for tooth' (Exodus 21:23–24 [NIV])/ 'Love your neighbour as yourself' (Matthew 22:39 [NIV]) demands protection of weaker allies through war.

For Jews, there are three types of war: obligatory (commanded by God), defensive (including pre-emptive strikes against a potential enemy) and optional (fought for a good reason when all peaceful ways to prevent conflict have been tried first)/ Jews have rules about how a war must be fought, e.g. protect civilians and the landscape (Deuteronomy 20:19), and treat prisoners with dignity (Proverbs 25:21)/ wars should not be fought to build an empire, destroy another nation, steal resources or take revenge.

10. It is when individuals or groups restore friendly relations after conflict or disagreement/ it is important to build good relationships after a war so conflict does not break out again/ justice and peace must be restored to prevent further conflict/ to create a world which reflects God's intention in creation/ Christians believe they must be reconciled to others before they can worship God properly/ 'Therefore, if you are offering your gift at the altar and there remember that your brother or sister has something against you, leave your gift there in front of the altar. First go and be reconciled to them; then come and offer your gift.' (Matthew 5:23–24 [NIV]).

Reconciliation is a sacrament in the Catholic Church/ Christians believe it is important to ask God for forgiveness for sins/ reconciliation restores a Christian's relationship with God and other people.

Jews believe God sets the example for reconciliation, as God forgives anyone who asks sincerely in faith/ Yom Kippur offers an opportunity to express sorrow for sin and be reconciled to God/ many Jews work for reconciliation with Palestinians to bring about a lasting peace in Israel.

Test the 12 mark question

Suggested answers shown here, but see page 11 for guidance on levels of response.

12. Arguments in support

• Some religious people believe in the concept of a holy war/ a holy war is fighting for a religious cause or God/ probably controlled by a religious leader/ these believers think that it is justifiable to defend their faith from attack.

• Religion has been a cause of such wars in the past/ e.g. the Crusades, wars between Christians and Muslims, were fought over rights to the Holy Land/ in the Old Testament there are many references to God helping the Jews settle in the Promised Land at the expense of those already living there.

• There are many examples of conflicts that involve different religious groups/ e.g. Catholics and Protestants in Northern Ireland during the 'Troubles'/ Israeli–Palestinian conflict/ conflict in India and Pakistan between Muslims and Hindus.

• Some atheists claim that without religion, many conflicts could be avoided/ religiously motivated terrorism would cease.

Arguments in support of other views

• Religion is not the main cause of wars: greed, self-defence and retaliation are all more common causes/ academic studies have found that religion plays a minor role in the majority of conflicts/ most wars have many causes/ e.g. opposition to a government, economic reasons, objection to ideological, political or social systems/ e.g. political differences played a greater role in the conflict in Northern Ireland than religion.

• Christians today believe they should defend their faith by reasoned argument, not violence/ many Christians think no war can be considered 'holy' when there is great loss of life/ '"Put your sword back in its place," Jesus said, 'for all who draw the sword die by the sword"' (Matthew 26:52 [NIV])/ 'You have heard that it was said to the people long ago, 'You shall not murder […] But I tell you that anyone who is angry with a brother or sister will be subject to judgement"' (Matthew 5:21–22 [NIV]).

• Most Jews in the UK do not wish to respond violently to what they see to be religious offences or an attack on their faith/ Judaism condemns vengeance and teaches love of neighbour (Letivicus 19:18).

13. Arguments in support

• Religious people should be the main peacemakers because of their beliefs/ e.g. Christians and Jews believe in 'love your neighbour'/ the sanctity of life/ peace/ forgiveness/ reconciliation/ Jesus taught 'Blessed are the peacemakers'/ the Tenakh advises people to 'Shun evil and do good, seek peace and pursue it' (Psalm 34:15 [Tenakh]).

• Christian and Jewish pacifists believe that peace comes through religious faith supported by prayer/ following God's law/ by actively working to promote human rights/ prayer and meditation can bring inner peace to individuals/ this helps avoid quarrels with others/ peacemaking begins with each person.

• Many religious people are engaged in peacemaking in today's world/ e.g. the Anglican Pacifist Fellowship works to raise awareness of the issue of pacifism/ the 'Peace People' (Mairead Corrigan, Betty Williams and Ciaran McKeown) in Northern Ireland work to bring Catholic and Protestant communities together to stop violence/ Dr Marshall Rosenberg founded the Centre for Nonviolent Communication, which runs courses on non-violent communication to resolve conflict in a peaceful way.

Arguments in support of other views

• Religious people should be peacemakers, but not the main ones/ the problems of global conflict require global solutions that are beyond any individual to solve/ the United Nations should be the main peacekeeping organisation/ only large organisations or governments with powerful resources can hope to affect peacemaking in the world.

• Religious people can be peacemakers in their own families and support justice and peace groups locally, but they cannot take the lead as peacemakers/ their main duty is to their family/ people have jobs that do not allow them to stop violence across the world/ the most they can do is contribute to organisations which help.

• Everyone should take equal responsibility for helping to contribute towards peace, whether they are religious or not/ some situations might benefit from peacemakers who are not religious.

9 Religion, crime and punishment

Test the 1 mark question

1. A) Corporal punishment

2. C) Happiness

Test the 2 mark question

Suggested answers, other relevant answers would be credited. 1 mark for each correct point.

3. Retribution/ deterrence/ reformation/ protection.

4. Poverty/ upbringing/ mental illness/ addiction/ greed/ hate/ opposition to an unjust law.

Test the 4 mark question

Suggested answers, other relevant answers would be credited. 1 mark for each simple contrasting or similar point, another mark for developing each point, so a maximum of 4 marks for two developed points.

6. *Beliefs must be contrasting:*

Approved of by most Christians and Jews/ as allows offenders to make up for what they have done wrong/ helps to reform and rehabilitate offenders/ may involve counselling, treatment or education/ may include an opportunity to apologise to the victim/ no harm is done to the offender.

Not approved of by some Christians and Jews as it is not a sufficient deterrent/ it is too soft a punishment/ 'life for life, eye for eye, tooth for tooth' (Exodus 21: 23-24 [NIV]).

7. *Beliefs must be similar:*

It makes reoffending unlikely/ it brings justice as the punishment matches the fate of the victim/ it deters others from committing serious crimes/ 'life for life, eye for eye, tooth for tooth' (Exodus 21:23–24 [NIV])/ 'Whoever sheds human blood, by humans shall their blood be shed' (Genesis 9:6 [NIV]).

Test the 5 mark question

Suggested answers, other relevant answers would be credited. 1 mark for each simple contrasting or similar belief, another mark for developing each belief, so 4 marks for two developed beliefs, 1 extra mark for a correct reference to a source of religious belief or teaching.

9. Christians are expected to forgive those who offend against them and if they do God will forgive them/ forgiveness is not a replacement for punishment/ it should be unlimited/ 'not seven times, but seventy-seven times' (Matthew 18:22 [NIV])/ Jesus forgave those who crucified him and Christians should follow his example/ 'Father forgive them, for they do not know what they are doing' (Luke 23:34 [NIV]).

Jews believe forgiveness should not be automatic/ offenders should show remorse and ask for forgiveness/ forgiveness is a duty if the offender asks genuinely/ the Ten Days of Repentance are the traditional time to seek forgiveness in advance of God's forgiveness on Yom Kippur/ forgiveness is not a replacement for punishment.

10. Hate crimes are condemned by Christianity and Judaism/ hate crimes target individuals and groups perceived to be different/ Christians and Jews believe God created all humans equal in his image/ 'There is neither Jew nor Gentile, slave nor free man, male nor female, for you are all one in Christ Jesus' (Galatians 3:28 [NIV])/ hate crimes are not loving ('love your neighbour')/ hate crimes are not just/ Jews understand how important it is to condemn hate crimes as they are victims of perhaps one of the worst hate crimes in history: the Holocaust.

Test the 12 mark question

Suggested answers shown here, but see page 11 for guidance on levels of response.

12. Arguments in support

• Sanctity of life means life is sacred and special to God/ should be valued and respected/ the life of an offender has equal value to any other life/ the use of the death penalty does not respect life.

- Sanctity of life also suggests that only God has the right to take life/ this means it is not right to take another person's life/ this interferes with God's plan for a person's life.

Arguments in support of other views

- Murderers have already taken the life of someone else so their life should not be respected.

- Executing a murderer ensures they don't go on to kill again, thus preserving the sanctity of life/ the death penalty may deter others from killing and breaking the sanctity of life.

- For those who don't believe in God, sanctity of life does not show that the death penalty is wrong/ there are other reasons for why the death penalty is wrong/ e.g. it is not an effective deterrent/ it does not allow for the possibility of reformation/ it may kill innocent people.

13.   Arguments in support

- Committing crime is wrong whatever the reason/ all crime causes someone to suffer.

- People should obey the law/ God put the system of government in place to rule every citizen so it is his law that is being broken (Romans 13:31).

- Christians and Jews believe it is wrong to commit crime because of poverty/ people should focus on creating a fairer society where the need to steal because of poverty is removed.

- Those who commit crime through illness or addiction should be provided with treatment so they have no reason to commit crimes.

- People who want to protest against an unjust law can do so legally, e.g. through a peaceful protest.

Arguments in support of other views

- Society is not fair so crimes because of need/poverty are justified in some circumstances/ e.g. it may be better to steal food than allow a child to starve.

- Some laws are unjust and the only way to change them is to break them/ peaceful protest is not always powerful enough to change the law.

- All humans have a tendency to do bad things, including crime, because of original sin.

- Those who commit crime because of addiction/mental illness may not be able to help it.

10 Religion, human rights and social justice

Test the 1 mark question

1.   C) Unfairly judging someone before knowing the facts

2.   B) Promoting tolerance

Test the 2 mark question

Suggested answers, other relevant answers would be credited. 1 mark for each correct point.

3.   Unfair pay/ bad working conditions/ bad housing/ poor education/ high interest rates on loans or credit cards/ people-trafficking/ modern slavery.

4.   Christians and Jews should give money to the Church or synagogue/ to the poor/ make voluntary contributions to charities/ support food banks/ use their wealth to help the poor lift themselves out of poverty.

Test the 4 mark question

Suggested answers, other relevant answers would be credited. 1 mark for each simple contrasting or similar point, another mark for developing each point, so a maximum of 4 marks for two developed points.

6.   *Beliefs must be contrasting:*

Prejudice is always wrong because it is unjust to single out individuals or groups for inferior treatment/ some Christians and Jews believe any relationship based on love should be cherished.

Some Christians and Orthodox Jews think homosexual relationships are unnatural and against God/ cannot lead to the 'natural' creation of a child/ goes against God's plan for humans/ 'Do not lie with a man as one lies with a woman; it is an abhorrence' (Leviticus 18:22 [NIV]).

7.   *Beliefs must be similar:*

Sacred writings stress the importance of providing human rights to all people/ which includes creating a more just society/ 'Let justice roll on like a river' (Amos 5:24 [NIV])/ Christians and Jews believe it is not loving to deny people their rights/ rights are written into law, and the law is inspired by God so must be obeyed/ Christians and Jews have a responsibility to help provide human rights/ 'faith without deeds is useless' (James 2:20 [NIV])/ protecting human rights prevents exploitation and creates a more equal society.

Test the 5 mark question

Suggested answers, other relevant answers would be credited. 1 mark for each simple contrasting or similar belief, another mark for developing each belief, so 4 marks for two developed beliefs, 1 extra mark for a correct reference to a source of religious belief or teaching.

9.   Poverty is sometimes caused by injustice and Christians and Jews must combat injustice/ poverty involves suffering and Christians and Jews are expected to help relieve suffering/ e.g. the parable of the Sheep and the Goats/ people have God-given talents that they should use to help overcome poverty/ e.g. the parable of the Talents/ tackling poverty is good stewardship/ Jesus' teaching to 'love your neighbour' encourages Christians to help those in poverty.

10.   Christianity teaches that wealth can lead to traits such as greed and selfishness/ 'the love of money is a root of all sorts of evil' (1 Timothy 6:10 [NIV])/ focusing on wealth brings the danger of ignoring God and neglecting the spiritual life/ 'You cannot serve both God and money' (Matthew 6:24 [NIV]).

Jews see wealth as a blessing from God, so it should be used carefully and to help others in need/ wealth can distract people from following God's path and this distraction should be avoided/ greed is discouraged because it can take from the poor.

Test the 12 mark question

Suggested answers shown here, but see page 11 for guidance on levels of response.

12.   Arguments in support

- Discrimination is an action that can cause physical and psychological harm/ goes against the ideas of equality and justice/ which are central to Christian and Jewish ethics/ 'let justice well up like water' (Amos 5:24 [Tenakh]).

- Christianity and Judaism teach that all people should be treated equally because they are all made in God's image/ 'There is neither Jew nor Gentile, neither slave nor free, nor is there male and female, for you are all one in Christ Jesus' (Galatians 3:28 [NIV]).

- Positive discrimination is still a form of discrimination/ it would be better to treat all people equally.

Arguments in support of other views

- Positive discrimination helps to make up for centuries of negative discrimination against minority groups/ helps to make people aware of the need to rectify negative discrimination against minority groups.

- Positive discrimination helps those with disabilities to live more equally alongside people without disabilities/ shows love and compassion to people who are suffering/ so it can be supported by Christian and Jewish teachings.

- It is important to differentiate between the needs of different people/ not everyone is the same/ some people are better suited to certain roles than others.

13.   Arguments in support

- Freedom of religion is a basic human right/ 'Everyone has the right to freedom of thought, conscience and religion' (The United Declaration of Human Rights)/ in the UK the law allows people to follow whichever faith they choose.

- It is wrong to try to force someone to follow a religion/ or to prevent them from following a religion/ it should be a matter of personal choice/ this makes choosing to follow a particular religion more significant/meaningful.

- Forcing people to follow a religion or preventing them from following a religion could lead to more conflict and fighting between different religions.

- Being a Christian or not is a choice that any person can make/ Jesus taught people to show tolerance and harmony/ Jews are mainly born into the faith but converts are accepted and leaving the faith is permitted.

Arguments in support of other views

- If a religion teaches hatred and intolerance, there should be limits on how it can be taught or practised/ people should not be allowed to join it for the wrong reasons.

- Some people might argue that to show patriotism, a person should follow the main religion in their country.

- Some people might argue that when people are allowed to join any religion, this can lead to conflict and tension between different religious groups, whereas if everyone followed the same religion then there would be more harmony between people.

- Some people might unintentionally harm/upset others through choosing a particular religion/ e.g. by choosing a religion that is different to their parents'/ so perhaps it should not be so easy to switch from one religion to another.

All resources from
AQA GCSE Religious Studies A (9–1)

Student Books

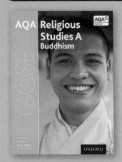

Buddhism
Student Book
978 019 837032 1

Buddhism
Kerboodle Book
978 019 837052 9

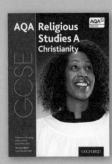

Christianity
Student Book
978 019 837033 8

Christianity
Kerboodle Book
978 019 837050 5

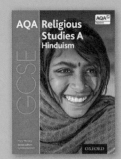

Hinduism
Student Book
978 019 837035 2

Hinduism
Kerboodle Book
978 019 837054 3

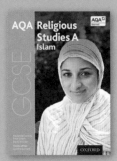

Islam
Student Book
978 019 837034 5

Islam
Kerboodle Book
978 019 837051 2

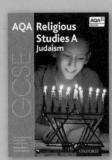

Judaism
Student Book
978 019 837036 9

Judaism
Kerboodle Book
978 019 837053 6

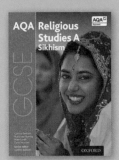

Sikhism
Student Book
978 019 837037 6

Sikhism
Kerboodle Book
978 019 837065 0

All student books are endorsed by AQA

kerboodle

Christianity Kerboodle:
Exam Practice and
Revision
978 019 837048 2

Specifications A and B

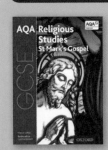

St Mark's Gospel
Student Book
978 019 837039 0

St Mark's Gospel
Kerboodle Book
978 019 841270 0

All student books are
endorsed by AQA

The Oxford Teacher
Handbook for
GCSE Islam
978 019 837047 5

Revision Guides   RECAP   APPLY   REVIEW   ✓ SUCCEED

Christianity
Revision Guide
978 019 842281 5

Christianity & Buddhism
Revision Guide
978 019 842285 3

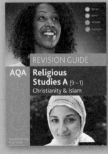

Christianity & Islam
Revision Guide
978 019 842283 9

Christianity & Judaism
Revision Guide
978 019 843254 8

OXFORD